PRAISE FOR
The Nazis Next Door

"Lichtblau brings ample investigative skills and an elegant writing style to this unsavory but important story. *The Nazis Next Door* is a captivating book rooted in first-rate research."
— Deborah E. Lipstadt, *New York Times Book Review*

"Engaging . . . Thanks in part to [Nazi hunters'] firsthand accounts, *The Nazis Next Door* provides an intimate and digestible introduction to a subject still very much in the news." — *Chicago Tribune*

"Fascinating." — Amy Goodman, *Democracy Now!*

"Riveting . . . Well-documented . . . Compelling . . . [A] gripping chronicle, informed by the reportorial skills of a journalist and impelled by the moral imperative to bear witness." — *Times of Israel*

"Grab a copy of Eric Lichtblau's new book and get your blood boiling."
— *Baltimore Jewish Times*

"Lichtblau's book is rich in detail and helps us better understand postwar American history. Moreover, it will mesmerize readers because of its interesting and fast-paced writing based on first-rate research . . . Reads like a suspense novel, with its often low-key heroes and unsavory villains. This important story should hold the reader's interest from the first page to its conclusion." — *St. Louis Jewish Light*

"Riveting . . . Lichtblau's book is an important, fascinating read."
— Jewish Book Council

"A disturbing new examination of this shameful moment in American history." — *Salon*

"Read[s] like a novel, offering suspense, interesting characters, both good guys and bad . . . It's all here . . . Excellent." — History News Network

"Lichtblau tells this story of unseemly patronage and moral accommodation, providing a highly readable account edged with a justified tone of indignation. He does a particularly nice job of showing that many of those most willing to climb into bed with former Nazis were themselves closeted—or not-so-closeted—anti-Semites." — *Irish Times*

"Revelatory." — *Sun Sentinel*

"Fascinating and infuriating corrective to the American mythology of the 'Good War.'" — *Kirkus Reviews*

"A fast-paced, important book about the Justice Department's efforts to bring Nazi war criminals in the U.S. to justice that also uses recently declassified facts to expose the secret, reprehensible collaboration of U.S. intelligence agencies with those very Nazis."
— Elizabeth Holtzman, former member of Congress

The Nazis Next Door

Books by Eric Lichtblau

Bush's Law: The Remaking of American Justice

The Nazis Next Door:
How America Became a Safe Haven for Hitler's Men

The Nazis Next Door

HOW AMERICA
BECAME A SAFE HAVEN
FOR HITLER'S MEN

Eric Lichtblau

**MARINER
BOOKS**

An Imprint of HarperCollins*Publishers*
Boston   New York

First Mariner Books edition 2015

Copyright © 2014 by Eric Lichtblau

Mariner Books
An Imprint of HarperCollins Publishers, registered in the United States of America and/or other jurisdictions.

www.marinerbooks.com

Library of Congress Cataloging-in-Publication Data
Lichtblau, Eric.
The Nazis next door : how America became a safe haven for Hitler's men / Eric Lichtblau.
pages cm
Includes bibliographical references and index.
ISBN 978-0-547-66919-9 (hardback)   ISBN 978-0-544-57788-6 (pbk.)
1. Anti-communist movements — United States — History — 20th century.
2. Nazis — United States — History — 20th century. 3. Refugees — United States — History — 20th century. 4. War criminals — United States — History — 20th century.
5. United States. Federal Bureau of Investigation — History — 20th century.
6. United States. Central Intelligence Agency — History — 20th century.
7. Espionage, American — History — 20th century. 8. Cold War. 9. United States — Politics and government — 1945–1989. 10. United States — Foreign relations — 1945–1989.
I. Title.
E743.5.L49 2014
324.1'3 — dc23   2014023543

Book design by Brian Moore
Map by Chris Robinson

Printed in the United States of America
22 23 24 25 26 LBC 10 9 8 7 6

For my mother, who taught me to keep asking questions

"The wrongs which we seek to condemn and punish have been so calculated, so malignant, and so devastating, that civilization cannot tolerate their being ignored, because it cannot survive their being repeated."

— *Robert H. Jackson, Nuremberg prosecutor (1945)*

"It is all forgotten. It's all over."

— *Jakob Reimer, former Nazi SS officer living outside New York City (1998)*

CONTENTS

A Name from the Past

July 12, 1974

LANGLEY, VIRGINIA

The old man sounded panicked. He was normally so cocksure and crafty, but now, as he related the strange events of the last few weeks, there was the squall of desperation in a voice left raspy by too many Marlboros. He was in trouble, Tom Soobzokov was telling his long-ago friend John Grunz on the other end of the phone line. Exactly why was still not clear; the words were tumbling out so furiously in Soobzokov's thick Slavic accent that Grunz could scarcely follow his helter-skelter story.

Crazy refugees from the old country were out to destroy him, the old man was saying. There was something about libelous stories in the newspaper. A hell-bent congresswoman was somehow involved, too. And did Grunz hear his old friend Tom right? Did he just say something about Nazi war crimes?

Slow down, slow down, Grunz urged. Whatever's going on, he said, we can deal with it. The assurances did nothing to calm Soobzokov.

You don't understand. My life is in danger.

Typical Soobzokov. He inevitably seemed to cloak himself in some bit of drama or other; there was always that element of intrigue. He was, as his secret psychological workups had concluded years earlier, a bold and impassioned man, "a leader type who can get things done," but volatile and scheming, too; "a skillful manipulator of people." His outsize, fill-up-the-room personality had defined him for as long as Grunz had known him.

But had his old friend, still rambling on the phone about Nazis and government probes, now turned delusional, too?

The two men, their lives once so tightly intertwined, had lost touch in recent years. Then came the cryptic message that an intermediary had passed along to Grunz just a few days earlier: someone named Soobzokov was looking for him. He wanted him to call as soon as possible. It sounded urgent.

Tom Soobzokov? Looking for him? It had been many years — fifteen, maybe twenty — since they had last spoken. What could he want after all this time?

Soobzokov, nothing if not resourceful, had gotten a friend in Congress to find Grunz's unlisted line and get the message to him. That wasn't as simple as it sounded, since Grunz had a way of making himself hard to find. He was, after all, a CIA spy.

Soobzokov knew a bit about spying, too. That was how he knew Grunz. Soobzokov had once been a spy himself for the CIA — not a particularly good one, but a spy nonetheless. Grunz had been his handler in the Middle East two decades earlier as they chased intelligence on the Soviets in the crazy Cold War days of the 1950s. Soobzokov's main mission was to recruit Russian émigrés and fervent anti-Communists — people like him — who might be willing to spy on their former homeland for America. He was always on the verge of turning the next big Russian agent, or so he claimed. It was in the Middle East that Soobzokov had picked up his CIA code name: Nostril, an unflattering allusion to his prominent hooked nose. If he minded the moniker, he never let on. He loved the cloak-and-dagger intrigue of the spy business. He also liked to brandish his agency credentials to friends and acquaintances, with a reckless bravado — not a good quality in a spy. As his handler, Grunz was sometimes forced to clean up the mess left by Nostril's indiscretions in far-flung places.

Now, so many years later, a frantic Soobzokov had put out word — through a congressman, no less — that he was looking for Grunz. No, don't give him my phone number, Grunz told the congressman's office. I'll contact him.

Whatever was going on, Grunz figured it couldn't be good.

He picked up the phone and dialed a 201 area code: northern New Jersey, where, if he recalled right, Soobzokov had settled when he emigrated from Europe after World War II among a mass of war-torn refugees.

Pleasantries were few, despite their long estrangement. Soobzokov needed help, and he needed it now, he told Grunz. His life — the American life he had cultivated so assiduously for himself, his wife, and his five children in the hardscrabble town of Paterson, New Jersey — was collapsing around him. Amid the flurry of wild-sounding events, Grunz was finally able to parse out enough of the details to fully appreciate his panic.

Maybe he wasn't so delusional, after all. People really were after him.

It had started with the whispers. For years, a bunch of Soobzokov's fellow immigrants who, like him, hailed from Russia's rugged western borderland in the North Caucasus, between the Black Sea and the Caspian Sea, had been spreading malicious talk about him, he said. He practically spat the words. They were obviously jealous of him — jealous of the political connections he'd built among state Democrats; jealous of the plum county job he'd landed; jealous of the reputation he'd earned in the immigrant community as a leader and fixer, a man who could make problems go away. When he walked into a room, people stood up out of respect. He was a man of stature, a man of influence, and his rivals in New Jersey obviously resented him for it.

Now their envy had turned truly vile. The outrageous things they were saying about him! That back in the old country, he had become the Germans' henchman in his village after Hitler's 1942 invasion. That he had turned on his own people. That he had worn the reviled Waffen SS uniform. That he had led roaming Third Reich "execution squads" that gunned down Jews and Communists.

That he was, in short, a Nazi.

Tall and lanky, with a bushy mustache, a ruddy complexion, and a handsome face that suggested any number of ethnicities, Soobzokov had gone by many names and identities since the war: his given name of Tscherim Soobzokov, or Tom, as he was called by the local politicos who had befriended him; Sergei Zarevich, or Kerim Lafsoka, as some of his official papers identified him; the vanilla-sounding alias of "Kenneth Desnew" on overseas spy trips; and, of course, Nostril, his code name in CIA files.

His accusers from the old country knew him by yet another name: *the Führer of the North Caucasus,* some called him.

It was slander of the worst kind, the old man insisted. At first, he had tried to write it off as just the vicious gossip of the immigrant community. Hadn't there been similar smears spread by the Communists against dozens of other good Americans since the end of the war? Good men, respected men, men like him. These were solid citizens who, like him, served their new country well but were accused of being Nazis nonetheless: German rocket scientists in Alabama, doctors in San Antonio, a successful business-man in Northern California, an Olympic coach in San Diego, an architect in Philadelphia, even a prominent bishop in Michigan.

All innocent, like him; all victims of lies, Soobzokov told anyone who would listen.

The public was largely oblivious to it all. For that, at least, Soobzokov was grateful. Even the powerful people who heard the whispers — the FBI, the INS, the occasional congressman — seemed blissfully uninterested. It was a brutal time, those war years, and whatever had happened was so long ago. No one cared, thank God.

Yet somehow, three decades after the war, his past was becoming quite public. The talk had gone from rumor to news, with his tiny hometown paper printing a few stories on the Nazi claims against him. TV newscast-ers had picked up on the innuendo, too. Soobzokov figured his rival — that scoundrel Dr. Jawad Idriss, a good-for-nothing fabricator who thought *he* was the real leader of their immigrant clan in New Jersey — must have gone shooting his mouth off again with his outrageous Nazi accusations. Grist for a lawsuit, perhaps.

That was bad enough. Then, just a few days earlier, Soobzokov was named in a story in the *New York Times* with a list of more than three dozen suspected Nazis living comfortably and quietly in America, divorced from their hidden pasts. The good name of Tom Soobzokov in the *New York Times!* Calling him a Nazi! Immigration officials, under pressure for failing to do anything about supposed war criminals living in the United States, had grudgingly turned over the list to a pesky New York congresswoman, Elizabeth Holtzman. A Jew, of course. Soobzokov didn't trust Jews. He had confided as much years earlier to the CIA; Soobzokov "would be ashamed to work for a Jew," a note in his file read. Now this Holtzman woman was demanding action and making his life miserable. He was seething as he told his old friend Grunz about all the accusations that were being slung at him.

There was talk of trying to take away his citizenship and send him back to Russia — back to the loathsome Communists who had taken away his father's land. What could be worse? And now the Jewish militants were planning pickets at his house, his friends inside the local police department were telling him. His political bosses in Passaic County, wary of all the publicity, were already threatening to suspend him from his county purchasing job. They were afraid of the political embarrassment. Cowards, all of them. And ungrateful, too, after all the votes he'd brought them from his fellow immigrants.

There'd been threats to his life, he told Grunz. *I'm a loyal American citizen. I did nothing wrong. I fought the Communists. I served my country. I served you — and the CIA.* As if to quell any doubts about his spy service, Soobzokov spoke ominously of the secret dossier he'd kept on his years of faithful undercover work for the CIA. There was a paper trail, he promised; a long one.

Lay low, Grunz implored. Don't say anything to anyone; that would make things worse. And whatever you do, don't mention anything about your work with the CIA. It will all blow over.

Yet in his own mind, Grunz wasn't so certain.

Now working at CIA headquarters outside Washington, D.C., Grunz knew he would have to inform higher-ups about the unnerving conversation with his ex-spy. They would no doubt want to sniff out senior officials at the Justice Department to see whether the CIA would be dragged into the muck by the accusations. Maybe they could get the INS to back off; this was a national security matter, after all.

Twice more in the next few days, Grunz spoke with Soobzokov. There'd just been *another* story in the newspaper naming him as a Nazi, Soobzokov told him, and he was growing more unwound with each bit of notoriety.

Grunz sat down to warn his bosses.

The CIA was facing a "significant flap," Grunz wrote in a long memo apprising them of what was happening in New Jersey. "Soobzokov has assumed a posture of outraged innocence (a posture he adopts quite convincingly) and has made numerous attempts to smoke out the nature and source of the various allegations."

The good news was that, so far, at least, Soobzokov was only looking for "advice"; nothing more. But to protect himself, Grunz warned, the ex-spy might well "begin to cash in what he considers to be certain 'chips' that he holds: namely, his record of clandestine cooperation with this or other agencies of the United States government."

Besides the CIA, those "other agencies" meant one in particular: the FBI. Soobzokov had worked not only for the CIA, but for the G-men at the bureau as well. As a confidential FBI informant, Soobzokov had thrown its investigators countless leads about suspected Communists over the years, essentially infiltrating his brethren in the immigrant community. FBI director J. Edgar Hoover had personally referred him for the job. Soobzokov was a Communist hunter, and a passionate one at that. If there were Soviet sympathizers in New Jersey, he worked to find them. Anyone was fair game. A few years earlier, in 1971, Soobzokov had reported to his FBI handler that a twelve-year-old boy in the neighborhood had voiced a vague interest in someday visiting Russia to see his family's roots in the Caucasus; Soobzokov suspected the boy might be vulnerable to Communist exploitation and advised the FBI to keep an eye on him. The FBI duly opened a file on the youngster.

Now, with his own name in the news, Soobzokov seemed ready to tell everything he knew. To protect himself from the curse of the Nazi label, he might fight back by blackmailing Washington's whole intelligence apparatus.

Grunz was worried. He could only imagine the headlines: *CIA Tied to Nazi Henchman.* The spy agency didn't need that kind of scrutiny, not with all the stories already bubbling up over the last few months about its ugly involvement in foreign assassinations, illegal spying on Vietnam protesters, and President Nixon's dirty tricks in Watergate. Now it might be in bed with a Nazi, too? Wonderful.

Grunz laid out the unattractive possibilities for the CIA if Soobzokov were to go public with his story. "If in defending himself," Grunz wrote his bosses, "he were to surface the fact that he had once worked for CIA, and given the present climate of intense media interest in anything having to do with CIA, it would seem likely that both the vote-hungry Congresswoman from New York and the Pulitzer-hungry journalist would very quickly zero in on the story and milk it for all it's worth."

How exposed was the CIA? Grunz couldn't be certain. Soobzokov's secret agency file from the 1950s had mysteriously gone missing, Grunz discovered after making a few calls. Even Nostril's colorful code name had somehow been changed. It was all very odd.

One thing was clear: the CIA wanted nothing to do with Soobzokov. Four days after his initial phone calls, Grunz got his orders from CIA attorneys: Soobzokov could get a private lawyer or "pursue whatever course of action he may think desirable," they said, but the CIA wouldn't help him; Nostril was on his own.

So was Soobzokov actually the Nazi war criminal that his neighbors were making him out to be? Grunz provided his higher-ups at the CIA no answer to that central question. Whatever insight the CIA's own files might provide — whatever America's foremost intelligence agency had turned up in all those years of background checks and lie-detector tests and psychological reports on its Communist-chasing spy — remained hidden away, or destroyed. But whether Soobzokov was a monster or a martyr mattered little at the moment to Grunz. What mattered right now was shutting this thing down.

This could get messy, Grunz realized. Very messy.

The Nazis Next Door

1

Liberation

Spring 1945

FÖHRENWALD DISPLACED PERSONS CAMP, OUTSIDE MUNICH

While the Nazis fled, their victims were left to languish.

These were the "lucky" ones: hundreds of thousands of Jews, Catholics, gays, Jehovah's Witnesses, Communists, Roma, and other "parasites" enslaved in Nazi concentration camps who, somehow, had managed to survive Hitler's genocidal killing machine. Yet even after Germany's defeat, the survivors remained imprisoned for months in the same camps where the Nazis had first put them to rot.

The names of their jailers had changed, with the dark Nazi swastikas now replaced by the bright-colored flags of the Allied victors flying above the camps, but the barbed wire fences and armed guards still encircled them. They were in a postwar purgatory, living in horrific conditions that a high-level emissary of President Truman would compare to those imposed by the Nazis themselves.

Jacob Biber, a Jew who survived the Nazi purge in the Ukraine, was among the masses confined in the American DP camp at Föhrenwald. "We felt like so much surplus junk," Biber would write of his confinement, "human garbage which the governments of the world wished would somehow go away."

The conditions faced by the survivors inside the Allied DP camps after Germany's defeat that fateful spring of 1945 were revolting in their own right. What made their confinement even more unthinkable was that, all the while, their Nazi tormentors were scattering to the winds. With few obstacles in their path, thousands of Hitler's helpers were heading to America, visas in hand, to start their lives anew. The flight of the Nazis, in the face of the survivors' brutal treatment at the hands of their Allied rescuers, amounted to one final, damning indignity.

The chilling irony could be reduced to simple math: every Nazi who managed to get a golden ticket out of Europe for passage to America meant one fewer "displaced person" in the Allied camps who would be able to get out. Visas to America, especially in the early months and years after the war, were precious and few; with more than seven million people across Europe left stateless, only forty thousand people were admitted to the United States in the first three years after the war, despite calls for America to open its shores. Lingering anti-Semitism meant the denial of visas en masse to Holocaust survivors crammed into the DP camps. Yet Nazi collaborators and even SS members in Hitler's reign of persecution, men who had proudly worn the Nazi uniform, were often able to enter the United States as "war refugees."

Thousands of Nazis sneaked in on their own, easily gaming the American immigration system. But hundreds more had help — from senior military and intelligence officials at the Pentagon, the CIA, and other agencies who believed that the new immigrants — despite their obvious Nazi ties, or sometimes because of them — could help vanquish the Soviet menace. No one hated the Soviets more than the Nazis, officials in Washington liked to say, and they wanted to exploit that enmity.

So it was that the United States became home to men like Jakob Reimer, a Ukrainian who settled in Queens and made a good living running a restaurant and selling potato chips. In coming to America in 1952, Reimer described himself as a German POW who worked an office job in the war years. Left out of his official biography were the more haunting aspects of his wartime service: raiding Jewish villages as a decorated SS officer, and training Nazi guards at Trawniki. American immigration officials did not press him to explain what he had done during the war, and he wasn't going to volunteer it. He got a visa with little difficulty, while Holocaust survivors in Europe struggled to find someplace that would take them. As an American prosecutor told a judge decades later: "He was never entitled to immigrate to the United States . . . There were only a limited number of visas back then, and Mr. Reimer took the visa of a real victim."

And so, with horror-ridden places like Warsaw and Trawniki and Auschwitz effectively whited out of their histories, Reimer and thousands like him were able to remake themselves into just the type of wartime refugee the United States was willing to welcome to its shores. They had become Americans.

The Allies had come at Hitler from all sides in those early months of 1945; the Russians from the east; the Americans and the British from the west. One by one, the Allied forces discovered scenes of horror and madness in concentration camps abandoned by the retreating Nazis. Inside the camps remained tens of thousands of survivors amid heaps of unburied corpses. Generations later, the mind's eye imagines the world embracing the survivors: the iron gates to the camps must have swung open at the arrival of the Allied forces, with a mass of bone-thin victims pouring into the awaiting arms of a world filled at once with shock, guilt, and joy over their rescue. Like trapped coal miners freed from a mineshaft, or a wrongly accused prisoner finally let out of prison, they were free at last. Home-cooked meals, warm beds, hot showers, and attentive doctors must have awaited them.

The reality was much darker.

Many thousands of the survivors did not leave the Allied camps; some not for months, some not for years, some not at all. Thousands died from disease and malnourishment even after Hitler's defeat. At Dachau, at Bergen-Belsen, and at dozens of DP camps like them, they remained jailed inside the walls that Hitler had erected. With the survivors surrounded by the stench of death and squalor, the liberating Allied forces, led by General Dwight D. Eisenhower, would not allow them to leave. The world didn't know what to do with them.

Crowded and ill fed, the survivors were left to wear their striped camp uniforms, the same uniforms that had become such a toxic symbol of Nazi oppression. In some DP camps, they were bunked side by side with Nazi POWs who were held there as well — people who, just months earlier, had been their wartime tormentors. Some Nazi prisoners were even put in charge of Jewish inmates at the Allied camps, ruling over them even in defeat. Exiled Jews in the camps who were originally from Germany, Austria, and other Axis nations were classified and treated by the Allies not as victims but as "enemy nationals" because of their countries of origin, no different from the Nazi prisoners jailed with them.

Just as remarkably, thousands of German doctors and nurses who had inflicted the Nazis' grotesque brand of medical care at the concentration camps were still being deployed at the DP camps — except now they worked for the Allies. At Dachau alone, more than six hundred medical personnel from the Germans' Wehrmacht military division — doctors, dentists, nurses, and orderlies — now counted themselves as members of the Allied medical staff, handling the survivors.

Many of the Germans had it better. At Allied-run camps reserved for German prisoners of war, ex-Nazi officers watched movies, played soccer, even took college courses. At Jewish DP camps, meanwhile, the Holocaust survivors fought merely to get extra rations of soggy black bread and coffee to make up for the starvation of the war years. American officials resisted; they complained that the Jews were getting "preferential" treatment and were using black-market systems at the camps to violate limits on food rations. The situation became so volatile that German police — with the consent of American officials — staged a raid on black-market activities in the Stuttgart and Landsberg camps in early 1946; rioting broke out, with police killing one Jewish DP. He had survived the Holocaust, but not its aftermath.

With word of the survivors' conditions filtering back to Washington, President Truman sent a special emissary, Earl Harrison, a former immigration commissioner who was dean of the University of Pennsylvania law school, to inspect the DP camps and assess the plight, in particular, of the Jewish refugees. The World Jewish Congress and other humanitarian organizations were protesting "conditions of abject misery." The reports seemed unbelievable. Could these horrific accounts of squalor, desperation, and mistreatment among the survivors — all in the wake of the Allied victory — really be true? Harrison was told to find out.

Harrison's blistering conclusions cast a pall over America's postwar euphoria. His findings were an indictment of the United States' refugee effort in the harshest terms he knew. "As matters now stand," Harrison wrote to Truman after touring the DP camps, "we appear to be treating the Jews as the Nazis treated them except that we do not exterminate them." The Nazis' victims, the dean found, were being victimized once again — but this time by the Americans.

General George S. Patton, the gruff war hero whose soldiers ran the American DP camps, fumed over Harrison's findings. Publicly, the general — Old Blood and Guts, as he was famously known — had adopted a posture of shock and revulsion that spring over the Allies' discovery of the Nazi death camps, and he urged journalists to see for themselves the horrors inflicted on the victims. Privately, however, General Patton held the surviving Jews in his camps in utter contempt.

"Harrison and his ilk believe that the Displaced Person is a human being, which he is not, and this applies particularly to the Jews who are lower than animals," Patton wrote in his diary after learning of the scathing report to Truman. Laying bare the rabid anti-Semitism that infected the American refugee effort, Patton complained of how the Jews in one DP camp, with "no sense of human relationships," would defecate on the floors and live in filth like lazy "locusts." He told of taking General Eisenhower to tour a makeshift synagogue that the Jews in the camp had set up to celebrate the holy day of Yom Kippur. "We entered the synagogue which was packed with the greatest stinking mass of humanity I have ever seen." This was Eisenhower's first glimpse of the DPs, Patton wrote, so it was all new to him. "Of course, I have seen them since the beginning and marveled that beings alleged to be made in the form of God can look the way they do or act the way they act."

Sadly, Patton's contempt for the Jews — from the man responsible for overseeing the survivors of the biggest genocide in world history — was not that unusual among Washington's elite. The Jews "do not desire to work, but expect to be cared for," one Senate lawyer wrote in seeking to limit the number allowed into the country after the war. "It is very doubtful that any country would desire these people as immigrants." President Truman's wife, Bess, did not welcome Jews in her home, and the president himself was known privately to deride "kikes" and "Jew boys." Still, with Britain blocking Jews from going to Palestine and the United States closing its own doors for the most part, Truman agonized over the situation in the DP camps. "Everyone else who's been dragged from his country has somewhere to go back to," Truman said, "but the Jews have no place to go."

The sense of hopelessness among the survivors trapped in the DP camps was overwhelming. They would sing old Yiddish folk songs with the children, with the words changed to reflect their plight. *Where can I go?* asked one song. *Who can answer me? Where can I go to? When every door is locked?*

Föhrenwald, near Munich, where Jacob Biber was held, was considered one of the more humanely run camps, with passable conditions and decent hygiene, yet the desperation among the prisoners was wrenching.

"A general malaise was growing as we realized how indifferent the world was to our tragedy," Biber wrote of his experience there. "Soon we began seeing men and women who had survived the worst tragedies imaginable during the war years suddenly killing themselves, often by hanging. Such events, added to the news that Palestine remained closed to us, guarded by British soldiers who were turning away DP's by the thousands, only added to our gloom."

And what of the Nazis?

While the Jacob Bibers of the Holocaust remained trapped inside the barbwired DP camps in the spring of 1945, thousands of Nazis were en route to Italy, to South America, to Australia, to Canada, and to America. With Germany's ultimate defeat foretold since early 1945, many of Hitler's henchmen had been plotting their escape for months, complete with fraudulent paperwork, fake names, hidden cash, and possible escape routes.

Rescuing themselves meant remaking themselves, erasing their pasts as persecutors and inventing new futures for themselves as supposed refugees. They would no longer be Nazis; they would become the victims. The more brazen among them might even pose as *anti*-Nazis. Otto von Bolschwing had been an influential aide in the Nazi Security Service's "Jewish Affairs" office before the war, but by 1945 he realized the days of the Third Reich were numbered. By war's end he was reworking his biography — claiming to be an opponent of Hitler who had tried to assassinate him — and volunteering himself as an informant to American military officials in Germany. His work was so well regarded that he was able to collect letters of reference from the U.S. Army praising him for the intelligence he provided on his former Nazi partners; within a few years, the CIA would take him on as a spy of its own, cleanse his Nazi record, and relocate him to America to begin a lucrative career in the export business. His Nazi past was long forgotten.

Many of the self-styled refugees cast themselves as apolitical, men without a state whose lives had been torn apart by someone else's bloody war. When Dmytro Sawchuk got a visa to come to America in 1951 as a refugee and start a new life in the Catskills, he told U.S. immigration officials that he had been a common farmer and woodcutter in Poland during the war. In fact, he had been an armed guard at three Nazi concentration camps, lording over prisoners who were forced to burn the corpses of fellow Jews, and he had taken part in a mass murder at a Jewish ghetto in Poland. It would be nearly four decades before his lies were revealed.

And Tom Soobzokov? The Führer of the North Caucasus, as some of his fellow countrymen called him, was reinventing himself as well. He was still wearing his Waffen SS officer's uniform when the Brits arrested him in Austria at the end of the war. But Soobzokov escaped from a truck full of Nazi prisoners and began a postwar journey that would take him from a DP camp in Italy to a refugee enclave in the Middle East and finally to a new life in Paterson, New Jersey.

In his official records, Soobzokov now listed himself as an ex–prisoner of war forced into hard labor by the Nazis. "Refugee + forced laborer," a relief aide scrawled after interviewing him in 1946 at the Italian DP camp. "Asks for help to emigrate . . . and help him financially," his file noted.

He, too, was now a victim.

Italy would prove a popular transit point for thousands of Nazis looking to make their escape from Europe — not just because of its easy access to the sea, but because of its politics. Italy, of course, had been one of Germany's original Axis partners under its fascist dictator, Benito Mussolini, and even after its surrender to the Allies in 1943, large pockets of the country remained in the stranglehold of the Nazis for the rest of the war. German was still the dominant language in some regions of northern Italy. Indeed, even after Hitler's defeat, it was tough to tell who was running some regions. "Did We Beat the Nazis or Not?" a headline in *Stars and Stripes,* the American military newspaper, asked days after the surrender, as uniformed SS officers were still roaming freely and running operations in the Tyrol region. With the Germans still in control, Nazi fugitives were able to navigate the area almost at will and make their escape out to sea and to points beyond.

They had help — from two of the most powerful institutions in the region. The Vatican and the Red Cross were each complicit in helping the fleeing Nazis gain shelter, travel documents, and escape routes from Italy, years of documentation would show. The Italian "rat line," as the escape route became known, was no secret to the United States. In 1947, two years after the war, a secret cable on the Nazis' flight from a State Department official based in Italy called the Vatican "the largest single organization involved in the illegal movement of emigrants," and concluded that church leaders had helped "former Nazis and former Fascists" to flee Europe for South America and elsewhere "so long as they are anti-Communist."

One Catholic bishop, a longtime anti-Semite named Alois Hudal, was so sympathetic to the Nazis, and so prolific in shepherding them to safety, that he became known as the Brown Bishop, an ode to the color of the Nazi uniforms. Church leaders like Hudal wanted not only to thwart the godless Communists, but also to expand their religious base — the "propagation of the faith," as the State Department cable put it. If expanding the faith meant protecting Nazis, so be it. "It is the Vatican's desire to assist any person, regardless of nationality or political beliefs as long as that person can prove himself a Catholic," the memo said. "This of course from the practical point of view is a dangerous practice."

With easy passage overseas, notorious Nazi war criminals like Adolf Eichmann and Josef Mengele, fugitives implicated in millions of murders during the Holocaust, were soon on their way to Latin America after the war ended. American officials knew that the Nazis had "easy entrée to South America" from Italy, with false documents rampant, but they decided not to press their allies to keep them out. There was nothing to be gained, U.S. officials concluded.

There was good reason to go easy on the Nazis' rat line. Not only did American officials know about its existence within a few years of the war's end, but they sometimes used the line themselves — through their contacts with another infamous Catholic clergyman, a Croation fascist named Krunoslav Draganovic. Father Draganovic ran a black-market operation smuggling war fugitives out of Europe, and American officials sometimes went to him for assistance. When U.S. Army officers needed help finding safe passage for a group of anti-Communist "visitors" in Austria who were wanted by the Russians — men who no doubt had ties to Hitler — they turned to the priest to hide them in "safe haven houses" in Italy and then get them to South America. "This, of course, was done illegally, inasmuch as such persons could not possibly qualify for eligibility" under refugee guidelines, an Army officer wrote in a top-secret memo. The rat line was a useful tool for American officials in their new Cold War struggle, but they couldn't admit that publicly. Officially, the United States needed to keep its distance from the priest, even as it was using him to shuttle fugitives to South America. Draganovic "is known and recorded as a Fascist, war criminal, etc, and his contacts with South American diplomats of a similar class are not generally approved by U.S. State Department officials," the secret cable said. "It is better that we be able to state, if forced . . . that we are not engaged in illegal disposition of war criminals, defectees and the like."

U.S. officials had a second powerful reason for wanting to play down the Nazis' escape route to South America. They knew that another lesser-known route, largely invisible to the public, was also being plowed, and it led straight to America. The United States, fabled refuge for the world's tired, its poor, and its huddled masses, was a beacon for Nazi war criminals as well. Even as the United States was casting blame on the Vatican for shepherding Hitler's minions to freedom, it was doing much the same itself, creating a safe haven for the Nazis in America.

Just months after Germany's surrender, U.S. Army investigators made a startling discovery: the flight of Nazis to the United States had actually started years earlier — during Hitler's rise to power. Four gunnysacks retrieved at a paper mill near Munich, filled with German war documents that were destined for shredding, led the investigators to a hidden trove of Nazi Party ID cards that cataloged Hitler's rank-and-file supporters. To the alarm of Army officials, nearly seven hundred of the card-carrying Nazi Party members had left Germany for America beginning in the mid-1930s; many of them were allowed into the country even after Hitler and the Nazis had invaded Poland in 1939 and set off World War II.

These were not Germans who were somehow "forced" into Nazi membership and were fleeing Hitler, the Army investigators concluded. These were Nazi Party members who had passed rigorous loyalty oaths, marched with the Nazis, and volunteered their support for the party and its racial ideologies. They were all listed with their names and new addresses in the United States. A banker in New York City. A chemist in Pennsylvania. A musician in Chicago. A pastry chef in New Orleans. A doctor in Oakland.

A student in Los Angeles. All had pledged their allegiance to Hitler and the Nazis, yet now called themselves Americans. Nothing was ever done about them.

With Hitler's defeat, the flight of the Nazis to America only accelerated. The true total of fugitives may never be known, but the number of postwar immigrants with clear ties to the Nazis likely surpassed ten thousand, from concentration camp guards and SS officers to top Third Reich policymakers, leaders of Nazi puppet states, and other Third Reich collaborators.

Some entered openly. In through the front door came more than sixteen hundred Nazi scientists and doctors, men who were eagerly recruited to the United States by the Pentagon. Military leaders wanted desperately not only to exploit their scientific and medical achievements, but also to prevent the Russians from seizing their work first. They provided the scientists with visas, houses, offices, and research assistants. Officially, the top-secret program — known as Project Paperclip — was banned to any "ardent" Nazi who took part in wartime persecution. But this was a fig leaf, a bureaucratic cover that was routinely ignored, as the U.S. government brought in professionals with direct links to Nazi atrocities and helped some of them "cleanse" their war records. The fact that a number of them had built rockets on the backs of slave laborers at concentration camps, or performed hideous medical experiments on concentration camp prisoners, was of little concern. Whatever moral baggage they brought with them was outweighed, military officials believed, by the promise of technological breakthroughs.

The most famous of these scientists was Wernher von Braun. At the very end of the war, at a ski chalet in the Alps along the German-Austrian border, von Braun, a committed Nazi under Hitler who used slave laborers in a mountain factory to build the V-2 rockets that bombed London, was already planning his exit to America as he listened to radio reports on Hitler's suicide. The war seemed far away. "There I was living royally in a ski hotel on a mountain plateau," he boasted years later from his new home in Huntsville, Alabama, where he had become an honored American scientist. "The hotel service was excellent."

Then there were the Nazi spies, hundreds of them, employed by U.S. intelligence agencies in both Europe and the United States. They came in through a side door — not formally invited to the postwar party, but welcomed eagerly nonetheless. Rabid anti-Communists like Tom Soobzo-kov in New Jersey and Otto von Bolschwing in New York, they had been recruited by American intelligence agencies, including the CIA and the FBI, to help get information on the Soviets. The intelligence that most of America's Nazi spies peddled to the government usually proved useless or, worse, flat-out wrong. But they were anti-Communist, and in the Cold War era, that was all that mattered. Like Hitler's scientists and doctors, the Nazi spies were now part of the American team, too.

And in through the back door came the biggest group yet: thousands of everyday SS personnel, war criminals and collaborators like Jakob Reimer, the SS officer turned potato chip salesman. They sneaked into America as reformed "refugees," with their only help from the American government coming in the form of an inept immigration system that made it easy for them to bury their pasts. They came because no one stopped them. False documents might get them entry, or a relative in America willing to vouch for them, or even a friendly American immigration interviewer who could coach them on what to put in a visa application — and what not to men-tion. Doing farm work during the war was a definite plus; wearing the SS uniform or serving in a concentration camp was not. "Better you don't put that in the papers," one Nazi SS officer at Trawniki was told by an in-terviewer after he claimed to be a lowly bartender at the concentration camp.

For Andrija Artukovic, getting into the United States was as simple as using a fake name. After he was granted what was supposed to be a ninety-day visitor's visa in 1948, Artukovic settled on a quiet beach south of Los Angeles and began working for a construction company that his brother owned. He ended up staying for nearly forty years. Had he used his real name, or had immigration officials dug deeper, it might have been evident that Artukovic was a top cabinet minister in the Nazi puppet government in Croatia, or that he had reputedly ordered the murder and imprisonment of some 600,000 of his countrymen, or even that Yugoslavian war crimes investigators wanted to arrest the man known there as the Butcher of the Balkans. But none of that was revealed. To immigration officials, he was simply another visitor traveling to the United States from Europe.

Like Artukovic, many Nazi collaborators came from Eastern Europe. Hundreds of fugitives with Nazi ties came from Germany, but many more who wound up in America were collaborators from Nazi-controlled countries like Lithuania, Latvia, Estonia, and the Ukraine. American immigration policies made it easy for them to come. In the first few years after the war, fully 40 percent of all the visas granted by the United States were set aside for war refugees from the Baltics. The Baltic immigrants — unlike the would-be Jewish immigrants derided by Washington policymakers as lazy and ungodly — were seen instead as hardworking, industrious, and, in the racist language of the day, "of good stock and good breeding," and they were welcomed eagerly to America. The bulk of the hundreds of thousands of Baltic immigrants claiming visas to the United States were no doubt legitimate refugees of war. But thousands among them were not. In vast swaths of Eastern Europe that had eagerly thrown their support behind Hitler, many of the people awarded visas from the Baltics were, as one immigration official put it, "individuals who served the Nazis as traitors and persons who committed atrocities against the Jews." These were Hitler's henchmen, collaborators who had greased the wheels of Hitler's killing machine as concentration camp supervisors and guards; as SS "death squad" officers and "liquidators" of Jewish ghettos; as regional police chiefs who issued the racist decrees and death orders for thousands of Nazi victims. They were "a thousand little Führers," as Robert Jackson, the Supreme Court justice turned Nazi prosecutor at Nuremberg, called Hitler's helpers. And yet, despite their dark pasts, they had little difficulty camouflaging themselves among the refugees seeking a haven in America. Immigration screeners were too ill trained, or uninterested, to spot them. A few immigration employees complained: ex-Nazis with the mark of the SS on their arms who had "committed atrocities against the Jews" were using fake papers to pass themselves off as war refugees and slip into America. Their protests went unheeded. The gates remained open.

For decades, the ex-Nazis lived American lives that were usually remarkable only for how quiet and uneventful they were. They were snapshots of the eclectic immigrant experience little different from those of millions of other immigrants. Whatever had happened during the war was now long passed. They became factory workers in Ohio and janitors in Illinois, car salesmen in New Jersey and life insurance agents in California. They raised children, sending them off to the military or to college. If their own wartime experiences in Europe seemed mysterious or unexplained, few noticed, and even fewer cared. A few muckrakers sounded a clarion call: there are Nazi war criminals living among us. But the gadflies were ignored or, worse, harassed by the FBI and the CIA for prying too deeply into America's dark secret.

Only grudgingly, in the late 1970s, more than three decades after the war had ended, would the nation begin to wake up to the reality that there were indeed legions of ex-Nazis living freely in their adopted homeland, unburdened by their past sins. The shame of a decades-long silence began to lift, and the government committed itself belatedly to trying to track down the Nazi fugitives. It proved a quixotic journey. Hundreds were investigated, and dozens deported. But with every success came another setback, as America's newfound desire to atone for the past collided squarely with the ongoing Cold War against the Soviets. America's notions of justice and due process were tested. It was an imperfect justice, and it would pit eyewitness against eyewitness, immigrant against immigrant, prosecutor against prosecutor, even Jew against Jew in the struggle to rid America of Nazi war criminals. The American justice system had never undertaken a challenge quite so daunting and complex, as it sought to hold its own citizens accountable for horrific crimes committed decades ago and an ocean away. This long after the war, many asked, why bother? Even if prosecutors could beat the long legal odds, was it really worth dredging up the past?

"It is all forgotten," Jakob Reimer, the ex-SS officer in Queens, said when confronted with the details of his Nazi crimes in an American courtroom more than a half century later. "It's all over."

2

The Good Nazis

March 1945

ZURICH, SWITZERLAND

The unholy alliance between the United States and the Nazis began with an ambitious American spy chief in Europe, a brutal Nazi general, a bottle of Scotch, and a secret fireside chat at a Swiss safe house.

Allen Welsh Dulles was America's top spy in Switzerland in charge of gathering wartime intelligence on Hitler. Nazi general Karl Wolff was the onetime right-hand man to SS chief Heinrich Himmler. Together, they sat by a crackling fire in the elegant library of a Zurich apartment for a pleasant conversation in early 1945. They spoke in German. America was still at war with Hitler, and the last shots of the Battle of Berlin would not be fired for another two months, but the two men — one the future director of the CIA, the other a leading Nazi general in the notorious Waffen SS — already had mutual interests to discuss. General Wolff realized the war was lost, and he wanted protection from the war crimes charges that were sure to follow him. Dulles wanted Wolff's help in getting the Nazi SS men in Italy whom Wolff controlled to lay down their arms early — before what appeared to be the inevitable German surrender. Perhaps just as important in the long term, he saw the "moderate" Wolff as an ally in confronting the next big threat: the Russians. Wolff and his motley crew of Nazi underlings in Italy offered Dulles the promise of developing a long-term source of intelligence that could be turned against Stalin and the Russians once a postwar Germany was formed.

The moment was a harbinger. In the coming years, Dulles and America's spy services would put to work hundreds of former Nazis as spies and operatives in both Europe and the United States as part of the new Cold War ethos. "Wolffie," thanks to Dulles, was the first big-name Nazi to help open the floodgates.

This rapprochement was a turn few could have predicted. For three and a half years, Hitler and the Nazis had been America's wartime obsession in the European theater. The Nazis were the tyrannical warmongers denounced by FDR for "acts of savagery" and "inhuman and barbarous activity." More than 185,000 American soldiers had lost their lives fighting in Europe. America's obsession with Hitler's aggression knew few limits. Fears reached such a fevered pitch during the war that, in one little-known operation, American officials even persuaded their Latin American neighbors to deport some four thousand ethnic Germans living in Colombia, Guatemala, and elsewhere — sending them to the United States to be imprisoned as "enemy aliens." Every German in the Americas, no matter how assimilated, could be suspected of plotting a "fifth column" attack on the United States. Few if any of the German natives had actual ties to Hitler, but FDR was taking no chances.

Yet now here was Allen Dulles sharing a fireside Scotch with Himmler's former chief of staff. To begin talks so abruptly with high-level Nazis was an astounding pivot. Even before Germany's ultimate surrender, the fear of all things Nazi was cooling quickly in the minds of American military and intelligence officials. As Hitler's war machine began to stall, the Nazis faded as the dominant threat they once were, and American officials were already beginning to plot how they would contain their new rival — the Soviets — in a Europe divided among the victors. A new mindset began to take shape: yes, there were ardent Nazi war criminals in Hitler's murderous regime, but serving side by side with them were moderate and "repentant" ones whose "heart had not really been in the Nazi cause," as one intelligence official said of none other than the notorious Nazi leader Hermann Göring. Perhaps America could tell the good Nazis from the bad, the thinking went, and turn the reformed ones to its advantage against the Soviets in what was to become a new cold war.

Dulles was a champion of the new mindset. With an ever-present smoking pipe in his hand and a bow tie crowning his tweed jacket, the Princeton-educated Dulles was the personification of a type: the Ivy League intelligence agent who came of age during World War II and went on to dominate the American spy business for generations. Beyond their blue-blood background, Dulles and his compatriots shared a single-minded contempt for the Soviet Union. Hitler was yesterday's enemy; Stalin was the existential threat that would outlive the war.

Dulles ran America's wartime intelligence operation in Europe from his perch in Bern, Switzerland. During the war, the secret spy cables he sent to his bosses in Washington were filled with intelligence not only on Hitler's military activities, but also on the ominous threat posed by America's wartime ally: the Russians. Again and again, Dulles would opine to Washington on Stalin's agenda and how it might affect the world balance after the war. Dulles appeared much less concerned about the everyday terror enveloping Europe. In Switzerland, he was getting regular reports about the Nazis' widespread massacre of Jews and European civilians, but his secret cables back to Washington included remarkably little on the topic. If reports of Jewish towns being evacuated and "liquidated" were mentioned at all in his cables, Dulles would pass them along to Washington either without comment or with an air of resignation. In 1943, his boss in Washington asked Dulles about a report that the Nazis had hauled four thousand children, some as young as two years old, in boxcars from Paris to "unknown destinations." Dulles responded that such reports "exist in all countries under German domination," but unless the United States was going to undertake a massive refugee program, "I do not see much that can be done in regard to this type of situation." Regardless, he said, the problem was outside his area of authority.

General Wolff was one of the senior SS leaders responsible for those massacres during the war. The general was a personal favorite of Hitler's; they were so close that the führer personally blessed Wolff's divorce and remarriage to his mistress after lower-level Nazis objected on principle. With a perpetual smile on his face, the blond, Nordic-looking Wolff would often appear at Himmler's side as the two men toured the concentration camp at Dachau, inspected French POWs, picked over antique Chippendale furniture and ornate rugs seized from Jews in occupied countries, or simply enjoyed a stroll in the countryside. The savagery of the camps was far from his mind. He "did not find the concentration camps pleasant," he conceded to one interviewer. Still, Wolff always made it a point to ask the prisoners how they were treated, he insisted; "none of them had ever complained." And what of those yellow Stars of David the Jews had to wear? "I had the impression," Wolff said, "that for the racially conscious Jews, it was an honor."

Prosecutors at Nuremberg weren't fooled by his shameless sophistry. Wolff, they concluded after the war, was Himmler's "bureaucrat of death." He had worked with steel-cold precision to help set up the network of boxcars used to "resettle" the Jews of Poland and herd them like cattle to their deaths. He watched the grisly medical experiments that Himmler wanted performed on prisoners at Dachau. He commanded the SS troops in Italy responsible for killing thousands of Italian women and children. Dulles's own spy agency, the Office of Strategic Services, in a report just months after the war ended, blamed Wolff personally for the "wholesale slaughter of populations."

High-level Nazi or not, General Wolff proved to be more an opportunist than a loyalist. He realized in early 1945 that despite Hitler's promise of a secret weapon to win the war, the defeat of the Third Reich was inevitable. So, for weeks, a small group of Nazi SS officers in Italy who were loyal to him — Members of the Black Order, they called themselves — held clandestine meetings at his direction with Dulles's men to discuss a possible surrender. Wolff's motives were plain: he and his men saw in Dulles the chance, as one of them said, to "save their skins."

This was a dangerous game for both sides. Wolff and his men faced execution if Hitler were to find out about their treasonous talks. Dulles, meanwhile, risked contravening the unambiguous declaration from FDR, Churchill, and Stalin at Casablanca two years earlier that the Allied powers would accept nothing less than an unconditional surrender from the Nazis. There could be no negotiated concessions from a regime as heinous as Hitler's, and "the monstrous crimes of the Hitlerites" would not go unpunished, the Allied leaders had insisted. Stalin would no doubt be furious if he knew of the secret talks between the Americans and the Nazis. Officially, Dulles could offer Wolff nothing in return for his cooperation; no leniency, no immunity, nothing. Just the chance to surrender, with no official promises. But unofficially, it was clear that the conniving General Wolff saw Dulles as his best hope to escape the gallows for his war crimes.

Dulles had personally approved the secret meeting. "An intelligence officer should be free to talk to the Devil himself," he would later write, "if he could gain any useful knowledge for the conduct or the termination of the war." For his part, Wolff was thrilled that Dulles had agreed to sit down with him. To prepare for the meeting, the Nazi general sent along a glowing curriculum vitae with his credentials, his wartime accomplishments with the Nazis, and even a list of character references. Among them was Pope Pius XII, whom Wolff had met in Italy a year earlier. The documents represented what the Nazis called their *Persilscheine,* or "detergent," meant to wipe clean the past. Wolff's record needed scrubbing.

Although Dulles was impressed by the material, some Allied officers involved in preparing for the talks were repulsed at the very thought of meeting with Wolff and vowed indignantly that they would never shake hands with the Nazi general. Dulles held no such reservations. As they met that day in Zurich under heavy guard, the two men greeted each other warmly. Sitting around the fireplace, they discussed a few mutual acquaintances before turning to the prospects for a military surrender in Italy. Dulles had the right man, the general told him. "I control SS forces in Italy," Wolff said, and he could get them to lay down their arms for him with the war all but ended.

The next day, Dulles sent a secret telegram to Washington recapping what he excitedly viewed as a breakthrough meeting with Wolff. Much of the memo was devoted to how impressed he was with the Nazi general, a rose-colored view that ignored the many atrocities he had directed. "Wolff is [a] distinctive personality," Dulles wrote, and "dynamic," too. "Our reports and impressions indicate he represents more moderate element in Waffen SS, with mixture of romanticism." The general's aim, Dulles cabled, was to help lead Germany out of war and "end useless material and human destruction." Wolff was handsome and trustworthy, too, Dulles added later, and the Allies would be able to work with him. Those who had met him could plainly see that Wolff was "no ogre."

Dulles was also duly impressed by Wolff's Nazi deputies, the senior Black Order officers who had arranged the meeting. He learned that Nazi captain Guido Zimmer, "despite his membership of the SS, was a devout Catholic ... Zimmer, somewhat of an aesthete and an intellectual, was moved by a desire to save the art and religious treasures of Italy" from ruin if the war continued, Dulles wrote. "Zimmer seemed to be a misfit in the

SS ... He was good-looking, clean-cut, not the way one pictures the typical SS officer."

Wolff sought no special protection from war crimes charges, Dulles insisted in his cable. But he did make one small request. It seemed that the general, while commanding his Nazi troops in Italy, had managed to acquire some three million shares of equity in Italian companies. Whether these shares were looted from the Jews, Dulles did not say. In any event, Wolff had asked Dulles what he should do with them. European finance was an area Dulles knew well. He had worked before the war as a lawyer representing major European banks and companies, and he seemed unfazed by the brazen request. "I suggested that if possible he make available to us [a] list giving numbers and names where registered securities involved and meanwhile do what he can to protect certificates from being sent to Germany," Dulles cabled Washington. Dulles would make sure that the Nazi general's financial interests were safe with him.

General Wolff — the right-hand man to Himmler — now had the Americans on his side. A few weeks later, when a group of anti-Nazi partisans seized him at a villa near the Italian-Swiss border, Dulles's men dispatched a team to rescue him. They got him out safely. A grateful Wolff thanked his American rescuers with a bottle of Scotch whiskey and packs of Lucky Strike cigarettes. Dulles had become the Nazi's protector. In a last testament written as a precaution as the fighting in Italy continued, Wolff expressed the gratitude of a condemned man looking to his patron saint for redemption. "If after my death, my honor be assaulted," the general wrote, "I request Mr. Dulles to rehabilitate my name, publicizing my true, humane intentions."

Dulles got what he wanted in the negotiations: Wolff and his men in Italy agreed to lay down their arms to the Allied troops. It was, at least on its face, a military and intelligence coup that proved a capstone in Dulles's ascendant career, helping land him the job of CIA director eight years later, under President Eisenhower, side by side with his brother, John Foster Dulles, who was secretary of state. Viewed with any perspective, however, the early surrender did not hold up as the momentous occasion that Dulles had envisioned it. Coming just six days before the full surrender of Germany, its military impact was blunted. Lives were saved in Italy, to be sure, but most of them were likely Germans and Italians, not Americans. Moreover, the success of Dulles's maneuverings was overshadowed inside Roosevelt's White House by the furious diplomatic fallout that his secret negotiations with the Nazis created in the waning days of the war, as Stalin and FDR exchanged a series of angry missives over what the Russians saw as an American double cross.

Stalin charged that the secret surrender talks in Italy were a ploy to get the Germans to turn their full aggression to the Russians in the east. FDR, denying disingenuously that any negotiations had taken place, bemoaned that "such distrust, such lack of faith" threatened to sink their wartime alliance. Just days after writing his third and final letter to Stalin on the contretemps, FDR died. (Wolff sent Dulles a personal note of condolence.) The president's warnings about the damage to U.S.-Soviet relations proved prescient. Indeed, some historians would come to view the confrontation over the early surrender engineered by Dulles and Wolff as the first major flare-up of the Cold War, fueling distrust between Washington and Moscow for years just as peace was at hand.

After the war, Wolff needed his patron saint. Allied prosecutors at Nuremberg, unimpressed by Dulles's star Nazi, named him among a select group of some two dozen "major war criminals" facing possible death sentences. Wolff was held in an Allied POW camp along with other senior Nazis. Even in custody, however, it was clear that Wolffie had achieved a special place of favor afforded to few others. Technically a prisoner of war, he was allowed to continue wearing his German uniform and carrying a gun, and he even went yachting with his family one weekend at a lake in Austria. Nonetheless, he was miffed. Official denials aside, he claimed that Dulles and his men had in fact promised him full immunity from prosecution — along with a cabinet minister's spot in the new German government — in exchange for the Italian peace.

Dulles was already working the Nuremberg prosecutors to see that his ally would not face charges. He prepared affidavits in his defense, kept evidence of his crimes away from prosecutors, and rallied support for his man. So many of Wolff's underlings from the Black Order were now also claiming protection from the Americans in Europe for their work with Dulles that policymakers in Washington had to decide what to do about all of them. Word soon came back that the United States and its allies "owe some moral obligation" to Wolff and his Nazi men for their help. Famed spy chief James Angleton was even more blunt. "Military honor dictated that we honor the promises made to these men," he wrote to the Army in 1946 about the need for protecting two Wolff SS officers from war crimes prosecutions. One of the SS men, Eugen Dollmann, not only escaped prosecution, but hooked on with the CIA, peddling Soviet intelligence of dubious value. And with little explanation, Wolff himself soon disappeared from the list of major war criminals at Nuremberg. Improbably, the top SS man became a mere "witness" to Nazi atrocities. There was little doubt who was responsible. "It is thanks to Mr. Dulles that you were not included in the first Nuremberg trial list," a Swiss diplomat told Wolff.

The bombastic Nazi general showed little gratitude. He was a leading general in the Third Reich, and he demanded to be treated like one. He was the true victim, he thundered to one Allied interrogator in 1947. His continued confinement as a POW — after handing Italy to Dulles and the Americans on a "silver platter" — was worse than anything the Jews ever faced under Hitler, he blustered. "A Jew is killed in the gas chamber in a few seconds, without having an idea or even knowing it. My comrades and I have been allowed to die once every night for 21 months. This is much more inhumane than the extermination of the Jews."

Ultimately, Wolff, one of the highest-ranking SS officials to survive the war, was convicted by a British court in 1949 as a "minor offender," the equivalent of a traffic ticket usually reserved for Nazi privates, not SS generals. He was promptly released. His four years already spent in custody as a POW, yacht trips and all, were punishment enough, the court decided. He resumed a lucrative career in the German advertising industry and collected a German military pension for his service in the SS. Even so, Wolff remained upset, complaining for years that Dulles and the Americans had broken their promises to keep him out of trouble altogether. He even sent the Americans an itemized bill for some $50,000 in lost time, clothing, and property, as well as legal expenses. Dulles was not amused by his wartime partner's hubris. Wolff, he said, "doesn't realize what a lucky man he is not to be spending the rest of his days in jail, and his wisest policy would be to keep fairly quiet about the loss of a bit of underwear, etc. He might easily have lost more than his shirt."

• • •

Wolff and his Black Order deputies in the SS were only the beginning. American military officials had their sights set on an even bigger target for recruitment: the Nazi scientists and engineers responsible for building Hitler's war machine.

General Patton, Old Blood and Guts, was among the scientists' biggest admirers. As commander of the American-run zone in Bavaria in the immediate aftermath of the Allied victory, Patton showed an odd, almost perverse fondness for the German POWs in U.S. custody. Even as he was castigating the Jewish survivors as subhuman "locusts," Patton was hiring Nazis as camp administrators and allowing them to keep their posts in the civilian government. His actions ran afoul of General Eisenhower's orders calling for the "denazification" of Germany, but Patton didn't seem to care. He admired the Nazis' technical competence, military rules be damned, and he wanted them kept in positions of authority in the camps. "Listen," Patton told one of his officers, "if you need these men, keep them and don't worry about anything else."

Weeks after Germany's surrender, General Patton visited a German POW barracks and sought out a senior Nazi prisoner who was being held there, a German general and scientist named Walter Dornberger. A leading German rocketeer, Dornberger had run the Nazis' V-2 missile program and had overseen the work of Wernher von Braun and the other technical experts who built the missiles that Hitler had used in Europe to devastating effect. "Are you that guy who was in charge of the development of the V-2 rockets?" Patton asked Dornberger. "Jawohl, Herr General," Dornberger answered with a nod. Patton, impressed, pulled three cigars from his pocket and handed them to his Nazi rival. "My congratulations," Patton said. "I could not have done it."

Germany's production of the V-2, the world's first long-range ballistic missile, represented both the soaring heights of the Nazi regime's technological achievements and the barbaric depths of its inhumanity. At the Peenemünde rocket site and its successor, a sprawling underground facility called Dora-Mittelwerk, Hitler aspired to create a weapon unlike anything ever created — at any cost in lives and treasure. To build such a scientific marvel of destruction, the Nazis brought in tens of thousands of slave laborers from nearby concentration camps — Russians, French, Italians, Poles, Roma, Jews, and more. At Dora, the laborers slept head to feet in giant, dank tunnels connected to the rocket factory, then made the trek each day at gunpoint to begin their toils. Tasked with erecting Hitler's missiles, the laborers were worked to exhaustion. They were routinely starved, beaten, stabbed, whipped, tortured, and brutalized. The boldest of the lot — prisoners suspected of plotting rebellion or sabotaging missiles — were hanged in the roll-call square, or sometimes in the factory from a giant crane; not in one fell swoop, but inch by inch, in slow, agonizing fashion. Nazi secretaries from the cavernous factory would come watch the spectacle for amusement. Prisoners were made to watch, too, as the limp corpses were left hanging for hours to warn the workers what would befall them if they interfered with Hitler's missiles.

Every day, twenty or so prisoners died from the diseases that were rampant amid the corpses, feces, and vermin in the tunnels. At the start of the day, a Nazi doctor would inspect the prisoners to determine which ones were strong enough to work on the rockets and which ones would be sent to a makeshift hospital set up to keep the laborers sufficiently alive to work. A French prisoner at the Dora-Mittelwerk camp, Michel Fliecx, recounted what happened when he came down ill one day in 1944. "I was transported on a stretcher from the tunnel . . . I was hoping they'd send me to the hospital. But no, they judged me still to be in too good shape; you had to be in the throes of death to get in now. I was again sent off . . . to the room reserved for those with dysentery . . . The first thing that hit me was a foul stench . . . On all sides, lying on disgusting straw mattresses, were skeletons, their dirty gray skin hanging from them."

The factory at Dora-Mittelwerk was an assembly line of death. The more V-2 missiles Hitler wanted to launch across Europe, and the more quickly he wanted them built, the more hellish the work conditions for the slave laborers became. The factories were a demonic testament to Hitler's determination to contort science and technology to fit his own twisted aims. "Leading men of science above all are to make research fruitful for warfare," Hitler had declared in 1942, "by working together in their special fields."

The victorious Americans saw the ballistic firepower that Hitler's team of experts had created. The impressive German war machine, from planes and rockets to tanks and submarines, had nearly subsumed Europe. Military officials were amazed that a country of Germany's size and relatively meager supply of raw materials had been able to achieve such battlefield dominance. They credited Hitler's scientists, and they were determined to claim the Nazi brain trust for themselves. American commanders saw it as a matter of survival in the postwar world. Russia, the new enemy, was already enticing German scientists to its side with all sorts of promises; there were even reports that Moscow was kidnapping unwilling scientists and bringing them across to the Russian occupation zone. The Americans wanted their share. For both Washington and Moscow, Hitler's scientists had become the spoils of war.

Even before Germany's ultimate defeat, as the Allies were driving the Nazis back from one stronghold after another, American scientific and military teams were dispatched to search through newly seized areas, confiscate the reams of research records left behind, examine the equipment and technology that had driven Hitler's brutal army, and interrogate Nazi scientists. A batch of SS chief Himmler's records on Nazi medical experiments, hidden in a cave, was among the troves recovered. But Washington had bigger plans. Military officials were intent on exploiting the Nazis' advances not just by seizing records and interrogating Hitler's scientists, but by bringing those scientists to America — as researchers for the United States military.

The secret program began almost immediately after the war, and it would ultimately bring more than sixteen hundred German scientists to America. Within the Truman administration, the idea was controversial from the start. State Department officials were adamant in their opposition, particularly over the idea of importing specialists who had produced the deadly chemicals used in Hitler's gas chambers. "We should do everything we consistently can to prevent German chemists and others from entering this country," warned one immigration official — to no avail. The military won out. In September 1946, President Truman gave the War Department the formal go-ahead to bring a limited group of Germany's top scientists back to America and put what they knew to use. The operation would have to be kept secret. If word leaked out that the military was bringing home Nazi agents — Hitler's "angels of death," one State Department official called them in protest — the public fallout in America and in Europe could be disastrous. The look of shock was plain on the face of another State Department diplomat when he learned that the military was looking to bring up to a thousand scientists into the country. It was clear from his reaction that State Department officials did not have "any idea such a number was contemplated and that this proposed number was not considered in the President's approval of a 'few' selected scientists," a military officer recounted.

The recruiting program became known as Project Paperclip, so called because officers reviewing the files of possible Nazi recruits would use paperclips to attach their German war records to their American papers. Their Nazi records and their American ambitions were now neatly joined as one. Within months, military officials had drawn up a list of twenty-four thousand German candidates from which to choose. These were not just rocket scientists. These were doctors and biologists; engineers and metallurgists; even a nutritionist, a printing pressman, and a curator of insects from the Berlin Museum. Nor were they all great scientists. "Their technical skills are only mediocre," a military officer wrote in assessing two rocket engineers assigned to an Ohio air base. One German scientist specializing in medical aviation, Dr. Konrad Schäfer, was brought to a military base in Texas even after Nuremberg prosecutors had linked him to Nazi medical atrocities. He was soon sent back to Germany — not because of his Nazi ties, but because he "displayed very little scientific acumen." The military could tolerate evidence of Dr. Schäfer's possible war crimes, but not his technical incompetence.

Some of the Paperclip recruits, in fact, weren't scientists at all. One, Herbert Axster, had been chief of staff to General Dornberger, the V-2 boss who earned Patton's admiration. Axster was brought to America not because of any technological expertise — he was a lawyer by trade — but because of his management experience helping to run the Nazis' missile plant at Peenemünde. He was as surprised as anyone to find himself bound for the United States. Imprisoned in Europe after the war and facing war crimes charges, he was startled to hear that he was heading to an air base in Texas with his colleagues von Braun, Dornberger, and other German scientists who had worked on the V-2 project. "I said, 'Why? I'm not a technician.'" An American colonel explained: "The US Army needs to know how Pennemünde was organized so we can organize our own rocket program."

Officially at least, any scientists who were active members of the Nazi Party under Hitler were banned. No war criminals need apply. "Generally speaking, these are outstanding men," a military officer bragged in a memo.

In practice, however, the supposed ban on ardent Nazis was a façade, and American military officials mocked the rules as meaningless. Bit by bit, the ban on Hitler's hard-core loyalists was washed away in a sea of bureaucracy. The background checks on the scientists' German affiliations were supposed to be completed before they were allowed into the United States, but for von Braun and hundreds of others, the reviews were not even started until long after the scientists were moved to housing at military bases around the country. Nazi Party affiliations would be allowed, the military finally decided, so long as the scientist submitted "a statement (of approximately one page in length) explaining such membership and extenuating circumstances, if any." If a scientist's first review came back negative, the military might simply do it again and change the result. "Ardent" Nazis suddenly became harmless ones.

Von Braun, the boy wonder of Germany's V-2 rocket program, was typical of the changing fortunes experienced by the Nazi scientists. At the close of the war, he was classified as a "potential security risk" because of his deep ties to Hitler and to the Nazi Party as a decorated officer. Within months, however, his hiring as a rocket scientist was suddenly reclassified as vital to America's national security. He was brought to Texas — along with his parents, his new bride, his brother, who was also a scientist at Peenemünde, and nearly a hundred members of his German V-2 team, now recongregated under von Braun at Fort Bliss.

Even with the standards for barring Nazi Party members virtually abandoned, military officials complained that their counterparts at the State Department and the Justice Department were still too slow to sign off on the scientists because of concerns about their Nazi records. Military officers fumed over the delays. The bureaucrats slowing the scientists' arrivals needed to bring "an iota of realism" to their task and to recognize that German scientists with Nazi links would ultimately have to be let in, the military's gatekeeper for the project, a Navy captain named Bosquet Wev, seethed in a memo in 1947. Echoing the views of other officers, the captain wrote: "In so far as German scientists are concerned, Nazism should no longer be considered a serious consideration from a viewpoint of national security when the far greater threat of Communism is now jeopardizing the entire world . . . To continue to treat Nazi affiliations as significant considerations has been aptly phrased as 'beating a dead Nazi horse.' Considerations such as these, which delay or prevent action being taken in the cases of scientists who can further the scientific research and development of the United States, are detriments which should be removed."

Soon enough, there was not even the pretense of keeping out Nazis, ardent or otherwise. The Air Force brought Emil Salmon, an SA Nazi troop leader, to an Ohio air base as a jet engineer, even after he was convicted in a denazification court of torching a synagogue. The military said it was "cognizant of Mr. Salmon's Nazi activities and certain allegations made by some of his associates in Europe, but desires his immigration in spite of this."

And so they came: German chemists from IG Farben, the notorious chemical company that supplied the deadly gases for the Nazi gas chambers; the rocket scientists under Dornberger and von Braun at the missile-building slave camps at Peenemünde and Dora-Mittelwerk; doctors at concentration camps who practiced their own brand of medicine on prisoners; and hundreds more. The professionals were generally paid six dollars a day in America and given comfortable housing, a laboratory with research assistants, and the promise of citizenship if their work proved valuable. Family members were welcome to join them later, too. The scientists were elated.

Despite the military's best efforts to keep the operation secret, word began leaking out within months of the arrival of the first batch of recruits in 1946. It was hard to hide a thousand scientists with German accents, even on a military base. As the State Department had warned, many Americans were outraged to learn that the military was bringing Hitler's scientists to live as their neighbors at military bases from Florida to California. Some objected on national security grounds: the Germans couldn't be trusted to stay loyal to America, they charged. Others voiced moral concerns; given their Nazi backgrounds, the scientists were "potentially dangerous carriers of racial and religious hatred," read one letter of protest signed in 1946 by Albert Einstein, Norman Vincent Peale, and some three dozen other noted Americans. One critic put out a mocking notice in a magazine: "Memo to would-be war criminal: If you enjoy mass murder, but also treasure your skin, be a scientist, son. It's the only way, nowadays, of getting away with murder."

With a backlash brewing, the military's PR people promoted feel-good stories in the media about the new German immigrants. Reporters in Texas were invited to watch as the recruits waited at the El Paso train station, flowers in hand, to be reunited with their wives, children, in-laws, and, in at least one case, a German mistress. The postal service even put out a stamp commemorating the Paperclip scientists' arrival at Fort Bliss in Texas. Such positive public images were essential, military officials believed, to counter the negative publicity generated by what one officer called "the natural Jewish bias against anything Nazi," and to ensure that Paperclip stayed on track.

Only on rare occasions did a recruit's wartime past surface. In 1952, influential newspaper columnist Drew Pearson wrote an article charging that one of the German medical scientists brought to Randolph Air Force Base outside San Antonio had approved "some of the ghastly medical experiments which the Nazis performed on hopeless victims." The scientist, Dr. Walter Schreiber, was implicated in exposing Polish girls to a gas form of gangrene. He had faced war crimes charges at Nuremberg, Pearson wrote. Yet the doctor was mysteriously "cleared" of the charges before the U.S. military brought him to America. Pearson's revelations caused no major outcry, no calls for broader investigation or congressional hearings into German scientists brought to America; just a few short stories deep inside the newspaper, and a letter of protest from a group of Boston physicians who said that the Air Force's employment of Dr. Schreiber was "a reflection not only of the moral standards of the medical profession but of the entire country."

At first, the military offered a tepid defense of Dr. Schreiber. The colonel who shepherded Schreiber's appointment insisted that the Air Force knew nothing about the horrific accusations unearthed by America's own investigators at Nuremberg. Regardless, the German doctor was the only person qualified to do the kind of medical research he was conducting in Texas, the colonel said. The defense was short-lived. Truman's people were unwilling to take the risk that a small, little-noticed news story involving a single Nazi scientist might mushroom into something much bigger that could sweep up hundreds of the newly arrived Germans. Within a few weeks of the column, the Truman administration announced that Dr. Schreiber was leaving America. The Air Force swooped him out of Texas — not to West Germany, where he might have faced trial for war crimes, but to safer confines in Argentina. Dr. Schreiber "indicated satisfaction with . . . his resettlement in Argentina," according to a secret Air Force account of the long-distance relocation. But the Nazi doctor did have one complaint over his treatment by his American handlers. He "voiced displeasure" that the military failed to give him any advance notice of the Argentine plan and was annoyed to have to read about it in the newspapers first.

The occasional embarrassment did nothing to slow the swelling numbers of German scientists entering the country. Military officials did everything they could to ease their transition and welcome them. German scientists in Alabama called one neighborhood outside Huntsville "Kraut Hill" because so many of them had found a comfortable home in the émigré community there. Sure, there were the occasional jokes. American officers at the base would laugh about the incongruity of hearing the Alabama rocket scientists singing German beer songs with a hint of a southern drawl, or of seeing the German doctors gallivanting through the air base in San Antonio in cowboy hats and western boots. But the connection to Nazi Germany was more a curiosity than any sort of scarlet letter. Colonel Paul Campbell, an Air Force doctor who helped bring some three dozen German doctors and medical researchers to Texas, promised the scientists there that "the day they took out their first American papers, we would no longer refer to them as Germans and would integrate them into our whole system, one way or the other." They would be "bonafide members of our American community," with their pasts safely behind them. And so they were.

Project Paperclip, as big as it was, was still just one pathway in America's Nazi rat line. Working side by side with the scientists were hundreds of Nazi operatives used as spies in Europe and America by the CIA and other U.S. intelligence agencies. There was no secret order, no formal presidential directive authorizing America's intelligence agencies to put these Nazis to work, at least not in the way that Truman and Eisenhower had done with the scientists. Opaque as always, America's spy agencies never mimeographed application forms or established guidelines to supposedly ban ardent Nazis, the way the War Department had with Hitler's engineers and doctors. But by the early 1950s, Allen Dulles at the CIA, J. Edgar Hoover at the FBI, and a handful of other senior American intelligence officials had in place around the globe a formidable network of their own of loosely linked and far-flung ex-SS men and Nazi operatives. They were the spy agencies' foot soldiers in the Cold War. In Europe, in the Middle East, in South America, and in the United States, hundreds of junior Karl Wolffs — ex-Nazis with ties to Hitler's brutality who were seen, nonetheless, as a bulwark against the Soviets — were now working for the Americans.

The network grew of its own momentum. One ex-Nazi agent recruited to work for the United States would lead to the next, and the next; one anti-Communist spy ring made up of scores of ex-SS men would produce another, and another. The field was dense by the time Eisenhower, the former World War II hero, became president in 1953. From Munich to New York and points in between, hundreds of Nazi officers who were the nation's sworn enemies just years earlier were now ostensibly on America's side as spies, informants, and intelligence "assets": fed and housed; paid and protected; dispatched and debriefed; code-named, cleansed, and coddled by their American handlers. That they had once worked for Hitler's Third Reich was of little concern.

"We knew what we were doing," said Harry Rositzke, a CIA officer who ran the agency's Soviet spy section in Munich in the early 1950s. "It was a visceral business of using any bastard as long as he was anti-Communist . . . The eagerness or desire to enlist collaborators means that sure, you didn't look at their credentials too closely." Wrote another CIA officer in 1953: "The West is fighting a desperate battle with the East, with the Soviets, and we will pick up any man who will help us defeat the Soviets — any man no matter what his Nazi record was."

As part of one secret spy program called Operation Happiness, the Americans provided a roster of newly freed ex-Gestapo officers with money, jobs for their children, promises of immunity, and a bevy of other enticements in exchange for their service. Even then, some of Hitler's men turned them down rather than work for Germany's conquerors. "A burned child avoids fire," remarked one ex-Gestapo leader, working as a watchmaker in West Germany a few years after the war, as he refused the Army's repeated overtures. He wouldn't work for them, the watchmaker told U.S. officials, "regardless of how much they would pay him." As badly as the Americans wanted the Nazis, the Nazis didn't always want them.

The zeal that the United States had shown at Nuremberg for punishing Nazi war criminals was already on the wane. For the first four years after the war, the United States on its own had tried and executed 277 German war criminals, imprisoning more than 700 others. Retribution was swift.

But within the newly formed West Germany, pressure was mounting on the Americans by the late 1940s to show leniency toward dozens of convicted Nazis already sentenced to the gallows or long prison sentences for war crimes. The Russian threat, as always, was at the center of America's calculations over what to do about the Nazis. With war breaking out in Korea in 1950 in a proxy fight between Moscow and Washington, the West Germans made their leverage plain: if Truman wanted their help in confronting the Soviets, the Americans would have to show Germans convicted of war crimes some forgiveness.

The decision on whether to grant leniency to the Nazis fell to John McCloy, a pragmatic Washington lawyer who led the American operations in Germany after the war. McCloy's seeming indifference to the horrors of the Nazis' genocide was already on display. As a top official in the Roosevelt administration during the war, McCloy in 1944 had rejected repeated pleas from Jewish leaders and from FDR's own War Refugee Board to bomb the train line from Hungary to Auschwitz, or the concentration camps themselves, in an attempt to disrupt the mass killings. Now, seven years later, with the West Germans pressuring him to extend clemency to convicted war criminals, McCloy complied. In January 1951 he announced that he was sparing twenty-one Nazi war criminals from execution and slashing the jail terms of dozens more, allowing them to walk out of prison to freedom. Among the beneficiaries were Nazi officers who had taken part in notorious war massacres; scientists involved in the medical experiments at concentration camps; and industrialists who had helped to build and finance Germany's gas chambers and missiles, profiting handsomely. The British and the French were outraged by the Americans' sudden generosity. The West Germans, of course, were thrilled; they knew they had the Cold War and the flare-up in Asia to thank. "Now that the Americans have Korea on their hands," smirked one German industrialist given his early freedom on slave-labor charges, "they are a lot more friendly."

The Americans' shift in attitude meant not just freedom for many of the accused war criminals in those early years after the war; it meant jobs and protection as well, as the American spy chiefs moved to exploit their newfound partners in the Cold War. So it was that America's network of "reformed," Communist-hating Nazis took root less than a decade after Nazi Germany's surrender.

In New York, a Nazi collaborator named Mikola Lebed worked with the CIA to stir Soviet resistance among Ukrainian immigrants in America. He gave anti-Soviet speeches, ran CIA front groups, and traveled back to Europe on occasion for covert assignments. During the war, Lebed had been "a well-known sadist and collaborator of the Germans" in the Ukraine, according to a witness account in the Army's own files, and was linked to the "wholesale murders" of Ukrainians, Poles, and Jews. Intelligence officials smuggled him into the United States with his wife and daughter anyway, and when the INS tried to deport him in 1952 over reports of his war crimes, Allen Dulles blocked the move; Lebed's spy work was of "inestimable value" to the CIA, Dulles wrote.

Outside Los Angeles, Andrija Artukovic, the top-level Nazi collaborator implicated in the murders of hundreds of thousands of Jews, Serbs, and Roma, became a friendly resource for the FBI in tracking Communist threats in America. With rival Croatian refugees accusing him of war crimes, Artukovic was happy to have the government on his side, and he made clear to agents "his deep appreciation of the FBI's interest in his safety."

In Washington, one of Hitler's top Russia aides, Gustav Hilger, was still shadowing the Soviets — but now as a secret analyst for the CIA. Although he was wanted in Europe for Nazi war crimes, senior State Department and CIA leaders intervened on Hilger's behalf and brought him to the United States under an alias, giving him high-level security clearance and the veneer of respectability through postings at Harvard and Johns Hopkins. Hilger made no apologies for his Nazi loyalties. "I feel no need to defend my actions or opinions; nothing urges me to make emphatic avowals or denials of my past life," he wrote in 1953 from his new home in America.

In Jordan's capital city of Amman, meanwhile, Tscherim Soobzokov trolled through immigrant hangouts on orders from the CIA to identify fellow refugees from the North Caucasus — White Russians, as they called themselves — who hated the Soviets as much as he did. As part of a classified covert program, his job was to recruit other immigrants from the old country who might be willing to spy on Russia for the Americans.

In Bavaria, Klaus Barbie — better known in Nazi-occupied France during the war as the Butcher of Lyon — was living with his family in a comfortable apartment provided by the Americans. He was earning a decent wage as a spy. Lounging poolside, he and other ex-Nazi operatives would use a municipal swimming hole in Bavaria as a convenient spot to meet their American contacts; they figured their comings and goings would attract less attention that way. When French authorities demanded his extradition — "Arrest Barbie Our Torturer!" implored one headline — the Americans refused to turn him over. As tensions with the French rose, U.S. agents spirited him out of Europe altogether, bringing him to Bolivia in 1951. Barbie seemed like an "honest man," one Army assessment concluded, and his value to the United States as an anti-Soviet agent was simply "too great" to give him up.

Nowhere was the postwar collaboration between ex-Nazis and American intelligence officials seen more vividly than in Germany itself. There, under a secret program code-named Rusty, some four thousand agents under the control of a well-connected ex-Nazi brigadier general named Reinhard Gehlen began spying for the Americans almost immediately after the war. With the United States and Russia maneuvering to control postwar Europe in a divided Germany and beyond, Gehlen's men would secretly lay surveillance cables along the Russian zones, monitor the Soviets' radio traffic, and toil along European rail lines to get intelligence on their movements. America's own spies did not know the German locales or the language well enough for such rudimentary spy-craft, so the Army and the CIA farmed out the work to Gehlen's men. "Now was the ideal time to gain intelligence [on] the Soviet Union if we were ever going to get it," said one American agent working with the ex-Nazi general.

Many of Gehlen's agents — at least a hundred, by one count, and probably more — had clear ties to Nazi atrocities; they were better described as "outlaws" than intelligence assets, one American military agent wrote in warning against hiring them. Gehlen's group, financed by the Americans, became a safe haven for war criminals of all stripes and levels. One of his couriers had served on a mobile Nazi killing unit linked to the murders of eleven thousand Jews. Another Gehlen man killed Russian political prisoners during the war. A third was responsible for recycling the clothing seized from Jews en route to the death camps in Poland.

Just how many war criminals Gehlen employed in his European spy ring was a mystery, however, because the onetime Nazi general at the center of the vast postwar fiefdom refused to give his military and CIA handlers the real names of his agents. Indeed, he ran his burgeoning network with impunity. The United States paid his group a half-million dollars a year in the early years after the war. Gehlen was even feted on a red carpet tour of America in 1951 that included a World Series game at Yankee Stadium. The general showed little appreciation. If he answered his handlers' queries at all, he would often feed them half-truths and disinformation, or play them off the French and the British, who were also vying for his services. Starved for information on the Russians, American intelligence officials continued working with Gehlen and paying him despite their frequent misgivings. Sometimes the Army officers chasing Nazi war criminals would press for information about the wartime activities of one of Gehlen's notorious agents. Back off, American intelligence officials told them; these were Gehlen's men. They were untouchable.

While their American handlers tried to airbrush their records for appearance's sake, some of the ex-Nazi spies did not bother to disguise their ideology, or their crimes. Theodor Saevecke, an SS officer who worked with Adolf Eichmann, had rounded up Jews during the war to send to slave-labor camps, and had admitted ordering the public executions of political prisoners in a town square in Italy as a demonstration of unflinching Nazi force. Even when he went to work for the CIA in postwar Europe, he was unrepentant — and brutally candid in a way that unnerved his American bosses. Most of the former Nazis in the CIA's employ at least tried to hide their criminal pasts, but their man Saevecke "still hankers back after the days when the [Nazi] Party was in the saddle," his CIA handler wrote in 1951. "He is convinced that the principles of National Socialism were sound."

When Saevecke faced war crimes accusations from survivors in Italy, he turned for protection, not surprisingly, to the CIA. Saevecke had two cards to play: besides his spy work for the agency after the war, he also claimed to have helped Allen Dulles and Nazi general Karl Wolff in the final weeks of the war to negotiate the early surrender in Italy. Dulles, who by now had risen to CIA director, didn't remember him, but he was willing to help anyway, if possible, just as he had with Wolff and a number of others. "Our attitude on [Saevecke] will depend on how bad he really was," Dulles wrote. "If his past [is] in any way defensible," the CIA would try to make the war crimes charges go away and allow him to continue his espionage work. If not, the CIA suggested, the agency could always find him a job at a private detective agency as "insurance" against something going wrong.

Lucky for Saevecke, it didn't come to that. With the help of whitewashed documents furnished by the CIA, the former SS officer was "exonerated" of war crimes accusations and remained a free man for another three decades, living off a pension from West Germany and dying of old age in 1988.

The Nazis' past crimes were of little importance, moral or otherwise, to their American intelligence handlers. The only real deterrent to using them as spies, though minimal, was the risk of political embarrassment or diplomatic run-ins should those crimes, and the Americans' knowledge of them, become known.

Wilhelm Höttl, a fervent Nazi and a notorious con artist, was virtually unknown outside the spy world in the years after the war. Inside the halls of the CIA, he would prove one of the most damaging of all the Nazi spies. An early supporter of Hitler and the Nazi Party, the Austrian-born Höttl was a senior officer in the Nazis' SD branch, the security division, working to deepen Hitler's hold over occupied Italy and Hungary. Self-assured and convincing, he emerged from the war largely unscathed — regarded as a "witness" to the Nazis' war crimes rather than a major player. Indeed, his testimony at the Nuremberg trials would produce one of the most wrenching and indelible moments, and a statement that would echo for decades. As a witness at Nuremberg, Höttl recounted a conversation in which the fugitive Eichmann had confided to him that the Nazis had killed six million Jews — four million in concentration camps and another two million elsewhere. But Höttl, despite his claims of innocence, was no mere bystander: his own involvement ran deep, as a top officer under Ernst Kaltenbrunner, a leading Nazi SS man who was ultimately executed after Nuremberg. Höttl himself was implicated in the deportation of hundreds of thousands of Hungarian Jews.

It was Allen Dulles, predictably, who first pursued Höttl as an American spy. At the same time that Dulles was working with General Wolff in Italy at the close of the war, he was also authorizing separate talks with Höttl in Austria. "H. is, of course, dangerous. He is a Nazi," an American intelligence officer wrote to Dulles in 1945, in reference to Höttl. As a result, any contact with him should be "as indirect as possible," the officer said. Still, Höttl made a "favorable impression" and appeared sincere and trustworthy, the officer wrote; using him as an American spy, even at a distance, seemed worth the risk.

Dulles agreed, echoing the assessment: "This type of source requires utmost caution." Höttl's wartime record with the SS "is, of course, bad," Dulles added. "But I believe he desires to save his skin and therefore may be useful."

As the delicate dance between Höttl and his handlers continued in the months after Germany's surrender, it was difficult to tell who had the upper hand — the Americans who had just won the war, or the vanquished Nazi officers who wanted to sell them their spy services. The Americans were desperate for intelligence on the Communists, and Höttl knew precisely which weak spots to hit in his dealings with Dulles. The British, he told one American interrogator, had a "well-established" intelligence operation in Europe, while the Americans clearly did not. Their intelligence operations in Europe were weak, he said, and they would inevitably have to turn to ex-Nazis like himself for information. "I believe that I can be of considerable benefit to the interests of the USA," Höttl said, sounding like an eager job applicant; his knowledge of the Soviets, he added, should not "be left unused in an internment camp."

Dulles and American intelligence officials took the bait. Even Höttl's Nazi bosses had not trusted him — one SS man in 1941 had declared him "a liar, a toady, a schemer, and a pronounced operator" — but the Americans were willing to take a chance on the man. Freed from custody, Höttl was entrusted by military intelligence and CIA officials over the next few years to run secret spy rings in Austria and Hungary that relied on former Nazi officers like himself. Other American officials who knew of Höttl's reputation were aghast to find out he was now working on their side. While there were "a few decent representatives of the former SD," Höttl was surely not one of them, a military official warned in an internal memo. "Should it eventually become known that Höttl is being used by the Americans, this would be incomprehensible to all decent Germans and Austrians."

For those who knew of Höttl's secret past, it was almost inevitable that the Americans' partnership with the ex-Nazi would implode. The intelligence he sold the CIA and the U.S. Army, based on his highly touted Soviet contacts, was often pedestrian, sometimes dead wrong, and occasionally even bogus. Public reports from newspaper or radio reports were passed off to the Americans as top-secret intelligence. Höttl could churn out much of the prized intelligence he was selling America, one U.S. assessment concluded derisively, "without interrupting his regular pattern of coffee house conversations."

His paltry output soon became the least of the Americans' concerns. Höttl, despite his claims to Dulles of "altruistic" motives, was plainly a man out for himself. At the end of the war, Höttl was negotiating with fellow Nazis to claim a share of the gold and jewelry looted from Jews in Hungary and hidden away via the so-called Hungarian gold train. There were reports that he had stashed looted Nazi assets in Switzerland as well. Once he started working for Washington, Höttl seized on the Americans as his next big moneymaker. He began embezzling massive amounts of cash from the Army, funds that were supposed to go to his U.S.-financed spy operations, American officials discovered. He was selling his intelligence elsewhere, too. Red-faced Army officials ended up paying another source about $3,000 in Austrian shillings for a thick stack of intelligence on Soviet activities in the region, only to learn that their own spy Höttl was the one marketing the secret documents in the first place. The revelations only got worse, as the Americans stumbled onto a number of Höttl's other secret customers. It turned out that Höttl — or Cheka, as he was secretly known in Moscow — was a Soviet double agent, and one of the Russians' most highly paid, too, according to evidence that would emerge from a KGB defector. Linked to a pair of American citizens in Vienna accused of spying for the Russians, Höttl was thought to have given the Russians intelligence on America and even the names of Allied agents. True to his reputation, the ex-Nazi was playing all sides.

In 1952, after years of unheeded warnings about their "dangerous" spy, Dulles and the CIA finally cut ties with Höttl for good. All the predictions about the damage the ex-Nazi might do to America had come true.

While the CIA's Dulles was the de facto ally of America's many Nazi spies overseas in battling the Soviets, J. Edgar Hoover at the FBI was his like-minded counterpart inside the United States — and every bit as powerful.

Hoover embraced the Cold War as his own. Like Dulles, he viewed the

Nazis through a lens tinted a bright shade of Russian red. And like Dulles, Hoover would intervene time and again on behalf of Nazi intelligence agents and allies inside the United States when they were accused of war crimes. His FBI worked with dozens of ex-Nazis as informants and intelligence agents against the Soviets. Their wartime records were largely irrelevant. Hoover himself, then at the apex of his power, invariably saw whatever evidence of war crimes that emerged against European immigrants in the United States as a concoction of Soviet propagandists meant to smear their American opponents for political gain.

"Since the war, there have been a great number of complaints that people aided the Germans during the war in persecuting the Jews," Hoover wrote in 1955, regarding a New Jersey immigrant suspected of executing Polish Jews. "Interviews in other cases have developed no substantiation of the allegations."

Hoover's tacit support for suspected Nazi war criminals reached the highest levels of the government. In 1962, the FBI learned from an apparent wiretap of columnist Drew Pearson that he might be planning to ask President John F. Kennedy about war crimes allegations against Andrija Artukovic, the Nazi collaborator in Croatia who became the FBI's anti-Communist tipster. Hoover saw the case against Artukovic as largely Communist propaganda. So the FBI alerted Kennedy's press secretary to help brace the president for possible questions at a news conference. Hoover didn't want the president ambushed by reporters demanding to know why a top Nazi collaborator from Croatia was living freely off the beaches of Southern California. Lucky for JFK, the question never came up.

When immigration investigators were trying to build a deportation case against another Nazi collaborator, an FBI informant in New Jersey named Laszlo Agh, Hoover came to his aid as well. With dozens of eyewitnesses testifying against him, Agh was accused of forcing Jews at a Hungarian work camp to throw themselves onto buried bayonets and eat their own feces, and he had made a damning admission to an FBI agent about his involvement with Hungary's Nazi-aligned Arrow Cross Party. But Hoover, in 1959, blocked his agent from testifying about Agh's admissions, effectively killing the deportation case against him. Agh was allowed to stay in Newark. At the same time, Hoover shut down a field investigation into the right-wing Hungarian American political group that Agh led. Agh and his group were seen as allies by Hoover, feeding anti-Soviet intelligence to the FBI for years, with some of it landing in Hoover's mailbox. The group's leaders "are known to have been connected with the Hungarian Nazi Party," Hoover admitted, but the organization "exhorts its leaders to be good American citizens and to report all Communist and subversive activities to the FBI." That, in Hoover's view, took priority.

Even when the FBI's own files held damning evidence of an immigrant's wartime atrocities, Hoover would defend him unabashedly. A Romanian bishop in Michigan named Viorel Trifa became so politically well-connected during the Eisenhower administration that he was given the honor of delivering the opening prayer at the U.S. Senate, and met personally with a sympathetic Vice President Nixon to urge support for his anti-Communist "brothers" back in Romania living under Soviet control. But he had a darker past. In Romania during the war, he was a well-known Nazi collaborator and leader of the fascist Iron Guard who gave a notorious speech in 1941 denouncing the "kikes." His fiery oratory helped set off gruesome pogroms in Bucharest that killed thousands, and he was sentenced to death in absentia after the war.

The FBI knew of the less inspirational elements of Bishop Trifa's history, because in its files was a copy of the so-called Trifa Manifesto, published in Romania during the war under the headline: "Death to the Masons and the Jews." But his past was irrelevant to Hoover. To him, Trifa was simply a loyal anti-Communist, and that made him an important ally. The Romanian Church under Trifa would send Hoover its literature attacking grand Communist plots, and when war crimes allegations surfaced against Trifa in 1955, Hoover defended him. He managed to scuttle a meeting that one of Trifa's main accusers was supposed to have with Vice President Nixon to press the war crimes allegations against him. In a note to Nixon, Hoover told the vice president that the accusations against Trifa were simply the result of "a factional schism within the Rumanian Orthodox Church of America." The bishop's accusers were Communists who lacked credibility, the FBI director assured Nixon. Besides, Hoover added dismissively, Trifa himself had denied any wartime involvement with the Iron Guard or the Nazis. That appeared to settle the matter.

The charges of Nazi collaboration against Trifa went nowhere, and the FBI soon closed its case against him. Eight years later, Trifa was able to return the favor to Hoover, when rumors surfaced that President Lyndon B. Johnson might sack the FBI director. Bishop Trifa, his staunch anti-Communist ally, was alarmed. "The American people," the onetime Nazi collaborator wrote in a letter to LBJ, "need men like J. Edgar Hoover."

3

"Minor War Crimes"

February 22, 1956

WASHINGTON, D.C.

The Russians were everywhere. Or so it seemed on a frigid Wednesday morning in Washington, as the capital was blanketed by talk of the Red menace, an atomic arms race with Moscow, and the escalation of the Cold War. It was George Washington's birthday, but save for a lone senator who read the first president's Farewell Address to a mostly empty Senate chamber, few lawmakers seemed to remember. History yielded to more modern-day threats, real and imagined.

At a raucous rally that night, Senator Joe McCarthy would rail against Communist "traitors" in Washington and "murderers" in Moscow. Congressional leaders would be meeting to find money for new ballistic missiles to keep up with the Russians, while the Pentagon pored over the results of a massive atomic assault it simulated the week before on the sands of Iwo Jima. And with Nikita Khrushchev delivering increasingly bold pronouncements almost by the day about Russia's global ambitions, President Eisenhower's aides would issue yet another dire warning about America's security.

A few blocks from the White House, a former Nazi SS officer with a cigarette in hand was doing his part to rein in the Communists as well. Tom Soobzokov was holed up inside the Statler Hotel, a fashionable spot frequented by presidents and celebrities. The CIA had given him a room at the grand hotel, along with seventy-five dollars in walking-around money, for the most important job interview of his life: he was vying for a spot as a spy on a top-secret team ominously called the "Hot War cadre." It was aimed at using anti-Communist refugees like himself to gather intelligence on their old country, stir discontent, and help overthrow the Reds.

It was a grandiose plan, more Keystone Kops than James Bond. But as Soobzokov figured it, this was a role he was born to play. If he got the job, it would put him in a position to not only help topple the detested Soviets, but advance his own outsize ambitions as well.

He was nothing if not ambitious. If the Soviets were thrown out of his native land in the North Caucasus, he saw himself in a leadership post in a new regional government along the Black Sea. He was brainier and more politically savvy than any of the other expatriates from his homeland, he volunteered to the CIA with smug pride. In his bold political vision, he imagined himself as a favorite son returning triumphantly to the Caucasus to lead an oppressed people back from the political wilderness.

It was heady stuff for anyone, much less a new immigrant to America still struggling to survive in the gritty, blue-collar streets of Paterson, New Jersey. Just days earlier, he had been selling cars there — a promotion from night watchman at the Plymouth auto lot. Now here he was sitting across from a CIA officer at a renowned Washington hotel, in line to become an American spy working on the most important issue of the day.

The CIA already knew a lot about him. Leaving Italy after the war amid a wave of refugees, Soobzokov had resettled in the Middle East with hundreds of fellow White Russians, and the agency quickly zeroed in on him in 1952 as a man with connections who could do some low-level spy work for the United States. They wanted him to be a "spotter" — someone who could secretly recruit other Russian refugees in the region who might then turn against the Soviets. The CIA had a keen interest in the Middle East at the time; working with Britain, the agency secretly overthrew the Iranian government a year later in a coup designed to ensure access to Iran's rich oil fields and to blunt Soviet influence.

The CIA saw great potential in Soobzokov as a spy. He spoke five languages. He was of Muslim heritage — but not religious enough to cause concern, the CIA reported favorably in one write-up. He was working for a well-connected energy company in Amman at the time. He had deep contacts among other disaffected Russian exiles from the Caucasus who had fled to the Middle East. He knew the Russians well, even studying at a Soviet military academy as a young man, according to his resumé. And, most important, he hated his old Soviet countrymen.

His marked antagonism "clearly indicated that he is prepared to join forces with any group working actively against the Soviet regime," the CIA noted in his file. Soobzokov was almost maniacal in his hostility toward the Russians, CIA psychologists would conclude. In the eyes of the agency, his "fanatic" hatred of the Soviets was an asset: in the Cold War era, there was no such thing as hating Communism too much.

His passion was what drew the CIA to him. His file described Soobzokov in wildly effusive terms: "sparkling and vivacious"; "a keen, alert mind"; "well poised"; "shrewd and practical"; a survivor with "animal cunning." Granted, his passion and lack of self-control could be a problem at times, the CIA acknowledged. (It was probably best, for instance, not to put him in the same room with a Communist, to avoid an anti-Russian outburst, one analyst warned.) But officials knew it was that brashness that made Soobzokov a leader.

CIA officials suspected something else about their new recruit, too. From their earliest dealings with Soobzokov, they suspected that he had fought with the Nazis during the war. Despite his claims to have been a prisoner of war for much of the fighting, the CIA knew better. This raised no alarms within the agency, however. It was deemed irrelevant. In fact, as they prepared to give Soobzokov his first lie-detector test in Lebanon in 1952, CIA officials wanted to make sure that Soobzokov — aka Nostril, his new code name — knew that nothing in his past would harm his prospects, and that he need not worry. His handler for the interrogations "may assure NOSTRIL," the CIA's top Middle East spy wrote, "that we are not at all interested in any criminal, moral or other similar lapses in his past and that such things will not be covered in the tests and interviews."

Whatever happened during the war was of no consequence to the CIA.

Soobzokov put in three years with the CIA in the Middle East, earning $150 a month, but his spy handlers had bigger plans for him. In 1955 the agency helped him, his wife, and their growing brood move to the United States. Within a year of his arrival, Soobzokov was put up for his new assignment: a member of the CIA's Hot War team. He would be trained to secretly stir discontent in the Soviet Union from the outside, recruiting other operatives from the Caucasus, disseminating "anti-Soviet propaganda" inside Russia, and engaging in what the CIA called "psychological warfare." At the same time, he would be readying himself to sneak back into Russia and jump into the fray inside the country if the need arose. This was a particularly sensitive assignment — and potentially hazardous — and the CIA wanted to determine whether he was up to the task before giving him the final go-ahead. For days and weeks, it would be peering into every corner of Soobzokov's life to determine his suitability for the job: two days' worth of interviews at the Statler, more than ten hours in all. Lie-detector tests. Psychological testing. A physical exam. Fingerprinting, photographing, a handwriting analysis, and background checks. If there were soft spots in his resumé, CIA's security officials were determined to find them before they took him on their team.

The day came that chilly morning in February for the start of his interviews. Soobzokov wasn't feeling great as the session at the Statler began just after 10:30 a.m. He hadn't gotten much sleep, he had a bit of a cold, and the four or five shots of whiskey he'd downed the night before weren't helping matters much. But what he lacked in energy he made up for in passion. For hours, as the interviewer pored through details of his life, Soobzokov regaled him with tales that demonstrated, in vivid hues, how he had come to so despise the Russians. He told how the repressive Soviet regime had seized his father's farm when Soobzokov was a boy, and how his father had died in prison. He told how he himself was jailed merely for trying to take some cloth for his destitute family. He told how he had deserted from the Russian army during the war and was shot in the shoulder during his escape. He told how he had led thousands of his fellow countrymen from the Caucasus by horse and cart to the Romanian-Hungarian border to seek refuge from the Russians. Finally, he told how he came to America for the promise and opportunity that it offered wartime refugees like himself.

It was a powerful performance, and Soobzokov, confident as ever, showed not the slightest hint of nervousness as he laid out his life story. That is, until the interrogator began to dig more deeply into what exactly had happened during the war after he deserted the Russian army. The ever-present sparkle in his eyes that the CIA psychologists had remarked upon seemed to almost disappear at the mere mention of the war. What exactly had Soobzokov done in those brutal years? The record in Soobzokov's file was murky; it seemed clear that he had connections to the Third Reich after the Germans invaded Russia, but precisely what he did, when, and for whom amounted to a black hole of vagaries and contradictions. His interrogator needed to plug the holes — if for nothing else than to ensure that this avowed Soviet hater was not simply some well-trained Russian mole who was now disguising himself as an anti-Communist.

So where exactly had he gone after deserting the Russians? the interviewer wanted to know. There were some indications from the file that he took sides with the Germans after they invaded the North Caucasus in 1942. Was that right?

Soobzokov squirmed.

Yes, he acknowledged, his tone defensive. He had switched sides to join the Germans, he said. He had turned on the reviled Russians, and he would do it again. He explained how he had deserted the Russian army, turned himself in to a German commander, and gladly offered to fight the Soviets.

And then? There was also the suggestion in the files that he had joined up not with the German fighting forces, but with the Waffen SS. These weren't "regular" army troops fighting in wartime; this was the brutal military branch of the Nazi security force created by Heinrich Himmler, responsible for countless war crimes.

Again, Soobzokov squirmed. Would he risk lying to the CIA? They obviously knew a lot about him — more than he wished. His CIA interviewers in the Middle East had never asked him such things. Yes, he finally acknowledged. That was true, too. He had joined the SS, not just the German military, and was made an officer — an *Oberleutnant* — and dispatched by the Nazis to Hungary and Austria. But it wasn't how it seemed. His job was merely to lure fellow Circassians to the fight. He was a recruiter with a fancy title. He had done some farm work for the Germans too, requisitioning food, Soobzokov said. He had little allegiance to the Nazis. It was all about helping his fellow countrymen and fighting the Soviets; nothing more, he insisted.

He seemed to grow more uneasy with each question.

Didn't these people get it? This was a war. You did what you had to do to survive.

The interrogator pressed on. What about the Nazi atrocities in his homeland — the widespread killings of Russian civilians, of Communists, of Jews? Was he involved in that, too?

No, no, Soobzokov said. There was none of that. He had never harmed civilians. Only soldiers. He had no problem with the Jews.

"All men are my brothers," he insisted.

Dutifully, the CIA interrogator noted the denials in his file. But he was skeptical. Soobzokov's explanations seemed too convenient, his manner too evasive.

On every other topic aside from the war years, Soobzokov had seemed "open and honest," the report noted. The stories flowed easily. Yet when the topic turned to the Nazis — particularly his murky duties with the SS — he grew nervous and was "somewhat reluctant to go into any details," the report said. Soobzokov had insisted "that he was not involved in any crimes against humanity generally attributed to the SS elements of the German forces operating in the USSR during World War II," the interviewer noted flatly. But his shifting denials "were not convincing." Indeed, the report concluded that "there is a strong possibility that Subject may have participated in unsavory activities for the Germans, which might well be categorized under minor war crimes."

Minor war crimes. It was a jarring choice of phrase, meant to ease concern. There was no fear of Soobzokov's involvement in "major" war crimes perpetrated by the Nazis, the interviewer was suggesting. If anything, these were Nazi war crimes that the CIA deemed somehow ordinary and run-of-the-mill.

If the CIA's lie-detector tests were right, another agency report concluded, Soobzokov was lying "regarding war crimes and is, no doubt, hiding a number of activities from us on that point." It seemed certain, the interviewer wrote, that Soobzokov was involved in some "minor" war crimes — again, that word — "but the major ones are unknown to us."

Whatever his crimes, they would not stand in the way of Soobzokov's employment. In fact, another CIA officer reviewing Soobzokov's file noted that if Soobzokov really was involved in Nazi war crimes and atrocities, minor or otherwise, it could actually work to the CIA's advantage: his fear of exposure could be used as leverage to ensure his loyalty, he wrote. He surely wouldn't want his war record exposed, the thinking went, and so he was more likely to remain loyal. His Nazi past could be used to the CIA's advantage.

A month later, the results of Soobzokov's assessment came back: he was CIA material. He had the job.

With his assessment complete, he would be signed on as a contract employee at the agency. He would keep his job in New Jersey at the Plymouth auto lot — it provided good cover for his intelligence work — but he would now have a new, $600-a-month post on the CIA's Hot War team to go with it.

The past was past. Whatever had happened in Europe, Soobzokov now had a future with the CIA.

For all the region's rugged beauty and rich history, the coastal highlands of Soobzokov's homeland in Russia's sprawling southwest corner have long been a place of battle and bloodshed. From the Middle Ages to the Cossacks and the Ottoman Empire, through to the Russian Revolution, the North Caucasus was a storied place of fearless warriors and epic clashes. But in the summer of 1942, the blood-red land of Krasnodar above the Black Sea, a settlement founded by Catherine the Great herself, met its most merciless enemy yet as Hitler invaded Russia from the west.

Armed with machine guns, Gestapo men in their notorious "poison green" uniforms stormed the region in tanks, horse-drawn carriages, and motorcycles. More than two thousand miles from Berlin, the Nazis occupied the region for six months of terror, scorching its rich farmlands, leveling its historic buildings and railroads, and killing many thousands, soldiers and villagers alike. Hitler's aims were never a matter of mere military objective. Mobile SS execution squads roamed the rugged countryside in search of the Nazi leader's undesirables. For reasons of ideological purity, in the North Caucasus alone the Nazis killed some twenty thousand Jews and thousands of supposed Communist "partisans" and Bolsheviks. Many were shot. Some were burned to death. Others were hanged from the majestic weeping willows so plentiful in the once-bucolic region.

Emboldened by the initial success of the biggest military invasion in history, Hitler demanded "severe" reprisals against any Russian who dared to support the "bandit gangs" of Communist partisans who continued to resist him. He put Heinrich Himmler in charge of the region-wide sweeps for enemies. By order of the Nazis, the death of any German soldier was to be met with the killing of up to a hundred Russians.

The killings grew more and more ruthless. In the Caucasus's Krasnodar region, roughly twice the size of Switzerland, the Nazis herded local Circassians — soldier and civilian, young and old, male and female — from homes, hospitals, and orphanages, and packed them eighty at a time into mobile killing machines unlike anything the world had ever seen. "The killer of souls," the villagers called the death trucks. Methodically, the victims would be loaded into airtight, windowless vans, with two specially engineered exhaust pipes winding their way back inside. After ten minutes or so, once the carbon monoxide had been pumped in and the futile cries for help had died away, the bodies of the victims, some just young children, were dumped in a dirt trench, a makeshift death pit.

Out of some sixty-seven hundred victims in Krasnodar, only one person, a nineteen-year-old worker named Ivan Ivanovich Kortov, was ever known to have survived the gassings. He was left for dead in the pit with all the others, after passing out amid a scene of horror that he could describe afterward only in a hushed voice. "The crushing confinement, the total darkness and the smell of exhaust fumes made people scream and cry and beat against the walls," Kortov recounted. "It was awful to watch the children's death struggle and be unable to help."

The Nazis did not act alone. They had help — help from some of the very Russians whose homeland Hitler had invaded.

It was a pattern that would play out in town after town, region after region, country after country, as Hitler's men swept eastward through Europe. From the Vichy regime in France to the Iron Guard in Romania and beyond, Hitler's brutal propaganda attracted throngs of collaborators — one million strong, by one estimate — by seizing on their simmering hatred of Communists and Jews and deputizing them as the Nazis' local warlords. Far from Berlin, the collaborators worked to imprison Hitler's enemies, staff his concentration and slave-labor camps, and carry out his genocidal plans. It was an alliance with grotesque results.

In Krasnodar, many Russians in the region fled or resisted the Nazis, urged on by Soviet radio broadcasts and newsreels calling on countrymen to stand up for "the Great Patriotic War." But in a region rife with ethnic divisions, a number of native clans cast their lot with the invading Germans, acting as macabre local tour guides to help identify enemies, round them up, and kill them. Some Russians manned the death vans. On one particularly savage day, others held villagers at gunpoint inside a burning farmhouse, with their neighbors screaming to get out. Perhaps the only group held in lower regard than the Bolsheviks in some local circles were the Jews, perceived as the political allies to Stalin. When the Nazis invaded the region — with their massive firepower, their brazen aggression, and their disdain for both the Jews and the Bolsheviks — they offered blood-soaked promises to do away with both groups at once.

So horrific were the atrocities in Krasnodar that the Russians, after wresting control of the region back from the Germans in 1943, made it the site of the first Nazi war crimes trials in all of Europe, even before the war had ended. Many Nazi collaborators had already escaped with the fleeing Germans, but eleven who were captured were put on public trial in a packed movie theater; the war crimes of the local collaborators were seen as almost worse than those of the Nazis themselves. It was there, in Krasnodar, that the accused Nazi collaborators first uttered the refrain that was to become the standard defense in such cases for years to come: the Nazis made me do it. "You see before you," one defendant said at his trial, "an abominable traitor who was forced to go this route by the actions of the loathsome fascists."

Eight of the eleven Nazi collaborators were ultimately convicted and sentenced to death. They were hanged from three wooden gallows in the town marketplace before some thirty thousand Russians, once their neighbors, who had gathered for the primitive spectacle. This was "the hour of retribution," a local newspaper declared. "Death to the traitors!" townspeople shouted. As the eight bodies swung listlessly in the wind, a church bell rang nearby, and a priest asked the townspeople to pray for the collaborators' souls. Few did.

Had Soobzokov been one of those collaborators in Krasnodar? What, exactly, had he done? These were questions that Soobzokov never really had to answer, even as he rose up the ranks within the CIA in the late 1950s. The CIA, unconcerned with any moral "lapses" in his past, did not press him explain what he did during the war, and he certainly did not volunteer it.

For nearly fifteen years now, ever since the end of the war, he had worked with a craftsman's zeal to create the façade that was to become his life story, caulking the cracks, buffing out the imperfections, adding a splash of paint to highlight the dramatic flairs. It was an immigrant's success story: the story of a man in search of freedom, a man of conscience who fought Communism and persecution in his native Russia at every turn; who led a wayward band of refugees through war-ravaged Europe; who came to America, made a new life for himself in New Jersey, and, as an up-and-coming young CIA undercover agent, worked secretly to help reclaim his native land from the Reds.

It was an inspiring tale, and whenever the storyline had prompted doubts from fellow immigrants he encountered, from the New Jersey politicians he'd befriended, even from CIA officials for whom he'd spied, his sheer force of personality had overcome them. When inconsistencies surfaced, he had explained them away.

Indeed, in his four years living in the United States, he had earned one stealth assignment after another from American intelligence officials. The CIA's suspicion that Soobzokov was guilty of minor war crimes had certainly done nothing to slow the work. In fact, the agency had sent him back to the Middle East in search of more intelligence on the Soviets and possible recruits among the Russian exiles there. He had trained with the U.S. Army in explosives and paramilitary operations as part of a secret anti-Communist operation. He'd even expanded his portfolio to include confidential work with the FBI. The CIA had suggested to their domestic intelligence partners at the bureau that Soobzokov could provide dirt not just on Communist sympathizers in the Middle East, but inside the United States as well; two New Jersey immigrants in particular had caught Soobzokov's eye as suspicious. The FBI jumped at the chance to use him, with J. Edgar Hoover writing personally in June 1958 to Allen Dulles. Yes, Hoover wrote, the FBI would be quite interested in making use of this Soobzokov fellow; please let him know that his men from the FBI would be in touch soon to find out exactly what he knew about the Communists, the director wrote.

Those were heady times for Soobzokov, a newcomer to America who was working for its two most famous intelligence agencies. But as he sat in a CIA interview room one November morning in 1959, answering questions from a stone-faced examiner for what seemed like the hundredth time, his life story was starting to chip away like paint from rotted wood. The results had just come back on his latest polygraph test — his seventh in just the last few years. Again, it was clear to the examiner that Soobzokov was lying to them. Over and over again. Particularly about the war years. He'd been given every chance to show his trustworthiness, but even now, he remained a cipher to the CIA, a ghost from a war long over. He had many faces, but no clear core, as he faced a barrage of skeptical questions from the examiner. It came down to this: Has *anything* you've told us about yourself for nearly the last ten years of your service been true? the CIA examiner demanded to know. And the most vexing question of all: What did you really do for the Nazis during the war?

The CIA's aim was not to determine whether Soobzokov might have been a Nazi war criminal; it had suspected as much almost from the beginning. No, what the CIA wanted to know was whether Soobzokov could be trusted or not. Being an ex-Nazi was acceptable so long as he could prove himself an honest and trustworthy one.

Soobzokov recognized the spot in which he found himself. This was his last chance to make things right with his bosses at the CIA if he ever wanted to work for the agency again.

How had the relationship come to this? Such skepticism, such distrust. Soobzokov was flummoxed. Hadn't he always been there for his bosses at the CIA, and they for him? They could count on him. Just two years earlier, they wanted him to drop everything, leave his pregnant wife and three young children in Paterson and do six months of secret, paramilitary training. He didn't ask why; he dutifully sent in his uniform measurements and shoe size as ordered, got on the train to Union Station in Washington on a scalding July day, and showed up for his assignment.

And when the CIA wanted him to take a leave from a new job he'd gotten with an insurance company and fly back to the Middle East for several more months on a risky undercover assignment? Again, Soobzokov was there for them.

Hadn't he proven himself by now a devoted CIA employee, a loyal anti-Communist? Sure, he loved the thrill and bravado of the spy's life, but he did it out of a sense of service to his new country, too. Whatever the CIA wanted, he did it.

The strange thing to Soobzokov was that his bosses at the CIA had always seemed so high on him. Soobzokov had become particularly close to John Grunz, the veteran CIA case officer who served as his handler, muse, confidant, and fellow Communist hunter. Soobzokov had reported to him during his time living in Jordan. After Soobzokov came to America, the two exchanged letters recalling their time serving together in the Middle East. Soobzokov would call Grunz collect to share Communist tidbits. He had Grunz's private phone line at headquarters, with instructions to identify himself to Grunz's secretary as "Mr. Tom." Soobzokov had shared everything with Grunz — all his tips about suspected Commie sympathizers in New Jersey, photos from a Russian émigré who seemed suspiciously smitten with the Bolshoi Ballet, and various theories on ethnic and political divisions back in Russia and in the Middle East.

Occasionally, in darker moments, Soobzokov would even share with Grunz the ugly, deep-seated biases that he kept hidden away from most of the outside world. There was the time a few months earlier when Soobzokov, looking to make some extra money on top of his part-time work with the CIA, was mulling over a job offer in exports with a New York firm. He talked over the position with an executive there by the name of Lansberg. But something worried Soobzokov about this Mr. Lansberg. He called Grunz for advice. Soobzokov wanted "to find out if the firm is reliable and whether Jews are involved. He would be ashamed to work for a Jew," the CIA dutifully noted in his file. "He thinks Lansberg is a Jewish name but Lansberg talked more like a German or a Dutchman," the file noted; those were "nationalities he wouldn't mind working for."

For a CIA officer like Grunz, each anti-Soviet spy he could count as part of his portfolio — even an inept one or an anti-Semitic one — was a prized commodity that would inevitably help to advance his own career. In that era at the CIA, you couldn't have too many Russian spies on your team. Grunz was willing to fight for his friend. "We must get him employment!" the handler scrawled in a handwritten note to his bosses after Soobzokov passed on the job with Lansberg, the Jew, and was struggling with money. Soobzokov "is willing to go on any type of mission for us at any time," Grunz wrote, "providing the objective is worth the risk in his opinion."

But as close as he had once been with Grunz and his other CIA spy bosses, the easy rapport began to fray by the time he was called in for his latest interrogation. For months now, the CIA's pesky internal security team had been asking him about unpleasant rumors that had surfaced during what proved a disastrous covert visit he took to the Middle East in the fall of 1957.

On the Middle East trip, he was supposed to spend three or four months secretly recruiting Russian exiles in the region as spies for the CIA. First he needed a cover story to explain his absence from home. Ironically enough, that cover came from his Nazi past. If fellow immigrants in New Jersey asked why he was going back to the Middle East for so long, he decided he would tell them that the German branch of NATO had sent him there, a story he figured would make perfect sense to those who knew his past. "I emphasized Germany because everybody knows I fought with the Germans during the war," he told his CIA debriefer afterward.

In the Middle East, Soobzokov still had many contacts among fellow White Russian refugees from the North Caucasus, and he was assigned to scout out some of his old immigrant haunts. With his cover story in place, and $1,800 in CIA money in his pocket to buy a car in Beirut, he was supposed to travel the region and discreetly work the refugees who might be willing to return to Russia as CIA plants. He would also be sending agents into Syria from Jordan on clandestine operations. He might even venture there himself.

The plan ran off the rails from the start. Instead of receiving intelligence on the Commies, CIA headquarters was soon getting back all sorts of unnerving reports about Soobzokov himself, and the dust storm he was kicking up during his stay. Word came that the CIA's $150-a-week covert agent had been openly flaunting his American spy credentials, insulting the locals with his arrogance, getting mixed up in Circassian politics, and offering to use his connections to help refugees emigrate to America. So disruptive was the trip that there was even talk among the locals that he might be a *Soviet* plant. Be careful of this man, Soobzokov's old countrymen were saying of the interloper; he was not who he seemed to be. One American official in Jordan became so fed up with Soobzokov's antics that he complained directly to Dulles, the CIA director. Within a week of the complaint, Soobzokov's trip was cut short, and he was pulled out of the country.

This wasn't the type of low profile the CIA expected from a covert agent. Indeed, the charges were serious enough that the CIA called in Soobzokov for a series of debriefings to explain how things had become so bungled on the trip. The situation might have worried another man. But Soobzokov, confident as always, believed he could explain it all away. Sure, he had heard the unpleasant gossip that followed him back from Beirut, but there was nothing to it, he assured the examiner at the outset of one CIA debriefing. These scurrilous charges were nothing more than "a small bothersome gnat buzzing around my head," he scoffed; just lies and innuendo generated by a rival from the old country.

The reason for the bad blood? It was all so silly, Soobzokov explained with an air of bemusement; it was all over a woman's virginity. After the war, he explained, when he was still living in Jordan among the Circassians, a friend had asked Soobzokov about a pretty young girl he'd noticed among the war refugees in town. As a self-styled leader of his refugee clan, Soobzokov liked playing the role of unofficial matchmaker. Yes, she was interested in marrying, and yes, she was a virgin, he told his friend after some inquiries. The two wed, but only then, Soobzokov explained matter-of-factly to the CIA examiner, did the groom discover his bride was no virgin. What's more, the girl had blurted out to her new husband in a moment of anger that it was the matchmaker himself — none other than Soobzokov — who had defiled her.

Ugly as it was, the episode had led to an understandable bit of ill will between the two men that had lasted for years, he acknowledged with some chagrin. So, Soobzokov explained, when he returned to Jordan from America on his mysterious "business" trip, and his former rival realized he was back in town, the bitter man quickly used the occasion to spread these malicious and baseless rumors — that Soobzokov was a Communist agitator and an untrustworthy man who had done all sorts of suspicious things during his stay. Few charges were more salacious among the White Russian war immigrants than calling a man a Communist spy. But there was nothing to the accusations, he assured the CIA. He was no Communist; these were just the lies of a vengeful man still upset years later because Soobzokov had deflowered his wife.

Remarkably, the CIA seemed to be satisfied with the grandiose explanation. Soobzokov had been "substantially truthful" in his debriefing and a polygraph, the agency concluded after hearing his explanations. The slew of accusations grew out of "jealousy and envy [by] his personal enemies," another analyst concluded. And the most damning accusation of all — the suggestion that Soobzokov was really a Soviet spy? It was "probably without foundation."

Soobzokov had talked his way out of trouble again, at least for now. Questions about the ill-fated Middle East assignment were put to rest. But then, just a few months later, another awkward encounter placed Soobzokov smack up against his past again, with the potential for even more damage to his career. The CIA and the military had scheduled him for six months of paramilitary training in southern Maryland in early 1958, as a member of the covert Hot War team. In Maryland, Soobzokov wouldn't just be focused on the softer side of spycraft, pedestrian stuff like recruiting Russian expatriates or spreading Soviet disinformation. No, at an army base at Fort Meade, Maryland, up the highway from Washington, D.C., he and other Russian-speaking members of the Hot War team would undergo training in the use of dynamite, grenades, weaponry, and a myriad of other tools of warfare to prepare for the possibility of being secretly dropped back into Russia at a moment's notice to conduct paramilitary operations.

Yet as titillating as the assignment might have sounded, the prospect terrified Soobzokov. He had always been able to use his powerful personality to wile his way through covert assignments, but dynamite and detonators? This was different. He wasn't sure the CIA, despite its confidence in him, had the right man. One scenario in particular paralyzed him with fear as he ran it over and over in his mind before leaving for Maryland, he later confided to a CIA debriefer in a moment of raw candor. As he imagined it playing out, the platoon of Hot War soldiers would be standing in formation at the army base next to an intimidating assortment of live demolition charges. The drill instructor would address him personally. "Soobzokov, I see from your biography that you graduated from a Russian military academy and were an officer in the Red Army against the Nazis," the platoon leader would say. "Why don't you show us how the Russians would execute a detonation like this?" Soobzokov, sweating, would then step out of line with two choices laid starkly before him. He could lose face in front of his instructor and his entire Hot War team by admitting that, his official resumé notwithstanding, he had never actually trained in explosives, had never been a Russian officer, had never attended the military academy, and, in fact, had barely even served in the Red Army before deserting. Or he could fake it, go ahead with the demonstration out of a "false pride," and risk "blowing himself up through ignorance," as he told his CIA debriefer. Neither option seemed terribly appealing.

He tried to reach his old friend John Grunz to get him to extricate him from the mess that the upcoming training mission and his fabricated resumé were creating for him. Unsuccessful, a panicked Soobzokov went to Fort Meade anyway as planned. It proved to be an anticlimactic time. He had worried himself for nothing; there were no confessions to make, no training sessions to lead, no life-or-death decisions to make by the light of an exploding grenade. In fact, his drill instructor at Fort Meade wrote afterward that the Hot War trainee impressed him as "intelligent, energetic and frank"; he was particularly struck by his "fanatic hate of communism." That was a huge plus for any Hot War cadet.

Nonetheless, the episode proved a moment of sober realization for Soobzokov. Each encounter with the CIA was now bringing him closer to having to admit that his official biography — from his supposed military officer's training in Russia to his wartime activities — was largely a sham. With his American citizenship application awaiting approval, his fabrications might even endanger his chances of staying in the United States permanently if they were to be exposed. Soobzokov had some cleaning up to do. So he went, again, to his confidant at the CIA.

"Dear John," he began typing. His recent assignment at Fort Meade had gotten him thinking, Soobzokov wrote, and he had "decided to ask you a small favour." He realized that there were some small inaccuracies in his official biography that perhaps he should now try to correct. "U.S. Congress passed a few months ago a law which allows immigrants to change some uncorrect dates when they were falsely writing them in order to come to the U.S.A.," he wrote. His own case seemed tailor-made for the new law, allowing him to amend the small mistakes in his biography and "become clean forever," he wrote. He was sorry to bother him with something so trivial, he wrote, but could John help him?

It was an audacious move: he was volunteering to fix the "small" misstatements in his history in order to continue hiding the big ones. Improbably, it worked — at least for a while.

On cue at his next debriefing, Soobzokov gave the CIA his "new" autobiography, with some of the smaller inconsistencies — when he was actually born, where he had lived, where he had gone to school — now effectively whited out and corrected. He explained to the CIA that these were minor misstatements that had helped him in Europe — making him seem older, better trained, and more experienced than he really was — and he kept repeating them even after the war for fear that admitting them might compromise his immigration to America. He always figured the lies would catch up with him, he admitted to the debriefer, but they never did, so he simply kept on telling them, again and again and again. "The Subject himself expressed astonishment at how simple it was to falsify to the American Intelligence incidents which in his opinion are very easily checked out and verified," the examiner wrote. When America's great spymasters failed to catch on to his bald fabrications, Soobzokov simply "continued to keep insisting [the misstatements] were true," the report added. He'd even written up an outline of his supposed biography just to keep track in his own mind of all the lies he'd told the CIA over the years, he admitted with some small pride. Indeed, there were so many lies that it was difficult to remember everything he'd said.

It was now clear, the CIA concluded, that Soobzokov's employment as an agent "was based on admitted lies and fabrications." The agency had a problem. It began to distance itself from its Russian spy as the questions about him continued to mount. "Nostril file burned last fall," read one cryptic memo at the CIA. The agency had no derogatory information on Soobzokov anyway, the memo lied, and his old CIA handlers were "not in contact with Soobzokov."

Soobzokov had one last chance, one final opportunity to regain the agency's trust, even after all the "admitted lies and fabrications," all the bungled assignments, all the melodrama about exploding grenades and deflowered virgins. The week before Thanksgiving in 1959, with Washington fixated on the new Communist revolutionary Fidel Castro, Soobzokov made another trip from New Jersey to Washington. This was to be his moment of reckoning. The agency was finally ready to challenge him on every aspect of his life story — both the small details he had already tried to correct, and the big ones he continued to hide. For the first time, the CIA had even done some digging of its own on the background of its troubled spy, using newly available war records on the Nazi occupation of Russia. For two days, he would face a top-to-bottom grilling by a CIA examiner who came armed with a thick stack of all Soobzokov's past debriefings and his spotty lie-detector tests — a record of everything he had told the CIA, everything he claimed to have done, everywhere he claimed to have been.

Less than four years earlier, interviewing for his big assignment with the Hot War team in that elegant hotel room at the Statler, he had answered the same basic questions about his life with no hint of skepticism from the CIA. This time, as he sat across from the CIA examiner at a much less decorous room at a covert outpost not far away, the mood was starkly different. Gone was the breezy, boys' club atmosphere. This felt more like an inquisition. Again, he was strapped up to the polygraph machine. The examiner put him on notice from the start. "He was cautioned," the examiner noted in his report, "that a repetition of his previous attempts at deception would not be beneficial to him or to his future." Any more lies and he was gone.

Soobzokov nodded his head in understanding and adopted his most earnest demeanor, his usual bravado gone. "Not one single word of untruth will come from my lips," he assured the examiner.

They began at the beginning.

So, what year were you really born? the examiner asked.

In 1924, Soobzokov answered.

Not 1918, as you'd told us before?

No, it was 1924.

How many times have you really married?

Twice.

You'd always told us once. Twice?

Yes, twice, Soobzokov repeated. There was a Circassian girl he'd wed named Khadizhet. It was 1942, if he remembered right. They weren't married long, maybe a few months, he said. She died. No, he didn't know how, Soobzokov said.

And what about the Russian military academy? Had he really graduated from the academy at a place called Ordzhonikidze as he had always claimed?

No, he admitted. He hadn't even attended the military academy, much less graduated. The farthest he'd gone in school was the eighth grade.

The examiner led him through all the other inconsistencies in his past stories, asking him about his father's farm, his relatives, his work record, a juvenile arrest, even a run-in with a girl from his childhood; all trivial in the scheme of things. But this was all just prelude, the CIA's version of foreplay, as the examiner walked Soobzokov toward that critical, opaque period nearly two decades earlier, in Europe's bleakest time.

Let's talk about the war, the examiner began. Tell me again what you did.

Soobzokov gave his stock answer — the same one he'd given CIA officials for years whenever he was asked about it. He had rehearsed it many times, using that same outline he had written up long ago. He had deserted the Russian army early in the war, Soobzokov began. He hated Stalin for everything he had taken from him and his family — the rich farmland they had seized, the liberties they stole — and after the Germans invaded in 1942, he was a prisoner of war forced to serve with other Circassians under Hitler's grip. It was one tyrant or the other; Hitler or Stalin. He did some farm work for the Germans, transporting hay. His main role, Soobzokov said, was protecting his fellow Circassians in his region from the ravages of the war, as their de facto leader. He'd worn a German uniform, but only as a formality. He'd never really served with the Germans.

Now it was the examiner's turn. From the clutter of documents in front of him, the CIA examiner removed a tattered, typewritten form and held it silently in front of Soobzokov; close enough for him to get a glimpse of its authenticity, but not to read it. This was by design. He didn't want Soobzokov to be able to see what it actually said. The examiner seemed to have been saving up the document for just this very moment. Just why, Soobzokov could not be certain.

The examiner began reading to Soobzokov: "Special order from German Field Command No. 548." It was a Nazi permit, stamped and signed the day after Christmas in 1942 in accordance with orders "issued by the commanding officer of the SS and SD Bureau in Krasnodar." In its cold, merciless Nazi bureaucratese, the permit gave legal authority to the only person named on it — Tscherim Soobzokov, born on January 1, 1918 — to "search all villages" in his area. Search for what? The form did not say exactly, but it did not need to. The answer was clear to the CIA and to any student of the Nazis' destructive path through western Russia. The order effectively authorized Soobzokov, as the CIA noted in his file, to "search the area of Toktamakai for Jews and Komsomol," members of the Young

Communist League. He was to be the Nazis' man on the ground in rounding up Hitler's enemies, going from one neighbor's house to the next to look for Communists and Jews in the region where he grew up.

Nothing like this had ever been raised before in all of Soobzokov's many debriefings. So, the examiner asked when he was done reading the document, how did he explain this?

Soobzokov was growing flustered, even desperate, the examiner wrote in his notes. This was hard evidence — typewritten by a Nazi regime meticulous in its barbaric record-keeping — that appeared to tie him directly to the roundup of innocent civilians in his own hometown. Where had the CIA gotten this document, and what else did they have on him?

It must be a mistake, Soobzokov insisted; a typo, a mixed-up name, maybe an out-and-out Russian forgery. He had handled only menial administrative tasks for the Germans, not the rousting of Jews and Communists from their homes, he insisted. And he wasn't even in that part of Krasnodar at the time the document placed him there, he said. The Nazi permit was simply wrong, he insisted.

The examiner didn't try to disguise his skepticism. It was obvious, he told Soobzokov, that he was lying. What was he supposed to tell his superiors at the CIA now? the examiner wanted to know. How was he going to explain to them all the different stories that he had given them over the years, one version contradicted by another and another?

Soobzokov was out of explanations. "Tell them that I'm lying," he said finally, "and that I can't logically explain these inconsistencies." The examiner wrote it all down.

Soobzokov had reached a breaking point. Yes, he finally acknowledged to the examiner, he had been lying to him about many things, just as he had lied to many of the CIA debriefers before him. But he was ready to tell the truth, he promised. He asked just one favor first from the examiner. Put down your pen, he said.

As he began speaking, the words seemed to tumble out of a dark place inside him, a place Soobzokov had not revisited in many years. It had all started with a Nazi officer named Hans, he told the examiner. He came to know him so well that he called him by his first name. When the Nazis invaded the region in 1942 and Soobzokov deserted the Russian army, he eagerly became Hans's eyes and ears on the ground in his hometown about a dozen miles from Krasnodar. His job was to keep security in town and help maintain the Nazis' stronghold. Even as the Nazis slaughtered thousands in the region, gassing them in mobile death trucks, burning them alive in a farmhouse, hanging them from the majestic willows, Hans was worried about what he euphemistically called "morale" problems: the resisters — Jews and Communists — who might dare to fight the invading army.

The Nazi commander looked to Soobzokov, as a de facto security chief, to secretly gather intelligence among the locals and alert him to any dissidents. No, Soobzokov admitted to the examiner, he was not the wartime protector and savior of the Circassians that he had always made himself out to be in his CIA interviews. Just the opposite: he was the Nazis' spy inside the gates.

It was an unofficial role at first, with Soobzokov playing the part of incognito informant for the Nazis. Then Hans came up with a more formal plan: Soobzokov was to join the Germans' 835th Battalion, made up mostly of Circassian prisoners of war in the region, in a covert effort to learn about possible uprisings and to spy "on his own people." He would report back to Hans on plots and any intelligence he picked up from the inside.

But the plan ran aground. As Soobzokov began surreptitiously asking so many odd questions about the other villagers and their true intentions, trying to root out the resisters, his neighbors came to suspect that he was secretly spying for the Nazis, Soobzokov explained. That was how the "special order" — the one that the CIA examiner was now holding in his hand — came to be. Hans issued it to Soobzokov. It bestowed on him the power to roam the town carte blanche and go through the houses — asking questions and searching for the Jews and the Communists seen as threats to Hitler's murderous regime. If the villagers were making trouble for the Nazis, Soobzokov was to find them. Whatever his neighbors thought of him and his Nazi alliance, no one could challenge his authority now.

And these people who were rounded up — what happened to them? the examiner wanted to know. The Communist "resisters," the Jews, the Nazi enemies — they were arrested? Jailed? Worse?

Soobzokov paused. Yes, there was one episode, Soobzokov said haltingly, still unsure exactly what else the examiner might already know. Some of the Russian townspeople and resisters were held in an encampment the Nazis had established in town, he explained. One man among the group was suspected of stirring trouble in the encampment, he said. The Nazis needed to deal with him. So, Soobzokov stated, he was put in charge of an execution squad meant to take care of the dissenter. He didn't explain how he had risen from a lackey and informant for Hans to the top leader of a Nazi execution squad, and the examiner did not ask. But the Nazis brought the man out, and on Soobzokov's orders, he was shot dead. Even as he told the grim story, Soobzokov seemed oddly insistent on one point: he himself never fired a shot. He simply gave the order to kill the man. This was important to know; in his own mind, it seemed to give him some absolution.

The examiner continued prodding. So were there other Nazi enemies who were "disciplined," others who were killed? It seemed hard to believe this was a onetime event.

Soobzokov paused. Yes, there was another episode that he remembered, he said.

Some other villagers in the encampment had purportedly hatched a plan to revolt, he recounted. They wanted to kidnap a Nazi platoon leader and turn themselves over to the Soviets with hostage in tow. Hans found out about the plot, and he was furious. He blamed Soobzokov for letting it happen; it was Soobzokov's job, after all, to keep security and stifle dissent. In a profanity-laced diatribe, Hans ordered him to find one of the central players in the supposed coup and bring him in. Quickly, all the local Circassians in town were called to formation, with the accused conspirators pulled out of line. Then — this time on Hans's orders, not his own — the men were shot dead by firing squad en masse, with the townspeople made to watch.

The spectacle, Soobzokov recounted to the examiner, was meant as "a lesson for any future conspirators."

The veil over his Nazi past was finally lifting. Soobzokov had spent the past seven years giving the CIA so many versions of his life that he had trouble remembering them all. But now, in just a half hour or so sitting across from the stone-faced examiner, he had revealed far more than he ever intended, telling how he had hunted down Hitler's enemies in house-by-house searches; how he had served the Nazis "as their informer against the Circassians (his own people)," as the examiner wrote; how he had ordered a Nazi execution squad to gun down a dissenter; and how he had been party to a mass killing ordered by Hans, his Nazi commander.

Yet if the confessional brought Soobzokov some sense of relief, the examiner was still not satisifed. For all that the interviewee had now admitted, the examiner believed there was still more to the story, much more. As damning as it was, large chunks of Soobzokov's wartime history — dates, locations, his supposed assignments with the Nazis — still didn't make sense. One of the biggest mysteries was what Soobzokov had done once he fled the Krasnodar region with the retreating Nazis in early 1943 in the face of the Russian counteroffensive. Soobzkov's accounts of what came next were always vague. He admitted to traveling to Poland, to Austria, to Hungary, and even to Berlin in 1943 and 1944 with the Germans as an SS officer, but his role, he insisted, was largely limited to recruiting his brethren Circassian prisoners of war as German soldiers and ferrying them to safety on orders from his superiors. He was the Circassians' helper and protector, he insisted. He did such a good job at it that the Nazis promoted him to *Oberleutnant* in the SS, the Germans' notorious security and intelligence branch.

A Nazi SS officer on a goodwill mission through Europe to help his fellow refugees at the height of Germany's power? It seemed preposterous on its face. One document in the CIA's own files showed that Soobzokov, as usual, had far more power with the Nazis than he was willing to let on. It was a certificate issued in his name in Hungary in November of 1944 — at a time when the Nazis and their Hungarian collaborators were rounding up some half a million Jews from the countryside and sending them to ghettos in Budapest and other cities to be kept in "Jews only" buildings identified with a Star of David on the front. Most would ultimately be sent by the trainload to their deaths at Auschwitz. The Hungarian certificate, not unlike the one issued to him in Russia two years earlier authorizing him to search homes for Jews and Communists, bestowed on him certain powers. "Soobzokow [*sic*] tsherim," identified as a "military commander" in a Circassian brigade, "has the right to reserve this building" for the military, it read. "The above mentioned building will remain under his reservation as long as this certificate is not withdrawn." Exactly what type of building, and what purpose it served, the order did not say. But the implications were jarring.

What else was he hiding? the examiner demanded to know.

• • •

Soobzokov had promised to finally tell all, yet here he was, in this dank, barren interrogation room, accused of holding out on the CIA yet again. He was growing more flustered with each question. They had been at it for hours — interrogator and witness, locked in hostile cross-examination — and Soobzokov begged for a break. It had been an emotional day. Just give him some time to compose himself and "consolidate his thoughts," he implored; he would spend the night "writing his autobiography." They were getting nowhere anyway, and the examiner acquiesced, bringing the day's interrogation to a close.

After a restless night, Soobzokov was brought back the next morning for a second day of questioning. He had scribbled down a few notes the night before to try to clear up some of the unfortunate discrepancies that had surfaced the day before, and he began to go back through the problem spots. But his new autobiography was largely a regurgitation of the old one he had given for years before. The examiner stopped him as he went through it. He was certain — "convinced beyond all doubt," he wrote in his notes — that Soobzokov had simply gone back to the outline he had long ago invented, freshening the details to shore up his crumbling life story. Again, the examiner confronted him. No, no; this time he hadn't gone back to the outline, Soobzokov insisted. This time it was the truth. The examiner scoffed. There was no point in continuing the charade. He ended the interrogation.

"It is the examiner's opinion," he wrote in his formal report weeks later, "that Subject is an incorrigible fabricator who is still attempting deception about his past."

Even now, Soobzokov was lying. Why? Why keep lying after he had already admitted so much? The fabrications may have made some sense when he first started inventing them, the examiner wrote; Soobzokov wanted to exaggerate his credentials to the people he was trying to impress — first the Nazis during the war, then the CIA afterward — and so he made up elements of his past out of whole cloth to make himself seem more important — more educated, more highly trained — than he really was. But why maintain the façade even now, even after he'd been caught? "The examiner can only draw one final conclusion about Subject and his unceasing deceitful attempts during interrogation," he wrote. "The reason why Subject is continuing deception about his background must be so important and pertinent to Subject's welfare that he cannot afford to tell the complete truth about his past without seriously jeopardizing his future."

Whether a minor war criminal or worse, Soobzokov had always been regarded by the CIA as a valuable spy — but only if the agency could trust him. Whatever he did during the war for the Nazis was of much less consequence than whether CIA officials could count on him to tell the "unvarnished truth." It was now clear they could not. What good was a spy if he couldn't be trusted by his own people? In the CIA ethos, that was the ultimate sin.

"Dear Mr. Soobzokov," began the official termination letter the agency sent Soobzokov seven weeks later. "I regret to inform you that the results of our interview on 19–20 November 1959, preclude the continuance of further mutual association. Further efforts to resolve the discrepancies are judged to be futile," the letter read. "Enclosed find a money order for $50.00 for the period 1 October thru 31 December 1959, as final payment for services rendered."

Nostril's days with the CIA were finally over.

4

Echoes from Argentina

May 11, 1960

BUENOS AIRES

The world's most wanted Nazi got off a ramshackle bus in a quiet suburb of Buenos Aires one evening in the spring of 1960 after working an uneventful shift as a foreman at an Argentine auto plant. Ricardo Klement began the short walk home to his wife and four children when a stranger approached. "Un momentito, señor?" the stranger said. Suddenly, two Israeli agents were wrestling the bespectacled man into an awaiting car and whisking him away to a safe house. There, the agents went through the assigned checklist to confirm Ricardo's true identity. The scar on his chest, the odd shape of his head, his size 8½ shoes, it all fit: this was Adolf Eichmann, the notorious architect of Hitler's Final Solution.

They had him; all that was left now was the escape. Days later, their final plans complete, his captors led Eichmann — once so feared; now doped and disguised as an El Al flight crew member — past unsuspecting Argentine airport authorities and onto a flight to Israel to face war crimes charges in one of history's most anticipated trials.

Eichmann's capture, fifteen years after he'd escaped Allied custody at the end of the war, riveted the world with its bravado, its intrigue, and its implausibility. But in New York City, in a well-appointed apartment along the East River, the episode carried a much more personal and harrowing resonance for a dapper fifty-one-year-old businessman who had immigrated to the United States just a few years earlier from Europe. For Otto von Bolschwing — "Ossie," to his friends in Germany — Eichmann was much more than a bold-type newspaper headline and a mythical Nazi fugitive. For him, Eichmann was a onetime pupil, a partner in persecution, and a hidden keyhole to his own dark past. As long as Eichmann had stayed hidden, von Bolschwing's Nazi secrets had seemed safe. With Eichmann now in an Israeli jail, everything changed. Von Bolschwing was terrified by the thought that he might be next. If the Israelis were to put Eichmann on trial and probe the Nazis' notorious Jewish Affairs office, it wouldn't be long, von Bolschwing feared, before they stumbled onto his own role. The Israelis might not even wait for a trial. Perhaps, he thought, they would simply kidnap him from the streets of Manhattan the way they had with Eichmann in the suburbs of Buenos Aires.

The well-heeled son of a Prussian nobleman, von Bolschwing had spent the postwar years reinventing himself with remarkable ease — first as a CIA spy in Austria, then as an international businessman in Manhattan. Trained in economics and law, von Bolschwing seemed to segue seamlessly into whatever new postwar role came his way. The CIA was often there to help him. But Eichmann's capture threatened all that. As hard as Ossie had tried to erase his past, those words that he had written so long ago — words of hatred and terror that he had written for the Nazis twenty-three years earlier as a primer on Jewish persecution — still shadowed him.

> A largely anti-Jewish atmosphere must be created among the people in order to form the basis for the continued attack and the effective exclusion of them ... The most effective means is the anger of the people leading to excesses in order to take away the sense of security from the Jews. Even though this is an illegal method, it has had a longstanding effect ... The Jew has learned a lot through the pogroms of the past centuries and fears nothing as much as a hostile atmosphere which can go spontaneously against him at any time.

Von Bolschwing was a twenty-eight-year-old SS lieutenant in the Nazis' Jewish Affairs office in 1937 when he wrote what amounted to an official Nazi white paper on waging anti-Semitism. His report was called *Zum Judenproblem* (On the Jewish Problem). In it, he laid out the terrifying bureaucratic arsenal — economic restrictions, special taxes, passport denials, systematic isolation, and more — that the Nazis could unleash to "purge Germany of the Jews." Heinrich Himmler liked what he read, and von

Bolschwing was put to work under an eager-to-please young officer named Adolf Eichmann. Still an unknown in the Nazi hierarchy, Eichmann was not even working on the Jewish "problem" at the time. He was toiling at the Freemasons section — another outcast group targeted for Nazi persecution — when von Bolschwing, a polished, well-spoken young man who exuded the confidence of his aristocratic upbringing, began his twisted tutelage of Eichmann, teaching him all he knew of Jewish persecution. With his mission at hand, von Bolschwing would write dozens of chilling memos and reports to Eichmann on how best to make Germany a place of abject misery for the Jews in the years leading up to the Holocaust. Seizing the Jews' money, labeling them on their passports, letting them leave the country but not reenter — he laid out all these tools of ethnic targeting and more for Eichmann.

"Heil Hitler," von Bolschwing signed his memos.

The Nazis had already been moving with brutal precision to ostracize and oppress the Jews since Hitler's rise to power in 1933. Four years later, what von Bolschwing was proposing went much further in its systematic campaign of terror. He didn't advocate killing the Jews outright. Instead he advised making their lives so terrifying and unbearable that they would be forced to flee Germany. Eichmann himself credited von Bolschwing as the "originator" of this idea; compared to the gas chambers that came a few years later, Eichmann said snidely, this was "the least of all evils."

As hate-filled as his words were, von Bolschwing seemed motivated less by deep-seated anti-Semitism — in the midst of the Holocaust, he married a half-Jewish woman — than by a thirst for power and self-promotion in the Nazi hierarchy. He was a man who had always craved glory and adventure. In the 1930s, he had ventured to Palestine in search of a cache of gold that, according to legend, the Germans had buried there during World War I. His rise in the Nazi Party under Eichmann seemed to offer him another gateway to power, riches, and relevance.

At Eichmann's side in the late 1930s, von Bolschwing began to put the building blocks of Jewish persecution in place — first in Germany, then in Austria, then in Romania. Tall and lanky, with a long, angular face and a receding hairline, he moved from an idea man to an on-the-ground practitioner. Dispatched to Bucharest in 1941 as the head of the Nazi SS espionage unit, von Bolschwing joined with members of Romania's fascist

Iron Guard. There he teamed with Viorel Trifa, the fascist student leader who riled a fiery crowd of demonstrators one Sunday, littering the January air with praise for Hitler, denunciation of the "kikes," and a promise to "eliminate [the Jews'] domination." The hate-filled oratory exploded into a particularly gruesome, days-long pogrom in Bucharest that left synagogues burned, Torahs defiled, and hundreds of Jews killed — dozens skinned and hung from hooks like carcasses at a slaughterhouse. When the spasm of violence had ended, von Bolschwing, the Iron Guard's patron in Romania, hid away Trifa and other militant leaders in a Nazi safe house in Bucharest.

Just a few years later, however, von Bolschwing realized that Hitler was bound to fall. So, like General Wolff in Italy and other senior Nazis, he decided to cast his lot with the Americans. He began secretly providing intelligence to the U.S. Army about his Nazi colleagues and about German military operations even as the war was still being waged. He pledged his "loyalty to the United States." Yes, he had been an SS officer, he admitted to the Americans, but he had turned against Hitler by the end, he insisted; he was an *opponent* of the führer and had tried to bring him down, he claimed. There was no mention of his work with Eichmann to rid Germany of the Jews; only of his newfound commitment to helping America defeat the Nazi scourge. Army officials were impressed. Von Bolschwing, his American handlers believed, was one of the "good" Nazis; one of the reformed ones who had denounced the evils of Nazism and could now be used to help the United States. His cooperation at the end of the war was "virtually indispensable," an Army colonel wrote in August 1945. There was no thought of investigating the SS officer for possible war crimes, only of finding more ways for the United States to utilize him. "It is with pleasure that I commend him for his fine work," the Army colonel wrote in one letter of reference, "and recommend him without hesitation to any Military organization with which he may come in contact in the future."

The glowing endorsements opened doors for von Bolschwing. In the early years after the war, with American intelligence officials scrambling to find any ex-Nazis they could to provide dirt on the Soviets, von Bolschwing showed up all around Europe. The former Eichmann aide worked for a time with the spy ring of Wilhelm Höttl, the Nazi SS leader who had convinced American intelligence officials that his knowledge of the Russians should not "be left unused in an internment camp." Von Bolschwing also caught on with Reinhard Gehlen's American-funded spy network — until Gehlen, the former Nazi general, dropped him for ineptitude and insubordination. The setback to his spy career was short-lived: the CIA picked up von Bolschwing in the early 1950s to run his own spy network informing on the Soviets in Austria. The Americans paid him some $20,000 a year to run a small group of ex-Nazi spies, with a "long overdue" raise promised to boost their "general morale." Von Bolschwing was now a valued American employee. When he developed stomach problems — the apparent result of stress from his spy work — the Americans ordered him to take a month's vacation to rest up. When he needed a car, they found him one. With a long record of anti-Russian work on his Nazi resumé, he promised the Americans a treasure-trove of secrets on the Soviets and their plans for Europe. But like the cache of gold he had chased in Palestine years earlier, his bold claims produced little but dust. Sometimes he even proved to be a liability. Once, on a train ride in Austria in 1953, von Bolschwing managed to lose a suitcase filled with classified American spy photos, film, and an incriminating letter exposing the identity of a fellow undercover agent. In a moment of what the CIA called "sheer foolhardiness," von Bolschwing had mistakenly swapped his suitcase for another bag on the train, this one filled with toiletries, a pajama top, and a dress shirt. Twelve days later, after a frantic search and a bit of blind luck, von Bolschwing managed to retrieve his bag with all the top-secret material still safely inside. The CIA breathed easier. "We are convinced, after this affair," his American boss wrote gratefully, "that there is a Goddess of Good, who must look over our left shoulder and does favor us with an occasional smile."

Some officials within the CIA, however, had doubts from the start about the agency's bungling, well-paid ex-Nazi spy.

What was known about von Bolschwing's war record with the Nazis "rests almost entirely on his own unsupported statements," an early CIA assessment of its new spy noted. Von Bolschwing was "self seeking, egotistical, and a man of shifting loyalties," and his claims to have been a Nazi opponent who tried to thwart Hitler didn't hold up to scrutiny. He was "a shady character," another CIA memo concluded bluntly. "Hold him with a tight rein," one assessment warned.

Yes, von Bolschwing admitted to being a card-carrying member of the Nazi Party before and during the war, but only as a way of getting government approval for a cement factory he wanted to build in East Prussia, he insisted. It was simply a business decision. The CIA knew better. Inside its own files was a mound of evidence linking him directly to Eichmann and top echelons of the SS. After the war, the agency noted in his file, "Bolschwing was denounced by a source believed to be reliable, as a member of the notorious SD Sonderkommando 'Eichmann' [team]." Another source in Poland identified him as the SS's top man in Romania in aiding the Iron Guard.

But the CIA stuck with von Bolschwing nonetheless. His membership in the Nazi Party under Hitler was "relatively inconsequential, particularly in view of subject's excellent service on our behalf," one assessment concluded.

Indeed, the CIA would rally to the ex-Nazi officer's aid many times over the years. When the Austrians inquired about von Bolschwing in 1950 because of war crimes suspicions surrounding him, CIA officials covered for him. The Austrians were told that there was "no file available." It was a lie of necessity, the CIA believed. One senior CIA official cabled: "Consider it essential [von Bolschwing] maintain present position and freedom of movement." When von Bolschwing ran into visa problems a few years later, the CIA tried to help get him citizenship in Austria, even after lying to the Austrians about his Nazi past. When that didn't work, they took another course that von Bolschwing had favored all along — to "realize his dream of becoming an American citizen." To get him into the United States, the CIA sped up his visa application and cleaned up his record — with instructions for von Bolschwing and officials at the CIA not to say anything to U.S. immigration officials about his Nazi affiliation. The extraordinary treatment was "a reward for his loyal post-war service and in view of the innocuousness of his [Nazi] party activities," the CIA wrote. The spy agency attended to every detail of the relocation. When Mrs. von Bolschwing, who feared flying, expressed anxiety about taking a plane to America, the CIA booked passage for the couple on the luxurious *Andrea Doria* cruise ship instead. With the family's "smooth landing" happily confirmed by the CIA on February 2, 1954, a military intelligence officer who had worked with von Bolschwing in Europe after the war was there to greet them and even to host them in his Boston home for their first few months in America. Less than a decade after the Nazis' defeat, Ossie had a new home and a new life.

It was a comfortable life, and a profitable one, as von Bolschwing used his expertise in international trade to become an executive for a series of big drug and chemical companies in America, including Warner-Lambert and the Cabot Corporation. He would travel back to Germany, back to the place where he had worked for Eichmann decades earlier, to consult on big projects like a carbon plant that Cabot was building in Frankfurt. If his colleagues knew anything about his true past, they did not say. He was so well-connected that he was even in line for a prestigious State Department posting in India as an American representative in international development. That is, until his old boss in the Jewish Affairs office was captured that spring day in 1960. Eichmann's capture threatened all that. Von Bolschwing feared that he was next. So he went back to the one place he thought could best help him: the CIA.

When the agency had brought him to America six years earlier as a reward for his good work, his handlers had ordered him — for his sake and for theirs — to break off all contact. He had been told to come back to his old CIA bosses only in a "dire emergency," a "life or death" situation. In von Bolschwing's mind, the capture of his old Nazi boss in Argentina qualified as just such an event. When he learned of Eichmann's brazen abduction, he went immediately to one of his old CIA handlers to ask for protection. His own name was bound to come out at Eichmann's trial, he predicted. (He was right; it did.) He wasn't worried about just the prospect that the Israelis would try to abduct him as they had Eichmann, he told the CIA; he was "afraid for his life."

So, after a six-year estrangement from its ex-Nazi spy, the CIA went back to work to help von Bolschwing. The agency had as much reason as he did to fear the possible fallout from Eichmann's capture. American intelligence officials had done little for years to find Eichmann, despite his global notoriety. By 1952, when the Austrians asked about Eichmann's status as a fugitive, America's waning interest was clear. "Prosecution of war criminals is no longer considered of primary importance to U.S. Authorities," an Army intelligence official wrote in an internal memo. Two years before the Israelis captured Eichmann, in fact, the CIA received a tantalizing lead that Eichmann might be living in Argentina under the last name "Clemens." The CIA did nothing. Not until the Israelis captured "Ricardo Klement" in Buenos Aires did officials at the spy agency realize — or care — just how close they had come to nabbing the world's most notorious Nazi.

Worse still for the CIA, von Bolschwing was just one of at least five ex-Nazis associated with Eichmann and the Final Solution who had worked with the CIA after the war in providing Soviet intelligence. The other four, unlike von Bolschwing, had remained in Europe, but their ties to the CIA ran almost as deep. CIA officials, alarmed by the implications of Eichmann's capture, combed their own files to determine how much damage von Bolschwing and the others might inflict. They were desperate to keep von Bolschwing's name — and his involvement with the CIA and with Eichmann — out of the newspapers.

West German agents, meanwhile, spent a month in Washington going through secret U.S. intelligence files on their own. Only then, CIA officials said in a string of secret, internal memos, did the agency unearth "voluminous information" about Eichmann that linked von Bolschwing directly to him and the Jewish Affairs office. Of course, much of the evidence linking von Bolschwing to Eichmann had been sitting in the CIA's own files for years, but officials at Langley played dumb, blaming von Bolschwing's dishonesty for their current predicament as they tried to assess the damage. The agent "failed to advise us that he had been involved with several war criminals," one internal memo said flatly. They knew von Bolschwing was a Nazi, CIA officials admitted; they just didn't realize how bad a Nazi he really was. For the CIA, it was better to appear duped by an Eichmann collaborator than complicit with one.

Von Bolschwing's pleas for help set off months of memos, in-house reviews, and handwringing at the CIA. Ultimately, the agency was willing to give the desperate von Bolschwing what he wanted: silence and protection. The CIA would not give him up to the Israelis, the agency assured him. Nor would it tell the U.S. Justice Department what it knew about his true Nazi past and risk a messy deportation case if prosecutors were to try to throw him out of the country. No one else even had to know that Ossie von Bolschwing was living the good life of an American businessman in New York City.

But the CIA's silence came with one condition, and it was not negotiable. Von Bolschwing was still being considered for the plum job in India with a State Department development agency, thanks to the support of a former governor in New Jersey who ran the export firm where he worked. He would have to drop out of the running for the post, CIA officials decided. Immediately. The agency could not risk the publicity the job was bound to bring him just as the case against Eichmann was ramping up in Israel. "It is our assumption," an internal CIA memo warned, that von Bolschwing "may be named as EICHMANN'S collaborator and fellow conspirator and that the resulting publicity may prove embarrassing to the U.S. if the subject becomes involved with [the State Department agency] or its activities." Without saying exactly why, the CIA pressured the State Department to drop von Bolschwing from consideration. That failed; he had too much support. CIA officials realized that they needed to get von Bolschwing himself to drop out. He needed to be told point-blank, the CIA decided, that unless he withdrew his bid for the job, the CIA would have no choice but to let his political supporters know all about his Nazi past and his ties to Eichmann — "with resultant unpleasantness to himself."

So, on a spring evening in New York City, two CIA officials who worked with von Bolschwing during his spy days in Eastern Europe sat him down to deliver the ultimatum: either relinquish the State Department job or risk the messy consequences. Despite the ominous message, von Bolschwing's visitors struck a conciliatory tone. The CIA, his old handler began, valued his "continued friendship." Agency officials did feel a bit duped by everything they were now learning of his close ties to Eichmann, his handler admitted, but no one was angry with him, he stressed, and the meeting wasn't meant as a punishment. "The purpose of the meeting, it was explained, was to draw his attention to the scandal that might result if he pressed his desire for employment" with the State Department, his handler wrote afterward. Eichmann's arrest had simply made it impossible for von Bolschwing to serve in a government post, they said.

Von Bolschwing protested. It was ridiculous for anyone to suggest that he had been Eichmann's collaborator, he said. He brought out a denazification certificate he had received in Austria after the war. Surely that was evidence of his innocence, was it not? He tried to walk his old CIA colleagues through his career with the Nazis — to explain how he'd been forced to join the party and played only a nominal role before turning against Hitler. They cut him off. They had expected his strident denials. They had read through all the new material linking him to Eichmann in the Jewish Affairs office. It was obvious, his handler told von Bolschwing, that he had told the CIA "far less than the truth about his Nazi activities." As much as he liked von Bolschwing, he said, it was impossible to believe from the SS records in their possession that he was anything but an active participant and full partner in Eichmann's operations in Nazi Germany. That was all likely to spill out into public view if he pushed ahead with the State Department posting, his handler warned him. The record of his SS activities with Eichmann, if it became known, would surely make him "a pariah" in America and Europe. There was the risk not just of a public shaming, but of a war crimes prosecution. Did he really want to go through "the anguish and expense of a legal trial before a West German or Israeli court?" his handler asked.

No, von Bolschwing agreed. He did not want to take such a risk. Realizing there was no way to press on with his job application, he agreed to withdraw his name from consideration for the post. He would cite personal reasons: his health, perhaps. The Nazi issue would not be mentioned. His handler would draft a telegraph to send to the State Department the following day, along with a letter to one of his congressional supporters who had strongly backed him for the job, they agreed.

Von Bolschwing was despondent over seeing his Nazi past suddenly thrown back at him fifteen years after the war. Twice he mentioned suicide to his CIA friends. He was particularly worried about how to explain to his wife his sudden change of heart over the India job. She had been depressed recently, and she was still recovering after a car accident. This would no doubt upset her even more, he confided. She knew little about his past, he said, and she wasn't the type who could live out her life with a "guilty secret." Grudgingly, he settled on a plan: he would admit to his wife that before the war, before they were married, he had worked for the Nazis in "emigrating Jews" out of Germany. His work was now being subjected to unfair "misinterpretation" in the wake of Eichmann's capture, he would tell her, and he was pulling his name for the State Department job as a result. That was all she needed to know.

And what about his American citizenship? Von Bolschwing was worried about that, too. He had received his citizenship papers only two years before. Was his immigration status in danger too? The CIA couldn't make any guarantees, his handler told him, but the agency would do what it could for him by working to ensure that no one else outside the CIA's security channels found out about his deep ties to Eichmann. Von Bolschwing's dark secrets were safe with the CIA. No one else needed to know.

Von Bolschwing was satisfied. As upset as he was over the sudden turn of events, his mood seemed to brighten as he and his old CIA friends agreed on a course of action to contain the damage from this ugly episode. "He showed surprising resilience and apparent courage," his handler wrote admiringly. Von Bolschwing "is tough and resourceful," he was glad to report; the ex-Nazi would no doubt soldier on. He was already looking to the future and seemed intent on "clearing his record and reinstating himself as a first-class citizen."

5

Tilting at Swastikas

May 19, 1963

CHICAGO, ILLINOIS

Eichmann's capture proved more a blip than a turning point. The broad global manhunt that Otto von Bolschwing had so feared never really materialized, and he and thousands of other ex-Nazis in America lived with little fear of scrutiny in the era of Camelot.

But a blue-blooded Quaker from Philadelphia was determined to change all that.

His name was Chuck Allen, and on a drizzling spring day in Chicago in 1963, he stood at the center of a raucous crowd of protesters and denounced "the Nazi war criminals in our midst." Even before the white mice were let loose and the neo-Nazis showed up, the day's event was shaping up as one of the odder protests that Chicago had seen in quite a while.

A diverse crowd of left-wing demonstrators — card-carrying Communists, an Orthodox rabbi, black civil rights activists, union leaders, and more — packed into a meeting hall to rally for a cause few outsiders even knew existed: expelling Nazi fugitives from America. Allen was their unlikely young leader.

A writer, activist, and provocateur, Allen was a celebrity among the Chicago protesters, almost a folk hero, thanks to a searing forty-two-page exposé he had just published in *Jewish Currents,* a tiny Communist-affiliated magazine in New York. In it, he made a startling charge: at least fifteen ex-Nazis were living openly in America, some of them right here in Chicago. He realized that his was a lonely cause. "What can a single journalist say about the story of the war criminals living among us?" Allen wrote. "We as a people are quite responsible for letting this happen, and are now doubly obligated to resolve this deeply moral issue. Now just what are we going to do about it?"

The righteous indignation was typical for Allen. A modern Don Quixote, armed with a poison pen instead of a lance, he tilted not at windmills, but at swastikas. A gifted athlete who played semipro football after college, Allen was known to his friends as Baby Bull. It was as much for his aggressive personality as his athletic build. He had no time for niceties. Long-haired and loquacious, Allen figured that if Americans were blind to the Holocaust and its aftermath, he would strongarm them into remembering.

Allen was ready to back up the sensational charges he was making. One of those named in his report was a leading figure in Chicago with the Catholic Church — a bishop from Lithuania named Vincentas Brizgys who was widely admired for ministering to war refugees in America. Allen unearthed a document prepared by American prosecutors at Nuremberg fifteen years earlier on the Nazi occupation of Lithuania and the bishop's long-hidden role there. The American prosecutors portrayed the bishop not as an exile of the war, but as a Nazi ally who cast his lot with the "liberating Germans" after they overran his country. Citing a secret SS report on the murders of some sixteen hundred Lithuanians in 1941, the Nuremberg report included a particularly chilling line on the clergyman's wartime role: "Bishop Brizgys has forbidden all clergy to aid Jews in any way."

In his exposé, Allen declared the bishop a war criminal. He made no distinction between the Nazis themselves and an apparent Nazi sympathizer like Brizgys; Allen was never one for nuance or subtlety in his writing, and he made no pretense of sober journalistic objectivity. His screed was a call to action, a boldface indictment of America's complicity in allowing ex-Nazis and their collaborators to live in their adopted homeland with impunity. The three-part series, accompanied by wartime photos and reproductions of documents like the Nuremberg SS report on Bishop Brizgys, was so voluminous that the editors at *Jewish Currents* printed it as a separate pamphlet and sold it for a quarter a copy. It caused a sensation among left-wingers, and the magazine had to order more printings to meet the demand.

Yet within the "establishment" that Allen so detested — mainstream newspapers, political organizations, and prominent Jewish advocacy groups — his report went essentially unnoticed. Those even aware of what he was writing dismissed him as a Russian mouthpiece who was parroting Soviet disinformation in order to damage the reputations of staunch anti-Communists. Who was Chuck Allen, they asked, to be making such outrageous charges? He was an outlier, a man with a political bias, no credibility, and a tiny audience.

It became easy for his critics to dismiss him not only as a loudmouthed know-it-all, but a Marxist-spouting ideologue as well. Allen didn't care; he made no attempt to hide his lefty views. While he always denied being a member of the Communist Party, he refused on principle to sign the loyalty oaths popular at the time; his stance cost him several jobs in journalism, and he struggled to find anyplace that would print his stories as a result.

"My principle has always been that I'll work with you — no matter who you are, including a raving Communist — so long as you are anti-fascist, anti-Nazi, anti-racist, and anti-anti-Semite," he once said. Allen reveled in the attacks against him: the tougher the fight, the better. He got up every morning "looking forward to doing combat against these wahoos," he once remarked.

Nothing in Allen's Christian background suggested he would become one of America's first Nazi hunters or, for that matter, that he would end up in the FBI's crosshairs because of it. If Americans thought at all about Nazi fugitives after the war — and few did — the image of the relentless Nazi hunter was embodied across the Atlantic in the slight, balding frame and thick Austrian accent of Holocaust survivor Simon Wiesenthal.

Chuck Allen was different. A self-described WASP, Allen wasn't Jewish, and he traced his ancestors not to war-torn Europe but to early settlers in America in the seventeenth century. He came to the Holocaust by chance in college at Swarthmore, when he fell for a Jewish refugee from Germany. They would read together late into the night, and the wrenching stories she told him of Kristallnacht, the notorious night of terror for German Jews in 1938, obsessed Allen long after the two parted ways.

What Allen lacked in Holocaust pedigree he made up for in an outsize passion for social causes, a trait he credited to his grandmother, a Pennsylvania Quaker who worked as a physician and pushed for women's rights.

As a journalist for left-wing publications in the 1950s, Allen wrote about McCarthyism, racial injustice, the KKK, and Nazism long before such topics were in vogue. He often came across — both in person and in his writings — as bombastic, self-righteous, abrasive, and hot-tempered. In college, a classmate analyzed Allen as the subject for a psychology paper on "natural superiority complex." He couldn't disagree with the assessment. Like a district attorney giving his closing argument, Allen would announce with dramatic flair, "I have proof that . . ." or "now it can be revealed that . . . ," as he spoke before audiences, launching into the evidence he had gathered against another accused Nazi in America.

Allen worked out of his small apartment in Manhattan, surrounded by dozens of boxes and a steamer trunk packed with material he had gathered over the years: war crimes documents from Nuremberg, alphabetical filings on the accused Nazis he was chasing, notebooks from interviews he conducted, letters from Holocaust survivors he'd contacted, photos from concentration camps, and macabre Nazi memorabilia. In the weeks and months before his big Nazi series ran in 1963, Allen trekked to dingy apartment buildings, a church, even the U.S. State Department, to try to locate the men he was about to name as war criminals. Some of his targets had been dogged by rumors of Nazi ties for years, with their names appearing in published reports before. Others faced war crimes accusations for the first time when they opened their doors to the intimidating stare of Chuck Allen. Almost to a man, those who spoke to Allen blamed the accusations against them on "Communist lies," and invariably, Allen would press them for more. So where had they actually been during the war? Did they serve with the Nazis? How had they gotten into the United States? He was more hardball detective than inquiring reporter. He tracked down the phone number for a New Jersey immigrant who, he learned, had been convicted in absentia as a member of a Nazi execution squad in Byelorussia, and called him up, demanding to know not only about the immigrant's Nazi past, but also the current whereabouts of another ex-Nazi who came to America from the same concentration camp. "Listen, mister," the man shot back. "You bother me any more and I get the FBI on you!"

The men Allen named publicly as war criminals had little reason to fear scrutiny in the United States, no matter what he wrote about them. One of them, the high-profile Hitler aide Dr. Gustav Hilger, was even listed in the

Washington phone book by his real name in the 1950s as he traveled seamlessly between the worlds of academia, diplomacy, and intelligence as an undercover "consultant" to the CIA. A decade earlier, as the Nazis' top specialist on Moscow, Dr. Hilger had been with Hitler in the Nazis' headquarters for the eastern front after Germany's murderous invasion of Russia. He was implicated in the roundup of Jews in Italy as well. After the war he was wanted in Europe for war crimes. Yet George Kennan at the State Department and Frank Wisner at the CIA had arranged in 1948 to spirit him and his family away to safety in Washington, where he became an éminence grise on all things Russian. "We were very glad he was here because we were worried that if we didn't [bring him over], the Soviets would get him," Kennan said. At the CIA, Hilger met secretly with analysts every two weeks to assess the latest developments in Moscow, and he could often be found at the Library of Congress, researching his memoirs as part of his CIA cover story. Raul Hilberg, a leading Holocaust researcher, would sometimes spot the ex-Hitler advisor working nearby in the federal archives, whereupon Hilberg would walk out in silent protest. The scholar finally decided to send Dr. Hilger a letter posing a series of uncomfortable questions about his role with the Nazis. Not surprisingly, he never heard back.

Allen, however, managed to reach Hilger on the phone one day as he prepared to go to print with his Nazi investigation.

"Hilger?" Allen barked when he picked up the phone.

"Ja?" came the answer.

Never one for the conventions of mainstream journalists, Allen didn't bother to identify himself as he launched into a series of pointed questions about Hilger's past activities in Germany and his role in Washington with the U.S. government.

"Just a minute! Who *is* this?" Hilger asked.

"Look, you are Dr. Gustav Hilger?" Allen responded. "Dr. Hilger, what precisely is your work with the U.S. State Department?"

"I have nothing to say. Nothing to say."

With that, he hung up. The next day, he had a new, unlisted phone number.

Few people outside the far left paid much attention to Allen's writings. Nor did many outsiders notice when, in the wake of his "Nazi War Criminals Among Us" series, Allen and his band of supporters formed a group calling itself the National Committee Against Nazism and Nazi Criminals. In Brooklyn, in Chicago, and in Los Angeles, the group organized rallies protesting fugitive Nazis — the first protests of their kind anywhere in America. It seemed an unobjectionable cause on its face. Yet at the Chicago demonstration, dozens of counterprotesters turned out to picket, many of them local immigrants from Latvia, Lithuania, Estonia, and other Eastern European countries occupied by the Nazis during the war. The picketers had heard about the journalist's crusade and believed their countrymen were being unfairly smeared by accusations of Nazi collaboration. Defending their homelands, the counterprotesters saw Allen and his left-wing cohorts as troublemakers and interlopers.

In the midst of Allen's fist-pounding oratory from the podium, the demonstration was brought to a halt when one of the counterprotesters, a young Latvian woman, let loose ten white mice into the crowd, sending people scurrying in a momentary panic. It was a bizarre scene, but not unprecedented. A Jewish newspaper in Chicago noted bitterly a few weeks later that setting loose mice was "one of the cute tricks used by the storm troopers in Hitler's rise to power" as a way to disperse unfriendly crowds. Joseph Goebbels, the Nazi propaganda minister, had used the same tactic to break up a showing of the 1930 film *All Quiet on the Western Front* because of its hostile, anti-German theme. Arrested, the Latvian woman in Chicago with the bagful of mice was fined $200 for disturbing the peace. But she had made her point: Allen and his ilk weren't welcome in her town.

Indeed, the rally had barely picked up again when a group of young men standing unobtrusively amid the crowd removed their shirts to reveal Nazi uniforms adorned with swastikas. Even as Allen was calling for the expulsion of Nazi war criminals, the young men were there as proud representatives from the American Nazi Party — a new generation of storm troopers. Fourteen years later, the American Nazis in Chicago would set off a famous constitutional battle over free speech with a planned march in nearby Skokie. On this day, they set off a brawl as they marched toward the podium. Allen met one of them with a blow to the head that he later claimed, with pride, had broken the neo-Nazi's jaw. In his struggle to defeat Nazis past and present, Allen counted the moment as a rare victory.

• • •

The neo-Nazis weren't the only ones worried about Chuck Allen that day in Chicago. The FBI was secretly watching him too — that day and many more like it; in Chicago, in Washington, in New York, even in Europe. While the neo-Nazis were confronting Allen head-on, the FBI was watching him from the shadows.

Allen had always suspected the FBI might be trailing him. He would talk in code on the phone in case his line was tapped. He would tell friends about unexplained incidents — the time, for instance, when he met with an Eastern European source in Connecticut to discuss Nazi war crimes records and noticed that he and his contact were apparently being followed by two men in a 1976 Plymouth Fury. One of the men was taking pictures. Allen jotted down the New York plates — 51-DKL-1976 — and traced the vehicle to a rental fleet used by the U.S. government.

As suspicious as he'd become, even Allen was dumbfounded when he discovered years later the full scope of the FBI's surveillance. The government files on him — not just at the FBI, but at the CIA and other agencies as well — totaled thousands of pages. As the documents demonstrated, the FBI had waged a decade-long campaign against the Nazi hunter beginning in the late 1950s in the belief that he was a dangerous Communist agitator. With the FBI then at the peak of its monitoring of left-wing "subversives," the bureau had set its sights on much higher-profile targets like Martin Luther King Jr., Muhammad Ali, and Benjamin Spock, but its surveillance of Allen was every bit as aggressive. J. Edgar Hoover himself signed off on the extraordinary treatment. One secret memo "re Charles Russell Allen Jr.," signed by Hoover and sent to the Secret Service, laid out the legal pretext for the government's actions. Under FBI protocol for launching such operations, Mr. Allen needed to be watched, the bureau asserted, because he "is potentially dangerous; or has been identified as a member or participant in communist movement" or other groups "inimical to US."

In a cruel bit of historical irony, Allen had Hitler to thank, at least indirectly, for the powers the FBI claimed in spying on him. In 1933, the German Embassy in Washington turned over to the Americans an anonymous letter from someone in the United States threatening to kill Germany's newly named chancellor, Adolf Hitler. The FBI was put on the case. At the time, its power to investigate subversive activity inside the United States was limited, but with the death threat to Hitler as an opening, Hoover secured from FDR broad new authority to establish an intelligence branch and investigate insurgent activity not just by Americans trying to kill foreign leaders, but also by "Communists, fascists ... or groups advocating the overthrow or replacement of the Government of the United States by illegal methods."

And so Chuck Allen, chasing Nazis thirty years later, fell into the FBI's dragnet. At a civil rights rally at the Statue of Liberty, at an anti-Nazi demonstration in front of the West German Consulate in New York City, at the Nazi protests in Chicago and Los Angeles and elsewhere around the country in the 1960s, the FBI would send agents to spy on him and report back on everything he said and did. The bureau paid informants to infiltrate his organization. Agents showed his photo to known Communists to see if they could confirm that he was a member of the party. (None could.) The FBI dutifully cataloged the many articles in left-wing publications in which Allen was quoted. One FBI report, recapping a 1966 article commemorating the Warsaw ghetto uprising, noted: "Allen said that although the United States did not have a Nazi tradition it was engaging in genocide in Vietnam." It all went into his secret file.

The FBI had plenty of help from other agencies, including not just the CIA, but the U.S. Postal Service and the State Department as well. With Allen exchanging numerous letters and documents with sources in Eastern Europe as he gathered war crimes evidence, the CIA opened and photographed the documents, adding them to its burgeoning file on him. He was placed on a secret "Lookout" list, so when he would travel overseas the eyes of the American government would track his movements and report when he left and when he reentered the country. "Will ascertain subject's plans for travel to Russia and East Germany," promised one FBI memo in 1965.

The one thing the FBI was hesitant to do was simply ask Allen himself: Are you a Communist? The bureau thought about interviewing him directly, but decided the risks were too high. Because Allen was "a freelance writer and might well use this interview for one of his attacks on the impairment of civil rights, and harassment by the FBI," one early memo in his file noted, it was felt that "an interview might prove to be a source of embarrassment to the Bureau."

Besides, the bureau noted almost as an afterthought, "a review of the file does not indicate CP [Communist Party] membership for the subject, or that he is an officer in a front group."

In fact, the FBI didn't need to go to Allen to find out what he was doing. He came to them. Weeks before his 1963 series on Nazi war criminals went to print, Allen wrote to the Justice Department and Attorney General Robert F. Kennedy with his findings, along with all the detailed evidence he had accumulated in the United States and Europe. He was hoping to get at least a formal comment from the department to include in his series. Perhaps, if he was lucky, the government might even cooperate with him in ferreting out the Nazis living in America. Allen was in essence offering to share a trove of documents on Nazi war crimes unavailable in the Justice Department's own threadbare files.

Allen's overture did attract attention at the Justice Department, but not for the reasons he'd hoped. A top aide in Hoover's inner circle, a trusted FBI advisor named Deke DeLoach, read through Allen's plea for help. DeLoach was adamant in his response: ignore him. Hoover, of course, was already on record telling his aides years before that he found "no substantiation" to allegations that a large number of Nazi fugitives were living inside the United States. DeLoach, in an internal memo to fellow FBI officials in January 1963, sidestepped entirely the substance of Allen's letter to Kennedy — "the presence of alleged war criminals now living in the United States," as DeLoach characterized it. He focused instead on Allen's own nefarious background — his "connection with various Communist front groups"; his association with a prominent labor leader of the day; and his "militant" public opposition to a McCarthy-era law used to prosecute "subversives." Given his background, DeLoach concluded, "Allen most certainly deserved no reply to his request for assistance in connection with his planned series of articles."

Three months later, long after Allen had published his Nazi series with a "no comment" from the Justice Department, a top aide to Kennedy finally got back to Allen with a perfunctory response. "Dear Mr. Allen," the letter began. "The Attorney General has asked me to respond to your most recent letter regarding the 16 individuals about whom you inquired earlier. After reviewing the correspondence, I am afraid I cannot see what further information this Department is able to supply you."

Allen, as always, got in the last word. Perched at his typewriter, he rapped out a follow-up story for the next issue of *Jewish Currents* detailing the vague and unsatisfying responses he'd gotten from the Justice Department and other federal agencies.

"Our Government 'Replies' to Charges," the headline read. "State Department and Immigration Service evade issue of Nazi war criminals among us." Above the story was the familiar byline that so irked the FBI: BY CHARLES R. ALLEN, JR.

Despite Chuck Allen's best efforts to shake America out of its Nazi slumber, the country remained largely indifferent. But sometimes, a reminder of the United States' links to Hitler's minions became too jarring to simply ignore. Such a moment came in early 1964, just months after the raucous anti-Nazi demonstration that Allen led in Chicago. And it began with a chance conversation in an outdoor café in Tel Aviv.

Simon Wiesenthal, Chuck Allen's better-known counterpart in Europe, was there for a bite to eat when three middle-aged Israeli women heard him being paged over the loudspeaker. They hurried over to his table to speak with him. Wiesenthal had attracted a measure of fame recently after outing an active-duty Austrian police officer who, as a Nazi officer two decades earlier, had seized Anne Frank from hiding. Wiesenthal's three visitors at the café — all Polish natives who had survived the Nazi concentration camp at Majdanek in Poland — knew of his growing reputation, and they approached him now with a question that had haunted them since their emancipation: What happened to Kobyla?

Wiesenthal had no idea what they meant. What, or who, was Kobyla? Soon enough, the women's story poured out: at Majdanek, the Nazi graveyard for an estimated 1.5 million Jews and other undesirables, there was a female guard, an Austrian woman who, even by the camp's gruesome standards, was infamous for her sadistic treatment of the female prisoners. "She was the worst of them all," one of the women told Wiesenthal. They called her Kobyla — the Polish word for mare — because of the ruthless way she would kick the women with her steel-toed boots. Her real name, one of the women recalled, was Hermine Braunsteiner. They couldn't put her out of their minds. She would march through camp with a whip, they said, lashing the prisoners at will. Leading the prisoners to the gas chamber at Majdanek was not enough for her; she seemed determined to humiliate them first, robbing them of whatever human dignity they had left. She was particularly cruel to the children. One of the women recalled for Wiesenthal the time when a new prisoner was brought to the death camp with a toddler on his back hidden in a rucksack; Braunsteiner whipped the child to tears, then shot him dead.

Back at his office in Vienna, Wiesenthal checked his files and discovered that a Hermine Braunsteiner had in fact been put on trial after the war in Austria — right there in his own city. She was sentenced to three years in prison for kicking and whipping female prisoners — not at Majdanek, but at a different concentration camp in Ravensbrück. Three years for such savagery seemed like a pittance to him, with no punishment at all for what she did to those women and children at Majdanek.

What had happened to her? Wiesenthal didn't know. But he and a researcher soon managed to track her hopscotch travels from Austria to Halifax, Canada, and on to Queens, New York, where, the last anyone seemed to know, she was living with her American husband, a construction worker named Russell Ryan. It was an improbable journey that had led a notorious Nazi guard — a woman, no less — to America.

Even Wiesenthal didn't consider the United States much of a destination for Nazi war criminals. Only a small number of suspected Nazis had ever been identified publicly in America, despite Chuck Allen's best efforts, and there was little political will during the Cold War to do anything about those few who had been identified. Despite many formal extradition requests from Russia and its Eastern European satellites seeking to prosecute accused Nazi war criminals, the United States had never agreed to send any of them back to stand trial. But the case of Kobyla — the "mare" of Majdanek — seemed different to Wiesenthal, if nothing else for its raw brutality and the power of the eyewitnesses who survived the terror.

Wiesenthal went first to U.S. government officials with what he knew. Like Chuck Allen a year before, he heard nothing back from them. American officials seemed to have no interest in the case. But Wiesenthal was adept at working not only with myriad governments, but with reporters, Jewish organizations, and survivors' groups, often leveraging one against the other to get results. Where Chuck Allen was determined to fight the system, Wiesenthal adroitly worked within it. So he brought his tip to a *New York Times* reporter in Vienna who had just written a long and flattering profile of Wiesenthal a few months earlier under the headline: "Sleuth with 6 Million Clients." Within days, Braunsteiner's name, along with all the damning information Wiesenthal had compiled on her, landed on the desk of a rookie metro reporter in New York named Joe Lelyveld. Wiesenthal had narrowed down Braunsteiner's apparent whereabouts to a blue-collar, immigrant-heavy neighborhood of Queens called Maspeth, but he did not have an exact address for her. So the young reporter began looking in the phone books for Ryans — the married name she had taken — and started knocking on doors.

He got lucky: the first Mrs. Ryan that he approached knew precisely the Austrian namesake he was trying to find; she pointed him to an address nearby at Seventy-Second Street. There, a tall, big-boned woman with a stern face and thin lips locked in what seemed a perpetual pucker answered the door. Her blond hair, now turning gray, was in curlers, and she had a paintbrush in her hand; she'd been painting the interior of her house. She was friendly enough, until she found out who Lelyveld was and what he wanted. "Mrs. Ryan, I need to ask about your time in Poland, at the Majdanek camp, during the war," Lelyveld began. Braunsteiner, a house-wife who had become an American citizen just the year before, began sobbing. "Oh, my God, I knew this would happen," she said. Quickly, the tears were overtaken by an angry and rambling defense of her actions. Yes, she had worked at Majdanek, she acknowledged, but "all I did was what guards do in the camps now," she said. It was all so long ago, she said. "On the radio all they talk is peace and freedom. Then fifteen or sixteen years later, why do they bother people? I was punished enough. I was in prison three years. Three years, can you imagine? And now they want something again from me?"

She was just a guard, Braunsteiner said in a self-pitying tone; just a lowly guard who did what she was told. Lelyveld then told her of a letter that Wiesenthal had written about her case, with detailed accusations against her. The letter suggested she was not just a lowly guard, but something much worse. Emotion overtook her again. "This is the end," she said, pacing across her small living room. "This is the end of everything for me."

A few days later, a story appeared in the *New York Times* under the head-line: "Former Nazi Camp Guard Is Now a Housewife in Queens." It was written in the *Times*'s typically understated tone, with none of the rhetorical flair of Chuck Allen's anti-Nazi writings. But it carried a wallop in New York, and it drew the attention of law enforcement officials in Washington as well. The very next day, with a speed and aggressiveness hardly ever seen in two decades of periodic Nazi reports, U.S. immigration officials announced that they were opening an investigation into the woman who was to become known as the notorious Stomping Mare of Majdanek. The INS wanted to know whether Mrs. Braunsteiner Ryan had lied her way into the United States by concealing her Nazi past.

What, if anything, would happen to her was still uncertain. But for once, the country seemed to be taking notice. American officials could brush aside Chuck Allen's fevered ranting with no fear of political fallout. But now Simon Wiesenthal and the *New York Times* were on the story. The Stomping Mare of Queens could not simply be ignored.

6

In the Pursuit of Science

November 23, 1974

SAN ANTONIO, TEXAS

"Does 'Hubertus Strughold' mean anything to you?"

Chuck Allen shrugged. "No, why?"

It was 1974, and Allen, the rabble-rousing reporter, was meeting off the record with a former INS investigator named Tony DeVito about Allen's favorite topic. It had been more than a decade since the reporter's big exposé, and the collective shrug it generated had done little to dim his obsession with all things Nazi. In DeVito, he had found a kindred soul, a man almost as outraged as himself by the government's apathy in confronting its hidden Nazi problem.

DeVito, a pint-sized, gruff-talking New Yorker from Hell's Kitchen, had taken to the Nazi chase himself a few years earlier when he was put on the INS's investigation into the Stomping Mare. DeVito was convinced there were more war criminals out there like Queens housewife Hermine Braunsteiner Ryan. His problem was that his bosses at the INS didn't seem to give a damn about Nazis except when the stories hit the papers. They preferred to deport Communists and pot-smoking rock stars like John Lennon. A World War II veteran who walked through Dachau hours after its liberation, DeVito railed against the agency's lethargy. "Don't we owe an immediate inquiry to the six million Jews and some five million others who perished in gas chambers and crematoriums of concentration camps under the Third Reich?" he asked in one memo to his bosses.

DeVito was so frustrated by the INS's failure to throw the Nazis out of the country that he quit the agency after more than twenty years as an investigator. If the INS didn't care about Nazi immigrants, DeVito figured there was one person who would want to hear more about them, and that was Chuck Allen.

DeVito's current fixation was Dr. Hubertus Strughold. Allen had never heard of the man with the odd-sounding name before, but DeVito was about to tell him everything he needed to know.

"Until he retired, he was the chief scientist of NASA's aerospace medical division," DeVito began. "The press calls him the father of space medicine." Strughold had apparently come to America from Germany just a few years after the war, DeVito said, but exactly how he got into the country wasn't clear. "After Wernher von Braun, he's the top Nazi scientist who's worked for the government."

DeVito wasn't done. Strughold, he said, is "supposed to have been involved — from the top — in medical atrocities. High-altitude and freezing experiments on prisoners at Dachau."

Chuck Allen stared back at his tipster, the outlines of a blockbuster story already forming in his mind. Now DeVito had his attention.

Hubertus Strughold, a buttoned-up, bow-tied doctor of aviation medicine, was indeed a star scientist — first for the Nazis, then for the Americans. He was one of the U.S. military's most prized catches in Project Paperclip, the secret program that brought some sixteen hundred German scientists to the United States after the war.

No one rose to greater heights among the German scientists than von Braun and Strughold, longtime colleagues from their days together in the German military. By the time General Eisenhower became president in 1953 on the strength of his war record in defeating their homeland, von Braun and Strughold — though not yet American citizens — were already living in the rarified air of scientific royalty, a fairytale existence out of reach to all but a few of America's native sons. With America racing to catch up with the Russians in the space war, they were at the center of it all as scientific emissaries testifying before Congress, lobbying the military for money, and selling the public on the promise of space travel. At an air force base in San Antonio, Strughold would pose for photos and give tours of his flight simulator to VIPs like Senator Lyndon Johnson and the shah of Iran. From his new perch at the military arsenal in Huntsville, Alabama, meanwhile, von Braun wrote popular space novels, became lionized as the subject of a feature film, and even earned that high mark of American cultural status, a spot on the cover of *Time* magazine — as America's "Missileman." The German-born scientist had ready access to leaders throughout the Pentagon and the space program, and he learned to work the American political system as well as any Washington insider. If a military subordinate in Alabama came to him with a gripe about the rocket program, von Braun would dismiss it with a wave of the hand and say: "Go tell it to your congressman!"

Von Braun and Strughold were ex-Nazi scientists now standing at the cross-section of Hollywood and Washington; of comic-book fantasy and awe-inspiring reality; of America's wartime past and its boundless future. Von Braun made America's rockets fly, and Strughold kept its pilots alive. Together, they were poised to take America into space.

Strughold's newfound stature had crystallized in the fall of 1957, when he was sailing aboard the *Queen Mary* en route to Europe. Hollywood filmmaker Walt Disney happened to be aboard the stately ship with him. Disney, learning that a space scientist of some renown was onboard, quickly latched on to Strughold and arranged for a nightly tutorial. Disney had always been awestruck by the prospect of space travel, and with the Russians set to launch their Sputnik satellite into orbit for the first time in a matter of weeks, he wanted to learn all he could. So each evening after dinner, teacher and pupil, each in his fifties, would stroll the moonlit deck of the ship, with Strughold revealing to Disney the secrets of "zero gravity," cabin pressure, and everything his research had taught him about keeping a man alive in space.

On their last walk together before Dr. Strughold disembarked in France, Disney gazed up at the moon and reflected on all the advances in travel and technology he had witnessed in the twentieth century. "If somebody told me that during my coming lifetime that somebody will fly to the moon," he remarked, "damned, I'd believe it." Strughold shook his hand, and they said their goodbyes. Anointed as the father of space medicine, Dr. Strughold had met all sorts of big-name military officials and politicos, but this moment — pondering the future of space side by side with an American icon — topped them all for him. Giddy, Strughold hurried back to his cabin to write down all the details still fresh in his mind, and he told of his nightly walks with Disney for years afterward.

Von Braun did Strughold one better with a panoply of Disney moments of his own that same year — not for an audience of one, but for millions. With Walt Disney's help, Dr. von Braun became a celebrated televangelist for space exploration. In 1955, when Disney's production company began airing what turned out to be a hugely popular series of television specials on the potential for space travel — to outer space, to the moon, and to Mars — von Braun was a natural choice as an on-air expert. With his slicked-back blond hair, his chiseled, ruddy face, his finely tailored double-breasted suits, and his worldly, debonaire charm, von Braun could have passed for an actor, at least until he began speaking into the camera. His voice — small and nasal, with a heavy German accent — was decidedly un-Hollywood. But he held the country's attention as he unlocked the secrets of rocket propulsion and demonstrated an atomic shield designed to protect the crew members — "zuh cruuuuuh membuhs," as he pronounced it — from dangerous radiation.

On camera, von Braun clutched the nose cone of a shiny, four-stage rocket prototype, a futuristic version of one he was designing at NASA's Marshall space center in Alabama. "I believe that a practical passenger rocket could be built and tested within ten years," he predicted. (In fact, it would take only six.) Disney's theme song, "When You Wish Upon a Star," played fittingly in the background.

The Disney series, part schoolhouse cartoon and part scientific documentary, introduced mainstream America to Dr. von Braun, solidifying his reputation as the father of rocket science. President Eisenhower received a private White House screening of the show. There was even a tie-in to a Mars ride at a new amusement park in Southern California called Disneyland.

Von Braun's focus was squarely on the future; there was little talk of the past or of the wartime legacy that had brought him to such a lofty place in American history. In Disney's retelling, the V-2 missiles that von Braun built became symbols not of destruction in Europe, but of technological prowess. "The V-2 emerged at the end of the Second World War," the Disney narrator remarked in one of the TV specials, "as the most successful rocket yet devised by man." Hitler was not mentioned. Even the most obvi-

ous remnant of the V-2's role in the war — the swaths of London and Ant-
werp reduced to rubble and the thousands of civilians killed by the missile's
unique firepower — did not merit notice.

Omitted, too, was the brutal story of just how von Braun and the Nazis actually built the rockets. There was no mention of the slave laborers
hauled from concentration camps; or of the prisoners from Dora routinely
whipped, beaten, or hanged for shoddy workmanship; or of the twenty
thousand prisoners in all who died of disease or malnourishment at the
missile factories in what von Braun himself acknowledged were "hellish"
conditions.

Nor was there mention, by Disney or any of von Braun's many admirers in America, of more than a dozen tours von Braun had taken of the
rocket factories during the war to inspect his prize invention. No mention
of the meeting he attended at Mittelwerk with senior factory administrators to discuss the need for requisitioning "another 1,800 prisoners" from
the camps. No mention of the high honors bestowed on him by Nazi leadership for his good work at the factories. And certainly no mention of the
personal briefings he gave on rocket production to Adolf Hitler, a man von
Braun likened after the war to a "new Napoleon" for his "astounding intellectual capacities, the actually hypnotic influence of his personality." American viewers saw none of this. They saw only the pictures of the smiling,
photogenic von Braun posing with Walt Disney next to one of his rocket
prototypes, not the grainy wartime images of him in a Nazi officer's uniform with a swastika on his arm.

After the war, Von Braun held onto a few photos showing slave laborers
at work at their stations at the underground missile plant. But these earlier
images, so stark and brutal, were not for public display. They were best left
buried in the rubble, like the slave laborers themselves. They did not fit the
Disney motif.

These were not state secrets, even in the 1950s and 1960s. Articles and
books in Europe were already beginning to tell the story of how von Braun
had used many thousands of slave laborers to build the V-2, and von Braun
himself practically gloated about it in an interview with the *New Yorker* just
six years after coming to America. He spoke almost wistfully about his use
of slave laborers in Nazi Germany as he mused about the ease with which
Stalin and the Russians, America's new rivals, could produce workers to

build their bombs. "Working in a dictatorship can have its advantages, if the regime is behind you," von Braun said. "I'm convinced that the man in charge of Stalin's atom bomb just has to press a button and he'll be supplied with a whole concentration camp full of labor. We used to have thousands of Russian prisoners of war working for us at Peenemünde." It was said not with shame, but with pride.

Sometimes, one particular rival of von Braun's in the American space program, bitter over the immigrant scientist's growing fame and funding, was known to complain drunkenly to his fellow scientists about "that damned Nazi." But such reminders of von Braun's ties to the Third Reich were generally verboten in Alabama and Washington, only mumbled under one's breath, if at all. Whatever skeletons his closet held, von Braun was too powerful and too revered to attack directly, at least not in America, and he certainly was not anxious to revisit the war himself. For the most part, von Braun took the advice of an American officer who told him that if anyone asked about his Nazi days, just tell them that it had all been investigated when he came to America.

The Germans, however, were not so willing to let it go. Von Braun, ironically, was not the Teflon figure in his homeland that he became in the United States. Just as von Braun was preparing for the crowning achievement of his career — America's moon landing in 1969 — he learned that the West Germans wanted to hear what he had to say about the hidden horrors of Mittelwerk. Nearly a quarter century after the war, prosecutors in Essen were putting on trial three SS officers at Mittelwerk for executing one hundred prisoners at the missile plant, and they wanted von Braun, the chief scientist for the project, as a witness. Von Braun, understandably, worried about damage to his own reputation and to the Apollo space program. He certainly didn't want to go back to Essen; witness or not, he was worried what the West Germans might do to him on their soil. Besides, he had nothing of relevance to add to the tribunal, he assured the court.

After a round of awkward negotiations, NASA arranged for its star scientist to stay on American soil and give a deposition in New Orleans, not in West Germany. If they wanted to know what he had to say about Mittelwerk, the Germans would have to come to him.

Von Braun finally sat down with German prosecutors in early 1969. He stated with no sign of reservation or nervousness that he knew from the very start of production in 1943 that the SS at Mittelwerk was using thousands of slave laborers to build his famed missiles. He had visited the plant some fifteen times to inspect the factory, and his own brother worked there as an engineer, von Braun acknowledged. But he insisted he had never seen firsthand what he euphemistically called the "special treatment" of workers: prisoners being hanged. "I never saw a dead person on my visit to Mittelwerk," von Braun told the prosecutors calmly. "Nor did I see any abuse or anyone killed ... I heard rumors that prisoners in the Dora camp were abused and that some in the tunnels were hanged for sabotage. I never saw that personally." He wouldn't have been surprised if the rumors were true, he said. The SS general who ran the camp was a reckless and brutally ambitious man, he said — but even so, von Braun did nothing about it. He had missiles to build.

He left the deposition with "a clear conscience," he said afterward, and he was relieved that the whole matter seemed to disappear with practically no attention in America. Months later, Neil Armstrong landed on the moon. Von Braun's supporters in Alabama hoisted him on their shoulders in the street in celebration. His star shone brighter than ever. "In regards to the testimony," he wrote later to his old friend, the Nazi general Walter Dornberger, "fortunately I have heard nothing more."

Von Braun voiced few regrets. "The working conditions there were absolutely horrible. It was a pretty hellish environment," he acknowledged. But he was stoic about his own responsibility. His overriding aim, in Germany as in America, was the pursuit of science, he said. It often seemed to be his *sole* aim. "We felt no moral scruples about the possible future abuse of our brain power," he said in explaining how he first came to build rockets for the Germans. "We were interested solely in exploring outer space. It was simply a question of how the golden cow could be milked most successfully."

Besides, he reflected, if he hadn't built missiles for Hitler, someone else no doubt would have. "The same things would have happened at Pennemünde without me," he said. "Do you think scientists should be blamed for wars?"

Dr. Strughold was, in many ways, von Braun's opposite. The aviation doctor had none of von Braun's Hollywood panache or charm. Von Braun could be lecturing on rocket science one day, then playing classical piano or scuba diving off the coast of Southern California the next. Strughold, with his white lab coat, bow tie, smoking pipe, and thinning white hair, was the picture of the bookish intellectual who seemed to crave little else but science. Where von Braun was a visionary with an almost cultlike following, Strughold was a tactician, slogging through his space research in San Antonio one test at a time.

But Strughold and von Braun, for all their personality differences, did share an astute ability to rewrite the past. Like von Braun, Strughold was portrayed unflinchingly by his admirers in America as a man advancing the cause of science; his ties to the Nazis were either minimized or forgotten altogether. Typical was an official Air Force biography in 1958, which declared: "Hubertus Strughold, M.D., survived the ruin of his nation in war, emigrated to another land, invented a new career for himself in a field of human endeavor as fresh as tomorrow, and became internationally renowned as the living sage of Space Medicine."

When he came to America as part of Project Paperclip, Strughold, like the other German scientists, had to establish for the official record that he was not an "ardent" Nazi. He dutifully explained that while he had in fact been a member of an aviation group affiliated with the Nazi Party, it was not out of any political loyalty, but rather because it would have hurt his career otherwise. Interrogators suspected his ties went deeper: his "successful career under Hitler" in the German Luftwaffe, one American investigator wrote, suggested he was "in full accord with Nazism." He was soon approved anyway, and in 1947, he began life anew as a top aviation medicine scientist at an air base in San Antonio. At the start of his stint, Strughold still had thoughts of returning to Europe in a few years. But after his first taste of Texas, he told friends, he liked America so much that he decided to stay.

Strughold's pioneering contributions to space medicine totaled thousands of pages in American military annals. He had, quite literally, written the book on space medicine: the first big project given to him in Texas was to compile the Nazis' aviation research into a monumental two-volume review for his new bosses in America, a glowing account called *German Aviation Medicine in World War II*. In his editing of the research, Strughold took out the references in the original data on how the Nazis had actually conducted their aviation studies and reached their findings. It was deemed irrelevant; what mattered were the results, not how they were obtained.

It was a notable omission. Normally, Strughold was not shy about touting his hands-on approach to scientific experiment. He was never one to limit his work to banal theory; he believed in conducting as many real-life tests as he could to answer the riddles of flight and put them to use. Before the war, when he was a young doctor making his name, he wanted to test the effects of altitude on the senses, so he stuck himself in the rear end with an injection of novocaine and went up in a plane to see how it felt. Another time, he set sail in a hot-air balloon and ran a battery of tests of his own ability to conduct basic tasks at high altitude; the hot-air balloon got stuck in a tree, but he had his results, and a jubilant Strughold popped some champagne he had brought along to celebrate the occasion.

He knew few limits in his work. As a young researcher in Cleveland during a stint in the United States in the late 1920s, he wanted to conduct cardiac experiments on dogs in which he would shock and restart their hearts. The Humane Society blocked him from using local dogs, so he brought in canines from Canada instead. Ethics weren't going to stand in the way of an important experiment.

By 1958, Strughold had graduated from dogs to people. He wanted to use his flight simulator in San Antonio to see whether a human being could withstand the pressures of space conditions for a full week. Some colleagues were hesitant; without more data, they feared it was too risky for anyone to attempt, and they urged Strughold to use a dog for the experiment instead. Strughold, realizing the political potential of the moment, stood his ground. Sure enough, when his subject emerged triumphantly from the simulator after seven days, an admiring Senator Lyndon Johnson, then an important friend to aviation research, was there to shake hands with the doctor and the test pilot as newspaper photographers snapped their photos. "I doubt that Lyndon Johnson would have been there to shake hands with a dog," a vindicated Strughold quipped afterward.

"Struggie," as he was known to friends, shared such stories freely with admiring military officers years later. But what of the war years? They made for a life-changing time when Strughold first established himself as a colonel in the German Luftwaffe and as director of a government-led research institute. But for all his prominence in Germany as a scientist, Strughold talked little about those days after he came to America. If Strughold discussed his time in Europe at all, it was inevitably to distance himself from Hitler.

"I had no affiliations with the Nazi Party," he told one military historian in the United States. "I have even had some Jewish friends."

For more than a quarter century, Dr. Strughold's place as the father of space medicine had been virtually unchallenged. Medical awards were named for him. His scientific writings filled libraries. Dozens of researchers in aviation medicine — American-born and German alike — answered to him as the chief scientist at the Air Force base in San Antonio. Even after officially retiring in 1968, he stayed on as a revered consultant to the space program and a beloved, grandfatherly figure at the air base. "One of the great minds of our time, perhaps of all times," a local newspaper columnist in Texas called him.

Chuck Allen was getting ready to challenge all that. The journalist had known nothing about Dr. Strughold when Tony DeVito first broached his name at their off-the-record meeting that day in 1974. But with his appetite whetted, he now wanted to find out everything he could about the doctor. Allen checked a listing of "active" INS investigations into suspected Nazis. Just as DeVito had promised, he found "Strughold, Hubert." Strughold, unlike von Braun, was not a household name, despite his prominence in the scientific world, and Allen had not identified him before now as anyone of particular significance in his own Nazi reporting. But DeVito had given him quite a rundown: *A leading space scientist with the Air Force in Texas... They call him the father of space medicine... Came to U.S. after the war and became a citizen in '56... A Nazi doctor in another life... Tied to human experiments at Dachau... Still working with NASA today.*

From what DeVito had described for him, Allen figured that Dr. Strughold certainly deserved a closer look. He knew instinctively that Strughold could prove much bigger than just a rank-and-file Nazi living quietly in America; bigger, certainly, than a Queens housewife from the notorious camp at Majdanek, and bigger than just about any other accused Nazi he had investigated over the years. Here was a man who, if his source was right, was brought to America by the military even after taking part in some of the Nazis' worst medical atrocities. If the lead checked out, if he could corroborate what DeVito was telling him, Allen figured Dr. Strughold might just be the most important Nazi in America.

A quick search of medical journals and newspaper articles made clear that Dr. Strughold was every bit as important in the medical field as De-Vito had made him out to be. He had earned all sorts of honors and awards, along with fancy-sounding titles with the U.S. military and the space program. It was clear, too, that he had worked for the German Luftwaffe during the war. But being in the Luftwaffe didn't necessarily make Strughold another Dr. Mengele. Was there really a link to Nazi atrocities? Allen went looking in a place that had proven a fertile hunting ground for him before: the Nuremberg war crimes files.

The historic war crimes trials at Nuremberg included a special set of medical cases against twenty-three Nazi doctors and medical personnel accused of taking part in the Nazis' experimentation on thousands of victims killed, maimed, or tortured. Himmler personally ordered a number of the most gruesome experiments, including a sadistic, sexually inspired test that involved placing a naked, unconscious, and nearly frozen man sandwiched between two naked female prisoners to see whether their body warmth would awaken him. The doctors were so proud of their work that they made a film to show to SS officials under Himmler.

The Brandt medical trial — named after Hitler's personal physician, Dr. Karl Brandt, one of the lead defendants — featured some of the most graphic testimony of any of the Nuremberg trials. American prosecutors told of a deli worker who was put in a flight simulator to mimic the effects of a sudden drop from an altitude of forty-seven thousand feet. He suffered violent convulsions, intense pain, and "the impression of someone who is completely out of his mind." The Germans wanted the altitude data to see how they could keep alive their own pilots under extreme flight conditions. Other experiments were designed to find the easiest ways to kill the elderly, the infirm, children, the mentally handicapped, and others. The doctors exposed test prisoners to yellow fever, typhus, cholera, and diphtheria. Sometimes the tests were conducted for no other reason than a morbid curiosity: 112 Jews were killed and defleshed, with their skeletons measured and sent to a museum in Strasbourg to be put on display in a collection. This was "no mere medical trial," the American prosecutor, Brigadier General Telford Taylor, told the panel of judges at Nuremberg. Under the guise of medicine, the Nazi doctors had engaged in "wholesale murder and unspeakable torture," he said, and had treated "their fellow men as less than beasts."

Ultimately, fifteen of the medical defendants at Nuremberg were found guilty, with seven of them sentenced to death for their crimes. They were just following orders, many of the doctors insisted. "It is no shame to stand on this scaffold. I served my fatherland as others before me," Brandt declared, moments before he was hanged in 1948.

From his postwar home at the military base in San Antonio, Hubertus Strughold followed the Nuremberg prosecutions with a personal interest. He had worked with virtually all of the doctors who were on trial — some as researchers working under him, some as colleagues who coauthored research papers with him, a few as his supervisors in the Luftwaffe. He held many in high regard. He even sent the Nuremberg judges letters in support of three of them. The chief medical officer for the Luftwaffe, who was ultimately convicted of medical atrocities at Nuremberg and sentenced to life in prison, was an "honorable, conscientious and self sacrificing" doctor, Strughold wrote. One of his own medical researchers on trial, Strughold wrote, was a "very humane and socially minded" young man. The doctor who wrote up the results on the deli worker tortured at forty-seven thousand feet — and even filmed the spectacle — was "a scientist of extraordinary experimental talent and ingenuity," Strughold wrote.

And what about Dr. Strughold himself? What was his role? He had been interrogated by the Nuremberg prosecutors while he was still in Germany after the war, and they suspected he had "covered up" his knowledge of the twisted experiments. But suddenly, without explanation, he was whisked away to Texas in 1947 as part of the exodus triggered by Project Paperclip. His "successful career under Hitler" was overlooked. He was given a spot as the top scientist in the medical aviation program in San Antonio. Strughold "was one of the first men anyone thought about trying to bring over here at the end of the war," one colonel said.

Now, in the fall of 1974, Chuck Allen was looking for anything in the Nuremberg records that might tie Strughold to the medical atrocities, not just through his troubling associations but through his own words and deeds. Searching through a cryptic document that the Nuremberg prosecutors had put together in their investigation, he finally hit on something.

Document No. 401 listed a roster of thirteen doctors "implicated" in the Nazis' discussion of "Experimentation of Human Beings" at the Dachau concentration camp. The fourth name on the prosecutors' list was "Prof. Dr. Strughold."

Strughold's ignominious spot on the list of doctors grew out of a macabre, two-day medical conference the Nazis had held in Nuremberg in October 1942. Luftwaffe doctors were meeting to explore "Medical Problems Arising from Distress at Sea and Winter Hardships." German fighter pilots who were shot down or crashed into the icy waters of northern Europe were dying from overexposure to extreme cold and harmful seawater. Nazi doctors wanted to see what they could do to keep their pilots alive, so they began doing research on extreme cold. Much of the data on hypothermia was drawn from grisly experiments the Nazi doctors were performing on prisoners at Dachau: submerging them in tubs of ice or keeping them naked outdoors for long stretches to see how long it would take them to die. The Nazi doctors wanted to see how much the human body could withstand. The hapless prisoners at Dachau were their human guinea pigs.

The Nazis' barbaric experiments were "clearly revealed" at the conference, causing a stir among the participants, the Nuremberg prosecutors reported. There at the conference was Dr. Strughold, a senior medical advisor to the Luftwaffe who ran a medical research clinic in Berlin for the air wing. The Nazis had even created top-secret "minutes" documenting their morbid discussions in starkly clinical terms. Nearly a hundred pages of minutes showed that Dr. Strughold not only attended the event, but gave a talk and commented on gaps in the medical research as it related to ice-cold ocean waters. "With regard to the experimental scientific research," Dr. Strughold said to the Nazi doctors at the conference, ". . . it is of interest to know what temperatures are to be counted on in the oceans concerned during the various seasons." Strughold seemed to be suggesting that the Nazi researchers go back — back to the human guinea pigs — and get more precise data to resolve the cold-water dilemma.

At a minimum, the notes from the conference seemed to establish that Dr. Strughold knew of the experiments as they were going on in 1942. This alone was significant, Allen realized. On those rare occasions when Strughold discussed the human experiments at all after coming to America, he always insisted that he knew nothing about them until after the war, when a radio report first alerted him. Now, in the graying pages of an official Nazi document, Allen had evidence that Strughold was lying.

Beyond the cold-water tests at Dachau were other, equally troubling, wartime experiments connected to Strughold. At the medical research clinic in Berlin that he ran, researchers would place epileptic children from a nearby asylum in a high-altitude chamber and subject them to sudden changes in oxygen levels. The Nazis' aim was to see if the conditions would trigger seizures in the children in the same way they did in rabbits. (Fortunately, they didn't.) In a separate pressure chamber at Dachau referred to as the Sky Ride Machine, prisoners were locked in an airtight ball. Like the deli worker driven mad, they were subjected to sudden changes in pressure to simulate rapid drops from high altitudes. Prisoners killed as a result of the experiments were dissected under the guise of collecting research data.

Strughold was mentioned by name sixty-one times at the medical trials at Nuremberg, usually by his fellow Nazi scientists in discussing the medical experiments. His name surfaced dozens of times in the interviews leading up to the trials as well. In one interview, long hidden away, a Nazi doctor convicted at Nuremberg for medical atrocities had implicated Strughold in the experiments both at Dachau and at Strughold's own medical institute in Berlin. A war crimes investigator grilled the Nazi doctor, Hermann Becker-Freyseng, about precisely what Strughold knew of the deadly experiments. Strughold knew all about the research, Dr. Becker-Freyseng asserted. He'd received all the medical team's reports and advised them in particular about high-altitude testing. And if Dr. Strughold objected to conducting the human experiments on prisoners, the investigator asked, did he have the power to stop it? "Of course," Dr. Becker-Freyseng answered. "He was the director of the institute. He could do what he wanted there."

Then there were the medical experiments focused on the hazards of drinking seawater. Another Nazi doctor testified at the Nuremberg trials that during the war, Strughold had told him about a young associate at the Berlin institute who had finally "solved the question" of how to make seawater safe for downed Luftwaffe pilots to drink — by adding traces of silver. As exciting as the breakthrough appeared, Strughold made no mention of just how his colleague had tested his theory: with Himmler's approval, the researcher first starved "asocial gypsy half-breeds," then gave some of them specially treated seawater while force-feeding others with putrid water until they became violently ill or died.

The deeper he dug into the Nuremberg files, the more convinced Allen became that Dr. Strughold — the noted alumnus of Project Paperclip — was directly connected to Nazi war crimes of the worst variety. Ten years earlier, Allen might have simply published the exposé in the same small Jewish magazine that had printed his 1963 report, without much notice or reaction, a tree falling silently in the forest. But now, Allen was looking for a bigger splash. So before he wrote anything, he went to the *New York Times* and offered to share with "the newspaper of record" what he had found out about Dr. Strughold. A young reporter at the *Times* named Ralph Blumenthal, who had returned to New York a few years earlier from covering the Vietnam War, had been working to uncover World War II secrets as well, writing a string of recent stories about suspected Nazis in America and the rising tensions they were creating within the INS and Congress. Blumenthal's Nazi stories rarely made it onto the front page of the *Times,* but he had no complaints; at least the stories were running somewhere, even deep inside the paper, which was more than many newspapers could say.

Allen had noticed Blumenthal's frequent byline on Nazi stories; he seemed like one of the few reporters out there with any interest in the issue. Allen called him from time to time to pitch an idea for some Nazi story or other, always with the same earnest intensity. "Ralphie!" he would chirp on the phone in his high-pitched, mile-a-minute voice. "It's Chuck Allen!"

When Allen told him about the Nuremberg documents he had found on Dr. Strughold, Blumenthal was immediately intrigued. The collaboration produced a story in the *Times* a few days before Thanksgiving in 1974 — deep inside the main news section, as always, on page 48 — with a large photograph of Dr. Strughold staring off into the shadows, his mouth slightly agape, looking almost as if he had seen a ghost. The story examined the ongoing delays at the hidebound INS in investigating recent Nazi accusations, and it used the new evidence against Strughold as its centerpiece. Allen was credited with unearthing the documents that listed Strughold among the thirteen doctors "implicated" in human experiments and that placed him as a participant at the Nazi medical conference in 1942, where the tests were discussed. Now, the article reported, the INS was investigating Strughold among several dozen suspected Nazis in the United States.

Before going to print, Blumenthal tried for days to reach Strughold and get his side of the story, but the Air Force closed ranks around its star scientist. Strughold, the article noted, "has ignored repeated requests from the *Times* for an interview."

Back in San Antonio, Strughold was livid over his newfound notoriety. The notion that he was somehow connected to medical war crimes, he told a local reporter, was "idiotic." It was "nonsense and false to even think that I had ever been a Nazi," he fumed. "It is so fantastic. I always have allied myself with the enemies of Hitler in those days in Germany. I sometimes had to hide myself because my life was in danger from the Nazis."

Strughold had important defenders in the Air Force and in Congress, and they were angry as well. The doctor was a revered figure in San Antonio. His local congressman, Henry González, quickly came to his aid. So did Senator John Stennis, the powerful leader of the Senate Armed Services Committee, a military hawk who was a strong advocate for the Pentagon. There was little sign that the INS investigators had done any actual digging into Strughold's past, or had even looked at the documents collected by the Nuremberg prosecutors that referred to him. Still, the mere mention of his name on a list of supposedly active Nazi investigations by the INS was reason enough for his supporters to worry. The two Washington lawmakers demanded to know why the immigration agency was interested in Dr. Strughold. González went on the House floor to denounce the investigation. Strughold was "a distinguished scientist of international reputation," the Texas congressman said. "This is hardly the kind of life a man would choose to lead if he had anything to hide." For Strughold to come under public suspicion made the INS "no better than the oppressors we abhor," he said.

Just as abruptly as it was opened, the INS inquiry into Dr. Strughold came to an end as the immigration service beat a hasty retreat. The inquiry, brief as it was, had found nothing to substantiate the allegations against Strughold, immigration officials assured González. "Our inquiries were terminated," the INS commissioner wrote, "and we consider the matter closed."

In San Antonio, the Air Force and its star scientist could rest a little easier. The doors to Dachau had closed once again.

7

Out of the Shadows

September 20, 1978

PATERSON, NEW JERSEY

Tom Soobzokov sat out on the front porch of his aging, World War II–era row house one autumn evening in 1978, a defiant look on his face as he surveyed the crowd of people angrily shouting his name in the street. On normal nights, this was one of his favorite spots, out here on the porch. He would sit in his appointed chair, cigarette in hand, drinking whiskey and laughing gregariously into the late hours with friends and neighbors who came to visit. Often, fellow immigrants from the old country would stop by to ask a favor, walking up the creaky stairs, past the faux-Roman columns, and up to the porch to see if Papa Soobzokov might have a minute to speak with them. Could he help with an immigration problem, they would ask, or might he know of a good-paying job with his friends at the Teamsters union? He would happily oblige, so long as they showed him the proper appreciation. Here, out on his porch, Tom Soobzokov was king, and this was his court.

But this night was different. His kingdom was under siege. On this night, marching up and down Fourteenth Avenue with fists clenched were dozens of Jewish protesters bussed across the river from New York. They were there because of him. DEATH TO SOOBZOKOV! their signs read. They had been sent by the Jewish Defense League, a militant group founded by the radical rabbi Meir Kahane with the aim of combating anti-Semitism "by any means necessary." The JDL's symbol was a Star of David within a clenched fist. The group now had its sights set on Soobzokov, who, at that moment, was New Jersey's most notorious Nazi. The JDL had been shad-owing Soobzokov for months, as details of his links to the Third Reich kept spilling out. The militant group's leaders had even come up with a death toll, plucked from the air, for the number of Jews they claimed Soobzokov had murdered in the Holocaust: three hundred thousand.

"How do we want Soobzokov?" a bearded JDL member shouted to the crowd. "Dead!" came the thunderous response from the men, women, and even a few children gathered in front of the house. The Israeli flags they waved created a cascade of blue and white bouncing off the streetlights.

On the other side of the street, an even bigger throng of counterprotest-ers, many of them friends of Soobzokov's and fellow White Russian im-migrants, turned out to meet fire with fire. They drowned out the dem-onstrators with boos and chants of their own and threatened bloodshed against anyone who dared try to harm the old man. WE LOVE SOOBZO-KOV, their own signs read. It had the makings of an ugly street brawl. Three police cars patrolled the scene, with officers pushing the two groups apart and breaking up a minor scuffle as things threatened to turn violent. After all the publicity surrounding Soobzokov the last few months, the last thing the police needed now was a melee in front of his house.

Soobzokov sat in stony silence on the porch, taking it all in. The cops wanted him to go back inside. His lawyer had urged him to leave the city altogether; go into hiding, go anywhere but here — out on that porch, in front of that angry crowd. Soobzokov wasn't going anywhere. A hot-tem-pered brawler all his life, he had to resist the urge to go after the protesters. Even in silence, he was going to stand his ground. He'd raised his five chil-dren here in this house. Back down to a lynch mob? They'd have to carry him away first.

This was what America's decades of resolute indifference to the Nazis in its backyard had wrought: a tinderbox in the gritty streets of Paterson, New Jersey, with one side demanding vengeance for historical wrongs, and the other rallying to the defense of an accused Nazi. The most striking thing of all about the scene was just how public a spectacle it had become for Tom Soobzokov. After decades spent in the shadows, first as a Nazi officer, then as a CIA spy, and finally as an FBI informant, Soobzokov was now a marked man living under the bright klieg lights of public scrutiny. There were no more camouflages to hide him. For more than four years now, he had been publicly identified as an accused Nazi over and over again — in the New Jersey newspapers, on local TV, in neighborhood coffeehouses, in the community halls favored by the immigrant community. He would turn on the TV, and there he was being mentioned yet again. Sometimes he would angrily pop in a VHS tape to record the offending program and document all the things being said about him. Other times, he would simply slam off the television and storm away. "They've got the wrong man," he would tell his bewildered children. Whether he was guilty or not — and most people in town had already made up their minds one way or the other — Soobzokov's days of mystery and seclusion were long over. He was out of the shadows.

Under attack, Soobzokov had adopted a pose of righteous indignation. He was no Nazi, he would tell friends, neighbors, reporters, and anyone else who would listen. He was innocent of these vile, hurtful accusations being slung at him by his Communist enemies. "On my side is God and truth, which is unbeatable," he said. He wore his pain like a crown of thorns. "Do you know what it does to a man's family to be put through something like this?" he would ask plaintively. "Torture," he said. "My family, friends, and kids have suffered much."

The stakes for Soobzokov were enormous. He was fighting not only for his good reputation, but for his status as an American citizen. The Jewish Defense League wasn't his biggest problem; its protests, embarrassing though they were, amounted to little more than public theatrics. No, his real enemies were the nettlesome federal officials who were threatening to take away his citizenship and throw him out of the country — if they could prove he really was a Nazi. Federal investigators were poking around, reporters were digging up records, a grand jury was hearing testimony from witnesses, and there was no telling where all this might lead. Soobzokov was worried.

In the span of just a few years, Soobzokov had gone from a man of stature in Paterson — an immigrant success story — to this: a man of notoriety known simply as "that Nazi." It was a dramatic fall. For many years now, Soobzokov had been a dealmaker in local ethnic, political, and labor circles, a man of power and connections who could fix problems for his fellow immigrants and deliver ethnic votes to local Democrats. His was an inspiring public story: an immigrant who would tell how he escaped fascism and persecution as a Nazi prisoner and a forced laborer during the war and went on to find freedom in America. From a meager start in New Jersey washing cars, he had become a car salesman, an insurance agent, and, ultimately, a civic leader and county executive who helped make Paterson a magnet for immigrants, particularly those from the Caucasus.

The image of a smiling Soobzokov — always so smartly dressed in suit and tie, with jet-black hair and neatly trimmed mustache, driving through the city in his sky-blue Chevy — became a sign of connections and possibilities in Paterson in the 1960s. Once known as Silk City for its textile manufacturing industry, Paterson had fallen into urban decay, and with times as tough as they were, Soobzokov was an important man to know. Local politicians made him Passaic County's top purchasing official at $16,000 a year. They put him on an influential planning board, and named him to lead a special panel to resettle new immigrants. He would go out to the port in New York to greet the newcomers arriving by boat from Europe and take them to New Jersey. The local Teamsters union called him a "distinguished servant of all mankind" and gave him a gold watch for helping hundreds of immigrants come to America and find jobs. His congressman honored him with a letter read into the *Congressional Record* recognizing all his good work in the face of adversity. His life, the local newspaper reported in a glowing profile in 1958, had been "a story of persecution," overcome by grit and guile.

But for all the praise heaped on him, Soobzokov had always had enemies in New Jersey. Many of them, not coincidentally, were the immigrants who came from the very same region of the North Caucasus as Soobzokov. They were the ones who knew of him during the war. The man they described, usually in hushed tones to one another, bore no resemblance to the one being feted for his civic work.

Occasionally, the rumblings about Soobzokov's past spilled into the open. In 1962, a Circassian woman in Paterson named Angela Stas was summoned to court in a domestic dispute with her estranged husband. Her husband was friendly with Soobzokov, but Angela had always detested him. Indeed, when she got to court and saw that the multilingual Soobzokov was there to act as her husband's interpreter, she grew furious and confronted him right there in the courthouse. "The second Eichmann!" she yelled — so loudly that the startled judge heard her screams. Soobzokov was irate; he threatened to sue Angela Stas on the spot for defamation.

The bad blood soon got the attention of the FBI, which felt compelled to send an agent to interview her after learning of the episode. "Angela Stas reported there were many people in the Circassian Colony, including herself, who despised Soobzokov," the FBI agent reported. "She claimed that there were many rumors concerning Soobzokov's activities in the Caucasus with the German forces in 1942–43."

This was a bombshell accusation that in another time, another place, might have triggered a frenzy of follow-up interviews to see if it was true. Instead, the report sat untouched in an FBI file cabinet for years.

Seven years later came a second report to the FBI, this one from another Russian immigrant in New Jersey named Mischeust Chuako, who lived just a few blocks from Soobzokov in Paterson. He went to the FBI with accusations of his own: During the war, Chuako maintained, Soobzokov was often seen in a Nazi uniform and "was a member of a Nazi execution squad," according to the FBI report. Soobzokov "personally took an active part in raids of population centers" and "took an active part in arresting people and killing them without any kind of investigation or [trial] — fair or unfair."

Again, nothing happened. The accusations went nowhere.

But Soobzokov's accusers would not let it rest. Four years later, in 1973, a third Russian immigrant in New Jersey went to the FBI with reports of his Nazi ties. "I am only trying to expose a former Nazi killer," the would-be tipster told the FBI.

And again nothing happened. The past was past. Hoover had made clear that he had no interest in having his agents wasting their time tracking down supposed Nazis in America.

Besides, Soobzokov was one of the FBI's own. The bureau already had a thick file on him — not as a Nazi suspect, but as an informant dishing out information on supposed Communist sympathizers. The CIA had broken ties with Soobzokov years earlier after branding him an "incorrigible fabricator," but the FBI had no hesitation about using him as an informant beginning in the late 1950s, with Hoover's personal approval. Soobzokov even had his own personal FBI handler, a street agent in New Jersey. He would pass on McCarthyesque leads to his FBI contact about whatever he was hearing in Paterson about immigrants with supposed Communist leanings. Since he was such a fervent anti-Communist, it didn't arouse much suspicion when he would go around town asking questions about local politics. What his fellow immigrants didn't know was that he was doing it as an undercover informant for Hoover's G-men, spying on the townspeople.

His FBI handler never really trusted Soobzokov; the man seemed slippery and always appeared to be involved in some financial scheme or other on the side. But Soobzokov did occasionally produce intriguing bits of dirt on the Commies, and dirt was dirt. When it came to Communists, that trumped all else inside Hoover's FBI.

In one disquieting episode early in his career as an informant, Soobzokov reported to the FBI that a twelve-year-old "half-Negro boy" in town had expressed an interest in visiting Russia. Soobzokov feared the boy could be used as Soviet propaganda, he told the FBI, so he started collecting the names of the boy's friends and even went to see the boy's doctor, a Jew from Russia who also struck Soobzokov as suspicious. Determined as ever, Soobzokov chatted up a nurse in the office, who agreed that her boss couldn't be trusted. "Jewish doctors were not reliable," she told him. Soobzokov dutifully passed what he'd found to the FBI, and it all went into the boy's file under the heading "Communist provocateurs."

The FBI protected its valued informant for years, sopping up all the Communist leads he fed the bureau while ignoring the damning reports in its own files about his reported Nazi ties. Things might have stayed that way, with the past kept safely hidden away, were it not for a tip to the Social Security Administration about a financial scheme that Soobzokov was rumored to be running in Paterson.

Even as Soobzokov was building up his reputation as a civic leader, there was always the suggestion of a shadier side to his Horatio Alger–like, up-by-the-bootstraps life story, and not just because of the Nazi rumors. Some immigrants whispered that, in exchange for a few hundred dollars or so, Soobzokov could make paperwork problems go away — changing a birthdate on a Social Security eligibility form, for instance, or greasing the skids for a would-be immigrant trying to get into the country. Soobzokov had heard the rumors, of course, and he denounced them as bogus. He had never taken a kickback in his life, he said, and the talk on the street was obviously the work of his rivals in the immigrant community, jealous of his success.

One day in 1972, a tip about one of Soobzokov's reputed kickback schemes landed on the desk of a Social Security investigator in Baltimore named Reuben Fier. He had been a police officer in New York City for more than twenty years, and he had loved the street cop's life. Now retired from the force and chasing Social Security cheats from a desk in Baltimore, Fier was bored and restless. He hated the slow pace and the banality of the work. But something intrigued him about the tip from New Jersey about this man Soobzokov. It was not simply the accusations of Social Security fraud, although a few interviews with Soobzokov's accusers had left him convinced there was something to them. No, it was the *other* issue that several of the immigrants who knew Soobzokov had mentioned to the investigator. They brought it up on their own, almost as an aside. *You know that he was a Nazi during the war, right?* No, Fier hadn't known that, but he certainly wanted to know more. A Nazi in New Jersey? If what these men were telling him about the Russian immigrant was true, it would make Fier's run-of-the-mill fraud cases look like jaywalking violations.

Fier organized a meeting of Soobzokov's accusers at the home of a New Jersey doctor named Jawad Idriss, a rival of Soobzokov's in the local immigrant community. Fier wanted to compare what they had to say not just about Soobzokov's purported financial scams, but about his war history as well. Ten men showed up, giving remarkably similar accounts of how Soobzokov, in German garb, had served with the Nazis and wielded extraordinary influence over prisoners in German-occupied zones, including his fellow countrymen. "I saw Soobzokov in an SS uniform in Buzov, Romania," said a war refugee named Isa Hoket. Soobzokov was the Nazis' point man in control of the many White Russian prisoners and refugees in the occupied area, trying to get them to fight for the Nazis and join a new front, he said. Hoket resisted his entreaties, he said, telling Soobzokov in one angry conversation that he was not his commander. Rebuffed, Soobzokov walked away and quickly returned with two senior Nazi SS officers, Hoket said. "The colonel spoke," Hoket recounted. "He asked me my name, and then said, 'Hoket, your *führer* is Soobzokov.' He used that very word: *Führer.*" Hoket told Fier how, twenty years after the war, a smiling Soobzokov welcomed him to New Jersey and, over lunch at a local diner in a much more serene setting, offered to help him resettle in his new country, just as he had with so many others. If Soobzokov remembered their prior encounter, he did not let on.

As Fier scribbled down the accounts from Hoket and the other New Jersey immigrants, the old passions that had driven him as a New York City cop were starting to rekindle. He saw the makings of a major investigation. His bosses, however, had other ideas. By now, an irate Soobzokov had gotten wind of the questions that Fier was asking around town. He went on the offensive, threatening legal action against anyone who had the audacity to accuse him of being a Nazi. These charges were nothing more than "un-American slanderous remarks and innuendos," he charged in a letter to the head of the INS. He even drove down to Fier's office in Baltimore to complain in person, and he brought along a powerful friend: Robert Roe, his local congressman from New Jersey. Roe was a longtime ally who, in one of his many gestures of support for Soobzokov, presented him with an American flag at a ceremony honoring his many civic contributions in Paterson. On this day, Roe's task in Baltimore was clear: get the government to back off. Why, the congressman demanded to know, was a Social Security investigator nosing around into a bunch of made-up Nazi accusations against an upstanding citizen like Tom Soobzokov?

Soon after, Fier was called into his supervisor's office for a dressing-down. The investigator was veering far outside his lane of authority, his boss advised him. He was supposed to be tracking down Social Security cheats, not Nazis. Besides, the statute of limitations on Soobzokov's supposed crimes had already passed. Stand down, he was told.

Fier was undeterred. He was going ahead with his Nazi investigation — with or without his boss's approval. On his own, he went to the Germans to seek war-era records on Soobzokov, digging up a document that identified him as a Waffen SS lieutenant at the end of the war. This was a critical piece of corroboration, he believed. He shopped the case to prosecutors outside his own agency. And he went looking for a new ally, a man he had heard was equally disgruntled over the government's bungled handling of fugitive Nazis. His name was Tony DeVito.

Fier had never met DeVito, the gruff-talking INS investigator from Hell's Kitchen who had bumped heads with his own bosses over the prosecution of Hermine Braunsteiner Ryan. But from all that he'd heard and read about DeVito, Fier thought he might find a partner in the INS investigator. DeVito knew nothing of all the drama quietly unfolding in New Jersey around Soobzokov until the day Fier drove up from Baltimore to

New York on his own time in April 1973, found DeVito during a recess in the Ryan trial, and sat him down at an immigration office cubicle for what turned into a lengthy off-the-books meeting. With three manila folders marked "Soobzokov" in hand, Fier gave DeVito a rundown of everything he was hearing in Paterson — and all the interference he was getting from his bosses. DeVito didn't need much persuading to take an interest. Here was another Nazi case that, somehow, seemed to have been ignored for decades. It seemed practically ready for prosecution. As he finished reading the files Fier had gathered, a smiling DeVito slapped his new Nazi-hunting partner on the back excitedly. "Jesus Christ!" DeVito yelled. "This case is made to order!"

Together, Fier and DeVito formed a rogue two-man cabal intent on tracking down evidence against Soobzokov. With DeVito's help, Fier redoubled his efforts, looking for more witnesses and more documents. They knew they would face resistance. They just didn't realize it would come from the agency that had secretly hired Soobzokov two decades earlier: the CIA.

Even as the two investigators were trying to build their case, the CIA was growing more and more nervous about the notoriety surrounding their onetime spy. The agency's dossier on Soobzokov was even thicker than the FBI's, and the spy chiefs at Langley had even more to lose if Fier and DeVito were to expose their years of clandestine dealings with him. For months, the CIA kept a secret running account of the growing public tumult surrounding their old agent, Tom "Nostril" Soobzokov. "We're hoping this will all blow over," one secret memo advised in 1974, after his name first surfaced publicly as the target of a Nazi investigation. The charges, one CIA official suggested, "stem from recent hysteria which appeared in U.S. press over congressional concern over number of former war criminals now living in U.S." But instead of blowing over as the CIA had hoped, the "hysteria" only intensified, and another secret memo a few months later — titled "Latest Development in the NOSTRIL case: An Approach by a Journalist" — warned that the accusations were "cutting closer to home" for the CIA.

A local reporter had come knocking on Soobzokov's door in Paterson to ask him whether it was true that he had been a spy for the CIA in the

Middle East two decades earlier. Soobzokov kept quiet, but the agency was alarmed to hear that the reporter was asking him — by name — about two agency operatives that he had contacted during his botched trip to Beirut in 1957. One of them was still working undercover seventeen years later. CIA officials feared the agent might be in danger, as they tried to shut down the leaks about Soobzokov. Then came another newspaper report in New Jersey suggesting that an unnamed Washington agency — it could only be read as the CIA — seemed to be protecting Soobzokov for reasons that were still a mystery. There were more questions arising publicly almost by the day.

With every turn in the case, the CIA was being drawn deeper into the muck, and its ex-agent was growing more nervous as well. Each new mention of his name in the press brought another frantic call from Soobzokov to the CIA. His old handler, John Grunz, reluctantly took the calls. He needed help, Soobzokov told Grunz in one call after another. He needed protection. The investigators, the reporters, even a member of Congress — they were all coming after him now.

For all his pleas, the CIA wanted nothing to do with him. Grunz let Soobzokov know that he was on his own. His continued contacts with the agency, he warned, would only end up hurting Soobzokov. Privately, Grunz and his CIA colleagues worried that Soobzokov was getting ready to "pinch" them for money— a demand for a payoff in exchange for his silence about his covert work with the agency. But even if the CIA could keep Soobzokov quiet, officials there saw little hope of silencing his growing phalanx of accusers in New Jersey, immigrants who seemed to know all too much about his checkered history in Europe. "He has certainly made plenty of enemies over the years," one CIA memo observed, "and Circassians do tend to run toward the long nursing of secret grievances and grudges."

Inside the CIA, the Soobzokov affair was now threatening to become a major political disaster for the agency at a time when it was already facing unparalleled scrutiny from Congress over its role in domestic spying and foreign assassinations. DeVito had helped persuade federal prosecutors to take a closer look at the case, and the Justice Department in Newark was now formally asking the CIA for any "derogatory" information it had on Soobzokov. If he really had been an agent for the CIA, as DeVito suspected, he wanted to find out what the spy agency knew of its agent's Nazi past that might buttress the case against him.

With the Justice Department asking for help, the CIA did what it had done many times before when facing Nazi accusations against one of its own: it closed ranks.

The CIA had plenty of derogatory information on Soobzokov, of course. Its files were crammed with his own admissions years earlier about his role in rounding up Jews and Communists during the war, taking part in the execution of supposed resisters, and spying for the Nazis on his fellow countrymen. Soobzokov was implicated in "minor war crimes," the CIA's analysts had concluded, and the "incorrigible fabricator" had concocted so many lies about his wartime record that the agency finally cut ties with him altogether in 1960. Fifteen years later, CIA officials saw all this and more spelled out in their own files. But they could not afford to reveal any of that to DeVito and the federal prosecutors. So when it came time to respond to the Justice Department's formal request for information in 1975, the CIA wrote flatly: "A thorough review of the Subject's file does not reveal any evidence of a derogatory nature concerning him . . . We have no evidence that Subject was involved in war crimes during his work for the German Army or at any other time."

One CIA official told a federal prosecutor bluntly not to expect any help from the spy agency. The Justice Department had waded in over its head in its investigation and should let it die, the CIA official told the prosecutor. "The greater good," he said, "is you guys oughtta back off. You don't understand these things."

The CIA's whitewashing of Soobzokov's file set back prosecutors' hopes for bringing a case against him. But the spy agency couldn't kill the story altogether. Soobzokov was already a notorious figure in northern New Jersey, but in 1977, his notoriety went national. He was one of a handful of suspected Nazis profiled in a book called *Wanted!: The Search for Nazis in America*, written by a *Village Voice* writer named Howard Blum. Young and ambitious, Blum had no particular interest in the Holocaust; he was simply looking for a compelling story that might make him the next Norman Mailer. He found it in the Nazis. There had been dozens of stories written since the war about accused Nazis in America, most of them little noticed or long forgotten, but Blum's book, written in a suspenseful style and an outraged tone — from its sensational title on through its dramatic narrative — captured an audience like none before it. It became a huge bestseller, and Tom Soobzokov's infamy grew with it.

Nazis in America were suddenly a hot topic. Robert MacNeil and Jim Lehrer, the newly formed news duo on PBS television, devoted a whole segment to it on February 1, 1977. Blum, the twenty-six-year-old author, appeared on the show, talking about all the accused war criminals — 143, by the INS's running count — who were still living freely in the United States. Tony DeVito was interviewed too, talking about the government's "cover-up" of the shameful saga. And there onscreen in the middle of it all, angry and unapologetic, was the former CIA spy and current Passaic County chief purchasing officer, Tom Soobzokov. Other men might have shied from the spotlight, but that was not Soobzokov's way. He would tell anyone who wanted to know — Robert MacNeil, Tony DeVito, Howard Blum, President Carter himself if he asked: he was innocent.

The charges in the book were "absolutely false," Soobzokov told Mac-Neil. "I can say it openly and irrevocably."

MacNeil tried to pin down some of the basics of Soobzokov's history. There was a document recovered in Berlin showing that Soobzokov was a second lieutenant in the Waffen SS. "Is that not true?" MacNeil asked.

"Let me put it this way," Soobzokov began, his Slavic accent as thick as the day he came to America twenty-two years before. "I wore that uniform but I never was any official. I never was in any service by the so-called Waffen SS ... I never executed any orders ... I never participated in any form or shape with the SS."

"But you did wear the uniform, you say?"

"Yes, I did."

"Why was that?"

"In order to save myself and about thirty-five or forty other people ... refugees who were hiding from the Germans and the advancing Soviet troops."

"Were you employed by the CIA after the war?" MacNeil asked the ex-agency spy.

"No, sir."

"You were not."

"No, sir."

The lies were now leaving Soobzokov's lips almost as fast as MacNeil could pose the questions. Some of his assertions came straight from the script of his life that he had written years earlier to keep track of all the different stories he had told his CIA interrogators. Some of the other claims he was airing for the first time, seemingly making them up on the fly.

So, MacNeil asked, was Soobzokov denying having served with the German forces in Europe or rounded up people for the Nazis, as Blum's book suggested?

"I had to laugh when I saw that," Soobzokov said. "I supposedly was rounding up the Communists and Jews. For the information of that young man who wrote that book, in our territory there was no Jews whatsoever." The Jews, he said, lived a few hundred miles away in a separate colony in the Caucasus, and no one ever harmed them. "They were saved like as in heaven," he said. "They never were our enemies."

It was a striking claim, and easily exposed as false. In Krasnodar and the North Caucasus, the Nazis and their local collaborators had killed thousands of Jews and Communists. Jews were gassed in roaming death vans, shot, hanged, or set afire in some of the worst massacres in any Nazi-controlled region in Europe. Yet the region, by Soobzokov's telling, was a safe haven for the Jews; a sanctuary where the Jews were "saved like as in heaven."

The denials struck Blum as ludicrous. He had spoken with Soobzokov for his book, and the old man's assertions seemed as thin now as they did then. But as he listened, Blum was struck by one surprising admission that Soobzokov had made. "I think tonight is the first time that I've ever heard Mr. Soobzokov say that he was in an SS uniform, that he even wore it," Blum told MacNeil. "What I've read in the papers, and what he told me when I interviewed him, he confirmed the report that he was a semi-forced laborer, a transportation worker."

It was indeed a puzzling moment. On national television, Soobzokov was admitting that he had worn the Nazi uniform as his accusers in Paterson had long charged. This was not the only surprise from Soobzokov on the show. That very night, his Long Island lawyer announced on the air, Soobzokov was filing a $10 million libel suit in federal court against Howard Blum, Tony DeVito, and the publishers of *Wanted!* for falsely accusing him of being a Nazi. Soobzokov was determined to put the American justice system to full use, and he vowed that the truth would come out.

For one inveterate reporter, the burst of publicity surrounding Blum's book was a moment of vindication. For years, Chuck Allen had been warning that there were "Nazi war criminals in our midst," and now, belatedly, the country seemed to be catching on. But *Wanted!* was also a source of some understandable resentment for Allen, a reporter who loved scooping the competition, even if no one noticed. He had spent years in obscurity chasing Hitler's men, and now a young kid from the *Village Voice* was reaping the fruits of his labor with a splashy bestseller. Allen felt he deserved more credit than he was getting for his groundbreaking work years before. In his view, *Wanted!* was a shoddy product, without the kind of documentation he favored in his own work. Miffed by all the publicity the book was generating, Allen wanted the chance to get back in the Nazi hunt with another big story. He found it in Tom Soobzokov.

On a sweltering September day in New York City, Allen walked into a gothic mansion in Manhattan's Upper East Side for a much-anticipated meeting. At the grand offices of the Soviet Consulate in New York, he sat down with Valentin Kamenev, a top official there, to talk about Tom Soobzokov. Months before, with publicity swelling over the accusations against Soobzokov, Allen had put a series of written questions to the Russians about what was known of Soobzokov's wartime record during the Nazi occupation. He was hoping to find records that might bolster the accounts of the Circassian witnesses in New Jersey. It would be another two years before the U.S. government reached a deal with the Russians to get access to their wartime records on the Nazis, but Allen already realized that behind the Iron Curtain lay a trove of documents and eyewitness accounts on Nazi atrocities in the Baltics. Many of the worst war crimes had occurred in the region. The Russians had long accused the United States of going easy on Nazi collaborators, and so they were eager to help Allen in his research.

At their half-hour meeting, Kamenev gave Allen a thick stack of Soviet documents detailing Nazi atrocities and wide-scale killings in the North Caucasus, including the notorious massacres at Krasnodar in 1942. The documents certainly looked authentic. Among the cache: eighteen sworn affidavits given after the war by Russian eyewitnesses, many of them placing

Nazi officer Tscherim Soobzokov at the scene of the killings. One of the affidavits was from Soobzokov's own father-in-law in Russia. Another was from his nephew, Yahkia Mosovitch Soobzokov, who testified that he last saw his uncle retreating with the Nazi troops in early 1943. "He still wore his German uniform at the time," the nephew testified.

Allen left the Russian Consulate with the documents in his hand and a bounce in his step. He'd found what he'd set out to find. As he walked out onto Ninety-First Street, he noticed a large blue van that appeared to be parked with a strategic view of the consulate's entrance. Allen had been through this cat-and-mouse routine with the FBI enough times the last few years to be suspicious. He jotted down the license plate — New York tag number 474-FZJ, which he later traced to an "unlisted federal agency." Peering in the front window, he saw a young man slumped in the driver's seat, apparently asleep. Allen tapped on the window. "You can wake up now," he said amusedly.

That night, Allen began contacting the major newspapers in New Jersey to tip them off to the documents he had obtained. "Soviets Provide Data on Suspected Ex-Nazi," the front-page headline in the *Star-Ledger* declared. Local reporters who had followed the case for four years speculated: Would this be enough to get the Justice Department to bring a case against Soobzokov? Two grand juries had already heard many days of testimony in the case, with investigations opened and closed. Yet for all the evidence gathered by Fier, DeVito, and others on the case, some prosecutors remained skittish. The Justice Department had never brought a denaturalization case like this against an accused Nazi. Was it really going to start now by taking on a prominent civic leader based on testimony that might be the result of bitter ethnic feuding? DeVito figured that all the witnesses might be dead before that happened.

The long delays in the case only fueled the simmering tensions in New Jersey. Immigrants in town had to be on one side or the other: those who thought Soobzokov was a Nazi, and those who thought he'd been wrongly accused. Soobzokov and the Russian witnesses against him were regularly filing claims and counterclaims with the police, accusing one another of all sorts of threats and confrontations. One of the witnesses against him even reported that a menacing Soobzokov had tried to run down him and his wife as they were crossing a busy street in downtown Paterson.

Soobzokov's neighbors and friends rallied to his defense, condemning all the attention he was getting. "When does World War II end for some?" a local newspaper asked.

"Never," came the answer from the Jewish Defense League. The group stepped up its demonstrations, wielding placards not just outside Soobzokov's home, but at the county office building where he worked as well. As the protesters chanted his name one summer day, Soobzokov went about his business, checking on a delivery of shirts to the local jail. "I can't let the hoodlums stop my duties," he said.

Death threats to his home and office became routine. "You are a nazi butcher of men, women, children and infants," read one signed by "a child of a survivor." The FBI had to put a tap on his home phone because of all the harassing phone calls and death threats he was getting. Then, someone mailed Soobzokov a package with a brown Te-Amo brand cigar box inside it. "Buddy, you didn't kill enough of them," a note read. Through the wrapping, Soobzokov could see what looked like a black button. He called the police, who had a bomb squad rush the package to a nearby rock quarry to blow it up. Among the fragments were a 9-volt battery, some yellow wiring, a few screws, and slivers of brown tape. It was a homemade bomb.

The situation was growing more volatile by the day. After four years of fits and starts in the case, the Justice Department was facing intense pressure from all sides to do something. Finally, on December 5, 1979 — nearly thirty-five years after Soobzokov became an SS lieutenant; twenty-four years after he'd come to America; seventeen years after a screaming neighbor called him the "second Eichmann" in a Paterson courtroom; four years after his name first surfaced publicly in a Nazi investigation; three months after someone sent a bomb to his house — prosecutors were ready to move ahead. A grand jury in New York had already declined to bring criminal charges against Soobzokov, but prosecutors in Washington brought a civil lawsuit seeking to strip him of his citizenship and remove him from the country. Soobzokov, the Justice Department charged, had "willfully concealed from the authorities his membership in the German SS during the war." The threat of being deported may have seemed like a small price to pay if Soobzokov was really the Nazi war criminal the reports made him out to be. But it was the best that federal prosecutors could do: there was no war crimes statute on the books in World War II that they could even seek to use against him thirty-five years later.

Facing formal charges for the first time, Soobzokov still had one card left to play. For three decades now, in CIA polygraphs, FBI interviews, court depositions, and newspaper interviews, he had offered a numbing and ever-widening array of roles he claimed to have played during the war, from hay-delivery man and forced laborer to local militia leader and anti-Nazi resister.

Now, Soobzokov put forth perhaps his most brazen claim, a story that was either preposterous or brilliant, or a bit of both. In a sworn deposition, Soobzokov acknowledged that he was an officer with the SS — not just in uniform, but in duties — but he claimed for the first time that he'd told the American diplomatic authorities in Jordan exactly that in 1954, before he ever set foot in America. He hadn't concealed anything or lied to anyone, Soobzokov insisted. Yes, he really was a Nazi, he admitted; but the Americans — and the CIA — knew all that and more before they ever let him into the country.

To Justice Department prosecutors, it was just another in a long line of outrageous claims from Soobzokov. The idea that the United States would have let an admitted Waffen SS officer into the country was preposterous, they thought. Yet the Justice Department had to do its due diligence and run the claim aground. "The State Department was undoubtedly well aware in 1955 that the Waffen SS had been found to be a criminal organization by the Nuremberg Tribunal," Joseph Lynch, a Justice Department prosecutor, wrote in an internal memo assessing Soobzokov's latest eyebrow-raising claim. The SS's crimes "were so widespread and involved slaughter on such a gigantic scale that its criminal activities must have been widely known . . . I am assuming, pending confirmation from the State Department, that Soobzokov is lying and never made such an admission re his SS membership to [U.S. authorities] in 1955."

He was right about the State Department. A report came back from Foggy Bottom that nothing had turned up. There were no records in Soobzokov's immigration file indicating that he had ever admitted his membership in the SS to the United States when he entered the country.

Lynch and the other Justice Department prosecutors were now set, with any last-minute doubts erased.

In a case already filled with improbable turns, that was when the unthinkable happened. With Soobzokov still claiming that he had told American authorities of his Nazi ties back in 1954 and hadn't concealed anything, his lawyer, Michael Dennis, went to the CIA with a formal demand: give us any records that would corroborate his claim that the United States knew all along that he was a Nazi. It seemed like another far-fetched gambit by Soobzokov and his lawyer. With an intensive search at the State Department already turning up nothing, there was little reason to think the CIA's search would turn out differently.

Except that it did.

The CIA produced not one but two 1950s-era documents showing that Tscherim Soobzokov, then working for the agency, had told American authorities of his collaboration with the Nazis and his role as a Waffen SS officer. One was a formal immigration form, known as a V-30 document. The second was an intelligence memo assessing Soobzokov's application to come to the United States. These documents were both created by the State Department, but somehow, mysteriously, had ended up in the records of the CIA, even though the State Department itself didn't have them.

Justice Department officials were flabbergasted. Some inside the building even suspected that the CIA might have fabricated the documents just to avoid a public trial that would have surely shed light on the agency's own twisted relationship with Soobzokov. But an examination of the typing appeared to show that the documents were authentic. Worse, they established that Soobzokov, remarkably, was telling the truth: when he had come to the United States a quarter century earlier, he had in fact told American authorities that he was a Nazi collaborator with the Waffen SS. They had let him into the country anyway. Joe Lynch was livid. The CIA's lawyers had been involved in monitoring the Soobzokov case step by step for nearly a year because of concerns about the agency's own role with their onetime agent Nostril, and now, at the eleventh hour, they had sandbagged prosecutors. Why hadn't we known about this? Lynch demanded.

The CIA's explanation was a model of bureaucratic legerdemain: the documents weren't the CIA's to turn over because, technically, they belonged to the State Department, the spy agency's lawyers explained. More-over, the CIA hadn't let the Justice Department know of the documents' existence because the Justice Department had never specifically asked about them. We didn't tell you, the CIA insisted, because you didn't ask.

Outraged though they were, Justice Department lawyers saw no way out of the fiasco the U.S. government had created for itself. Prosecutors did not believe they could move ahead in good conscience with a case against Soobzokov for concealing his Nazi ties, since he had actually admitted them to American officials decades before. Red-faced, Justice Department prosecutors went to court and asked a federal judge to throw out their own denaturalization case against Soobzokov. The judge acquiesced. "Some may find it ironic that we must terminate this litigation because the defen-dant admitted his affiliation with organizations loyal to the Third Reich," said Justice Department prosecutor Allan Ryan. "It is a step I take only after concluding that the law and the evidence leave me no choice."

Soobzokov had taken on the best lawyers the Justice Department could throw at him, and he and his own attorney had beaten them at their own game. It may have come on a legal technicality, with some last-minute help from his friends at the CIA, but the end result was the same. A quarter century after the United States welcomed an admitted Nazi SS officer, Tom Soobzokov was still an American citizen. He had won.

Outside the federal courthouse in New Jersey on a hot summer's day, a jubilant Soobzokov exchanged hugs with his tearful children in an emo-tional scene of vindication. Then he went home to celebrate with friends and neighbors at an impromptu party at his house on Fourteenth Avenue. "I was never afraid, because I knew I was innocent," he declared. "I am over-whelmed," he said, "not only for my sake, but for the sake of my belief in the Constitution and the justice system of the United States."

8

"An Ugly Blot"

July 10, 1980

WASHINGTON, D.C.

The stunning collapse of the Justice Department's attempt to throw Tom Soobzokov out of the country attracted little notice outside New Jersey. But in Washington, Elizabeth Holtzman was livid. The Brooklyn congresswoman had been watching the long-playing drama surrounding Soobzokov with keen interest, and she was seething over how it had ended. The CIA's eleventh-hour discovery of long-buried documents that had saved its ex-spy from deportation seemed almost too convenient to believe. If the 1950s-era documents really were authentic, that seemed almost worse: it would mean that the State Department and the CIA had decided to let into the country an admitted member of the Waffen SS. Either scenario was damning. The CIA sat Holtzman down for a briefing to explain its version of what had happened, but she was not mollified. "This once again raises the specter of connivance and collusion on the part of our government in admitting and providing sanctuary to suspected Nazis," she fumed.

For seven years, Holtzman had been waging a lonely fight in Congress to shine a spotlight on Nazis living in America. She had made more progress than anyone else, but too often, her efforts had fallen into the usual black hole of government inertia: one step forward, two steps back. It was inconceivable to her that an issue as black and white as Nazis living in America could be met with callous indifference or, worse, active obstruction. Yet this was where they stood: listening to Tom Soobzokov praise the virtues of the American justice system outside the courthouse in Newark because he had actually admitted years before that he was a Waffen SS officer.

When she was first elected to Congress in 1972, Holtzman had no inkling there were suspected Nazis living in America. Less than a year on the job, a midlevel official at the INS scheduled a confidential meeting with her to discuss something that was gnawing at him. The INS, he told her, had a list of dozens of suspected Nazis living in the country, and the agency was sitting on it. "It is doing nothing about them," the official told her. Holtzman was dumbfounded. The tip seemed implausible, but she felt obliged to follow up on it. At a House hearing not long after, she asked the immigration commissioner whether the INS actually had a list of suspected Nazis in America. She expected an outright denial. Instead, the commissioner acknowledged that, yes, there was in fact such a list. "How many names are on the list?" she asked, taken aback. "Fifty-three," he said. And what, she wanted to know, was the INS actually doing to investigate these people and deport them? The answer struck her as a maze of bureaucratic doublespeak. It wasn't clear what, if anything, the INS was actually doing. So Holtzman, a Harvard law school graduate and a future DA in Brooklyn, decided to visit the agency's Manhattan office to examine the case files herself. The files were laid out for her neatly on a metal desk, dozens of dusty folders with Nazi atrocities hidden inside. The first one contained accusations that an American immigrant had been a Nazi police officer involved in the massacre of Jews. That was about it: no follow-up by the INS, no witness interviews or record checks, no real attempt to corroborate such serious accusations. The rest of the files proved just as sparse. If INS agents did anything at all, they might knock on a suspect's door and ask a few cursory questions. Nothing more. Some of the cases had stagnated for so long that seventeen men on the list had died while the INS "investigated" them.

Holtzman's tipster was right: the INS really was doing nothing about the Nazis.

The congresswoman was determined to change that. Although she was among the youngest members of Congress, at thirty-one, Holtzman was already making a name for herself as a woman willing to ask unpopular questions. When President Gerald R. Ford testified at a dramatic televised House hearing to discuss his pardon of President Nixon after Watergate, the junior congresswoman pointedly asked the president whether he and

Nixon had struck a deal. Older lawmakers looked askance at Holtzman's temerity, but she did not shy away from a fight.

Holtzman, along with Congressman Joshua Eilberg, a senior Democrat from Philadelphia who ran the immigration subcommittee, began bombarding federal officials with questions about the INS's failure to investigate Americans with clear links to the Third Reich. The pair demanded documents, traveled to Russia to interview witnesses, dispatched congressional investigators to examine possible obstruction by the INS, and looked to fix the law to make it easier to deport war criminals. They were riding a surge of interest in the Nazis. An ABC miniseries, *Holocaust,* was bringing genocide into the open; the book *Wanted!* was naming names. Survivors were becoming increasingly vocal in demanding justice for Nazi fugitives.

After years in the shadows, new Nazi suspects seemed to be constantly emerging in the spotlight in cities around the country, and some of them, just like Tom Soobzokov, boasted protection from the CIA and the FBI. In 1976, reporters in San Diego went to the ranch home of a high-school track coach named Edgars Laipenieks and confronted him with evidence that he had collaborated with the Nazis as a police officer in Latvia. With a shotgun on the floor and two German shepherds at his side, the burly immigrant invited the reporters into his house and began showing them a stack of papers on the dining room table. The papers, he said, would clear him of any suggestions that he had killed Jews and Communist civilians as part of a Nazi-led militia. Midway through the stack, the reporters noticed three recent letters to Laipenieks — on official CIA letterhead. He was reluctant to let the reporters see the letters at first, but he finally allowed them to make copies. Laipenieks, the startled reporters learned, had worked with the agency after the war as a spy in anti-Soviet operations, and the agency was still in touch with him. Just months earlier, with the Nazi accusations bubbling up against him, the CIA had written to Laipenieks, a former Olympic star in Latvia, and assured him, with an apologetic air, that the INS was closing a war crimes investigation against him. "Thank you once again for your patience in this instance, and your past assistance to the Agency," the CIA wrote.

The CIA director, George H. W. Bush, was visiting San Diego the next month when one of the reporters asked him about the city's newfound Nazi. Bush admitted that the Latvian immigrant did in fact play a "minor" postwar role with the agency, but he was evasive when asked if the CIA had hired other purported Nazis as well. That was a confidential national-security matter. "If it were in my knowledge," the future president said, "I'm not sure I'd tell you."

But even the CIA could not keep a lid on the growing story that the Nazis had become. What Holtzman called "an ugly blot on our country's history" received its first full public airing at a remarkable series of congressional hearings in 1977 and 1978 at an ornate House hearing room. Holtzman and Eilberg could not understand how the country had arrived at this place: struggling to track down Nazis who had called America home for decades. "Why, after individuals were identified as having committed these crimes against humanity, were they allowed to remain undisturbed in the midst of our society, enjoying the very privileges they sought to destroy, protected by the same laws they violated?" Congressman Eilberg, a former prosecutor, asked at the start of one hearing. "I can only ask 'why?' Were the U.S. government agencies deliberately shielding these individuals? Were they so ignorant of the atrocities committed by the Nazi regime that they gave no significance to these persons being here?"

The hearings brought together an eclectic cast of characters who had been warning for years about the country's silent indifference. There at one of the witness tables, suddenly in the national spotlight as the long-ignored dean of Nazi hunters, was Chuck Allen. There, too, was Tony DeVito, the bitter ex-INS investigator, telling the lawmakers how he was blocked at every turn from going after suspected Nazis. With them was a parade of State Department and INS officials, wishing they were anywhere but behind the witness table as they tried to explain how all this had happened. And, of course, there was Holtzman, grilling the government witnesses with a prosecutor's eye for flimsy rationalizations.

No one had really cared about the Nazis before, Chuck Allen lamented. Fifteen years earlier, when he had published his forty-two-page investigation on Nazi war criminals in the United States, "there was no cry of rage, there was no indignation in the halls of Congress," he said. Now, he was happy to report, that finally seemed to be changing.

Tony DeVito, blunt and passionate as always, told the committee that he faced "obstructions galore" from his former bosses at the INS in investigating accused Nazis like Hermine Braunsteiner Ryan, the Stomping Mare of Majdanek. He had to take up a collection in the office just to cover the meals and expenses of a group of elderly Holocaust survivors who had flown from Israel to New York to testify against the ex-Nazi camp guard; the INS money had fallen through at the last minute. It was not just bureaucratic ineptitude, DeVito was convinced, but an actual government cover-up driven by the CIA and other intelligence agencies under the banner of protecting national security. "There was a fix just as sure as I'm sitting here now," he declared.

As for the famed Nazi scientists brought over in Project Paperclip, DeVito had heard all the justifications from Washington for importing them to America to keep pace with Russia's technological advances. The World War II veteran bristled at the notion that the Nazi scientists were somehow essential to national security. "If they were so brilliant," DeVito demanded, "how come they lost the war? We didn't need these people. We could have gotten to the moon without them, and this country would be better off without 'em."

A longtime INS lawyer named Vincent Schiano, who had worked with DeVito on Nazi investigations, testified as well. He didn't buy into his old partner's conspiracy theories. The two weren't on speaking terms, in fact, because of what Schiano saw as DeVito's overheated rhetoric about cover-ups. Still, Schiano shared DeVito's frustration over the INS's failure to move against suspected Nazis, whatever the reason. Schiano told the committee about his bosses at the INS pulling him off promising Nazi cases to work instead on the deportation of John Lennon. He shared the story of a particularly frustrating investigation into a notorious Nazi financier in Romania named Nicolae Malaxa, who immigrated to New York and became a friend and business associate of Richard Nixon's. Malaxa, who fled to Argentina for a time before returning to the United States, wanted to make an INS investigation into his Nazi connections go away. A friend of Malaxa's approached him, Schiano recounted, and mentioned that he had a few hundred thousand dollars to "dispose of this problem." Schiano told him to get lost.

For Holtzman, the litany of Nazi horror stories was affirmation of what she had suspected since her INS tipster came to her five years earlier to report the existence of a secret "Nazi list": the U.S. government, she told the committee, "allowed our country to become a haven for persons who were guilty of war crimes and atrocities." Even now, she said, the CIA and the FBI were blocking congressional investigators from finding out what the agencies' own secret files said about suspected war criminals. That information was classified, protected under the guise of national security. The bureaucratic mumbo-jumbo incensed Holtzman.

"National security can be used to hide a lot of things," she said pointedly. "I don't understand what people who engaged in mass murder could do that has anything to do with the well-being of this country, and I find it very hard to understand why the CIA and the FBI or any other agency would throw a cloak of secrecy over their connection with these people."

With the political winds at her back, Holtzman set out to change the immigration laws in ways that would prod the government to go after the Nazis after all the years of inaction. The first priority was to plug a startling loophole: in the late 1950s, immigration law did not ban Nazis from entering the United States. Hundreds, perhaps thousands, of Nazis and Eastern European collaborators exploited the loophole to gain entry, and the INS maintained that they had little power to deport them. Under what became known as the Holtzman Amendment, Congress authorized the INS and the courts to kick out any Nazis or Nazi collaborators who engaged in persecution in the war years, regardless of when they came to the United States. Lawyers for some of the suspected Nazis facing deportation howled. Congress couldn't just go back and make it illegal thirty-five years later for Nazis to come into the country, they insisted; that was the type of ex post facto law banned by the Constitution. But the courts came down on Holtzman's side, and the 1950s-era loophole was finally sealed.

The second step that Holtzman took was a top-to-bottom restructuring of the way Nazi cases were prosecuted. With the stories from DeVito and others fresh in her mind, she was convinced that the INS was unfit for the job. In the wake of public pressure, the immigration agency's small team had actually managed to try five cases against suspected Nazis in the late 1970s, but the results were a disaster. Prosecutors lost three of the five cases outright after embarrassing missteps in court. In one of the losses in 1978, a Holocaust survivor on the witness stand, when asked if he saw the man who had been a guard at Treblinka in the courtroom, looked past the defendant and pointed instead to an elderly man in the gallery, as listeners in the courtroom gasped. The only deportation case of the five that the government actually won — this one against a Polish immigrant in Chicago accused of having been a member of the Gestapo — had to be thrown out when it became clear that the prosecutors had the wrong man; one of the original tips about the defendant's supposed Nazi links came from a disgruntled former tenant of his who was angry over his eviction and made up the accusation.

The INS's Nazi-hunting efforts were a mess. Holtzman was determined to create an entirely new organization at a high level within the Justice Department to take over the task. The problem was that some officials in the Justice Department didn't want the job; the Nazi cases, as one lawyer put it, were "legal lepers," dangerous to any prosecutors who touched them. The resistance did not deter Holtzman. In 1979 Congress ordered the Justice Department to create the Office of Special Investigations within the Criminal Division to handle the Nazi cases, and it authorized more than $2 million for the work. The new team was to include lawyers, investigators, and historians to chase the hundreds of dormant leads that had accumulated over the years. Still, some skeptical Justice Department officials weren't convinced there were enough real Nazi cases out there to spend the money on. But like it or not, the job was now theirs.

Officials in the Carter administration hoped to give the new Nazi office instant gravitas by naming a former prosecutor at the Nuremberg trials, Walter Rockler, to lead the startup. Not long after, the Justice Department brought in Allan Ryan, a top appeals lawyer, to help lead the investigations. Bearded and professorial, Ryan had won a crucial case that affirmed the government's power to deport Nazi persecutors. With the government's dismal record for prosecuting Nazis, "that's one more win than anyone else," a Justice Department official told Ryan wryly when he brought him on. Ryan had another thing going for him that didn't show up on his resumé: unlike Rockler and a number of the other top lawyers in the office, he wasn't Jewish. It didn't get him the job, but it didn't hurt, either. As Rockler said of his Irish deputy: "A little seasoning wasn't a bad idea." The hunt for Nazis would always be inextricably linked with the Jewish victims, but the department did not want its Nazi hunters to be seen as merely an extension of Jewish activists. They needed to make their own name.

Expectations were high. This was supposed to be the moment when the United States got serious about finding Nazis, with a group of prominent, well-funded lawyers and investigators to lead the hunt. The Nazis in America had been hiding in plain sight for decades; now finally, the government was pledging to go after them in earnest. But the nascent effort, seeking to hold American immigrants accountable for crimes committed almost forty years earlier across the Atlantic Ocean, faced legal and political obstacles from the start. The Justice Department got an early taste of the skepticism it would face when one of Rockler's senior deputies, Art Sinai, traveled to East Germany to meet with top officials there about getting access to war crimes documents and witnesses to aid the American investigations. At a meeting at the foreign ministry, General Günther Wieland, the top prosecutor in East Germany, laughed as Sinai, through a translator, laid out the government's ambitious plans. "Oh, you're finally talking about Nazis?" the East German general said dismissively. "Why did it take you so long? All those scientists you brought over . . ." The general's voice trailed off. "Well," Sinai said, "it wasn't as many as your Soviet brothers." East Germany had plenty of Nazi war criminals of its own, Sinai noted. What did they do with all of them? "We shot them," Wieland answered.

One of the biggest roadblocks that the government's new Nazi-hunting efforts would face came not from overseas, but from right across the street from the Justice Department — inside the J. Edgar Hoover Building at the FBI.

J. Edgar Hoover himself, a defender of many accused collaborators in America, had been dead for six years when the Justice Department christened its new Nazi-hunting team in 1979, but resistance within the FBI toward Nazi investigations outlived him. Indeed, it was still sometimes difficult to know whose side the FBI was on when it came to prosecuting Nazis. Few agents at the FBI even knew what the Justice Department's new Office of Special Investigations was, or what it did. Not long after the Nazi office was opened, Art Sinai got a surprise visit from an agent in the FBI's 's espionage section. Sinai and another lawyer from the Nazi office had been spotted coming and going at the Polish embassy in Washington; the FBI had the place under surveillance as a Soviet bloc nation, and the agent had tracked them back to the Justice Department. Government lawyers sneaking around in a Communist embassy? "What were you guys doing there?" the G-man demanded. The lawyers explained that they were part of a new

Nazi-hunting unit and that they were meeting with the Poles to get access to war crimes archives. It was all part of their job.

Satisfied with the explanation, the agent left. But not all of the Nazi hunters' dealings with the FBI would end so neatly.

Soon after, officials in the Nazi office went to the FBI with what seemed like a routine request, as they began gathering material on hundreds of suspects whose files had grown musty over the years. The Justice Department gave the FBI a list of 239 names of Nazi suspects to see what information the bureau's own files might turn up. "We'll help you out any way we can," a friendly intelligence official at the FBI told Sinai when they met. But it turned out that there was a catch: sixteen people on the Nazi list had been confidential FBI informants over the years, often providing information on Communists in America and "domestic security." And the Nazi prosecutors learned that the FBI's informants were off-limits to them. These were people like Bishop Trifa and Tom Soobzokov, staunch anti-Communists who had worked with the FBI for years. Five people on the list, in fact, were still FBI informants — and the FBI wasn't willing to give up information on any of the sixteen, no matter what its files might say about their Nazi ties. The refusal was cloaked in typical government bureaucratese. "In accordance with our established policy of protecting the confidentiality of such sources of information to the fullest possible extent," a senior FBI intelligence official wrote to the Justice Department, "their specific identity is not being disclosed."

This wasn't supposed to happen, not anymore. When the Nazi office was created, the Justice Department declared that "every lead and every case will be vigorously pursued." The road to investigating the Nazis wasn't supposed to stop at the door of the FBI, with its own informants protected from scrutiny. But when it came down to a choice between investigating suspected Nazis or protecting the FBI's anti-Soviet informants, the fight against Communism still won out.

Rockler summed up the FBI's dismissive attitude toward his new Nazi office with four words: "To hell with you."

Months later, a Nazi office lawyer stumbled onto documents suggesting that the FBI had known about Nazi collaborators coming into America as far back as 1951, during the Hoover era. But when the lawyer asked the FBI to produce records on the issue, he got nowhere. "There may be reason to suspect the FBI of willful concealment of embarrassing material," the Justice Department lawyer wrote to his supervisor. "If the FBI is unwilling or unable to locate their own files when furnished with this much identifying information, then they damn well should let our OSI investigators go into the file room and do the job themselves." That never happened, of course.

In one of the Justice Department's highest-profile investigations, the deportation of the notorious Bishop Trifa in Michigan, the FBI destroyed perhaps the single most critical piece of evidence in the entire case: a copy of the "Trifa Manifesto," a virulent, Jew-hating screed that Trifa had put out in Romania in 1941 as the leader of a Nazi-supporting student group. Upset, the judge in the Trifa case ordered an investigation to determine what had happened. The FBI blamed a clerical error for the destruction.

Then there was the remarkable case of Ferenc Koreh, a former Nazi propagandist in New Jersey who had a whole band of FBI agents trying to protect him from deportation.

During the war, as an official at the Hungarian Ministry of Propaganda and as a newspaper editor, Koreh put out dozens of articles and official, anti-Semitic propaganda attacking the Jews as "traitorous, unscrupulous, cheating people" and calling for a "de-Jewification of Hungarian life" and "final solution" to the country's Jewish problem. (Some 440,000 Hungarian Jews were ultimately deported to Auschwitz and other Nazi camps.)

After coming to America in 1950, Koreh went on to become a vocal anti-Communist in New Jersey and an on-air broadcaster for the taxpayer-funded Radio Free Europe. When the Justice Department learned of Koreh's canon of wartime hatred thirty-five years later, prosecutors tried to denaturalize him. He fought the charges — and he had help within the FBI. His daughter was an FBI agent, as was her live-in boyfriend. The pair, along with other supportive agents in the FBI's New York field office, launched what amounted to a rogue investigation of their own into Koreh's case. They charged that the case against him was based on "forged" Communist documents. The daughter's boyfriend, meanwhile, wrote a forty-six-page single-spaced internal report on FBI letterhead attacking the case not only against Koreh but also against Bishop Trifa. The FBI agent insisted that the two men were not Nazi supporters, but victims of a pro-Communist disinformation campaign. His colleagues at the Justice Department, the agent charged, had been duped.

The FBI, in a quasi-official report from its own agents, was now on record defending two high-level Nazi propagandists. Furious, a Justice Department official called the bureau's conflict of interest "scandalous" and "so outrageous" that it threatened to compromise the integrity of the FBI as a whole. The Justice Department was trying to deport Koreh, while agents at its premier investigative arm — the FBI — were defending him.

The headwinds from the FBI muddied up the prosecution and delayed the deportation case against Koreh for years, while he stayed in the country. In the end, however, Koreh grudgingly acknowledged in court what prosecutors had charged all along: that he had published a slew of hateful, pro-Nazi propaganda that fueled the persecution of Hungary's Jews. He was denied his government pension and stripped of his citizenship. He died in New Jersey under the toxic label of Nazi propagandist. Even his powerful friends and family members at the FBI, as hard as they tried, could not save Koreh from his wartime past.

9

The Sins of the Father

February 2, 1981

SACRAMENTO, CALIFORNIA

Gus von Bolschwing didn't think much of it when he first got the call that day in 1980. A Justice Department lawyer in Washington named Jeff Mausner wanted to speak with him. That itself was nothing unusual. As a successful malpractice attorney in San Francisco, Gus got lots of calls from fellow lawyers. Except that this lawyer didn't want to talk to Gus about one of his malpractice cases; he wanted to talk to Gus about his seventy-one-year-old father, Otto "Ossie" von Bolschwing.

"Did you know," the Justice Department lawyer asked Gus, "that your father was a high-ranking Nazi in the SS?"

Whatever came after that was a blur; Gus couldn't quite process the words. This must be a bizarre mistake, he thought; maybe some sort of cruel hoax. "Are you kidding me?" he finally asked. No, he wasn't, Mausner explained. The Justice Department's new Nazi-hunting office wanted to ask Gus some questions about his father's activities during World War II. Prosecutors were conducting a formal investigation into newly unearthed evidence that Otto Albrecht Albert von Bolschwing — a retired international businessman, husband and father, American citizen for twenty-two years, and now an ailing resident of a Sacramento nursing home — had a hidden past as a top Nazi war criminal and an aide to Adolf Eichmann in Hitler's Jewish Affairs office.

Denial followed disbelief. In an instant, Gus's mind raced through everything he knew about his father, or everything he thought he knew. He tried to view his father through this dark new prism, twisting and turning what he knew of Ossie's life to see if he could recognize anything the Washington prosecutor was now telling him. His father had fought the Nazis in the underground movement in Austria. At least that's what Gus had always been told. Gus had never heard him utter a single anti-Semitic word. Not once. After he and Gus's mother had divorced, Ossie had even *married* a woman who was part Jewish. Ruth was her name, like the fabled character from the Old Testament, and her mother came from a prominent Jewish family in Austria. Ossie and Ruth, the baron and his half-Jewish bride, were married in Austria in 1942: in the midst of the war, in the midst of the Holocaust. Marrying a Jew could have gotten him killed by the Gestapo, but Ruth was "the love of my life," Ossie always said.

Gus flashed back to his arrival in America in 1954 as a boy of fifteen. His father arranged for him to go to a prestigious high school in Boston and live there with the Fleischners, relatives of Ruth's from Europe who had fled the Holocaust. They were a kind, generous Jewish family. They opened their home to Gus, giving him his own room. There was no hint of tension that Gus could recall, no sign that his father was suppressing any dark secrets. Sometimes, Gus remembered, his father would talk to him about the basic precepts of Judaism and Christianity, never disparaging one or favoring the other. Make up your own mind, his father always said when it came to religion. Find your own way.

This was the man the Justice Department was now calling a Nazi? And not just any Nazi, but a senior SS officer, the author of a hate-filled primer on "the Jewish problem," a man who signed "Heil Hitler" at the bottom of his memos to Adolf Eichmann, the architect of the Final Solution? *This* was his father, Otto von Bolschwing?

No, it wasn't possible, Gus von Bolschwing told himself. True, he and his father had never had a particularly warm relationship, and sure, Ossie could be many things: cold and aloof, moody, perhaps a bit arrogant and insensitive in the erudite manner one might expect of a man born a Prussian nobleman. But a Nazi? Was there any more vile pejorative to sling at a man, any man? No, this was not his father, Gus told himself. It couldn't be.

There were hundreds of Gus von Bolschwings scattered across America: sons and daughters of accused Nazis swept up in the rising tide of investigations brought by the Justice Department's aggressive new team of prosecutors.

Overwhelmingly, the children — many of them first-generation Americans and products of the war themselves — believed in their fathers and their innocence, even in the face of overwhelming evidence. It was simply too painful to do otherwise. The father's battle became the child's. As prosecutors tried to throw their fathers out of the country, the children kept vigil at their fathers' sides, protesting their fathers' innocence to judges, to journalists, to neighbors, and to anyone else who would listen. Hadn't the Nazi hunters at the Justice Department blown cases before, they would ask? Overzealous prosecutors could shade the evidence any way they wanted, they would insist. Elderly witnesses flown in from Israel were proven wrong sometimes, their memories skewed over what really happened in the concentration camps so many years ago. Nazi IDs could be forged, they would claim. Men could be wrongly accused, smeared because they came from a different land. Every child was convinced his father was one of the innocents.

That's the way it was for Diane Lavoie when she learned the Justice Department was threatening to deport her father, a Lithuanian-born factory worker in central Massachusetts named Vladas Zajanckauskas. He was accused of unthinkable crimes: leading the massacre of Jews at the Warsaw ghetto. The Washington lawyers were cordial enough, and they certainly looked professional, with their leather briefcases and fancy suits, as they came up from Washington for depositions and court hearings. But the lies they told about her father: the things they told Diane were impossible for her to believe. They wanted her to think that her father was a Nazi officer at Trawniki — promoted three times, in fact — and that he'd led a unit sent to Warsaw to "liquidate" the ghetto in one of the Holocaust's bloodiest episodes. Zajanckauskas's name, the lawyers explained to her, was right there at the top of a roster of Nazi officers at Trawniki sent to Warsaw. He went there, they said, as part of a Nazi unit that crushed the Warsaw ghetto uprising in a show of brute force notorious even by Holocaust standards. Nor was he just any officer, the prosecutors told her. He was a training officer; he schooled the rank-and-file Nazis at Trawniki in the tools of genocide. *This* was her father, they told her.

None of it made any sense to Diane. Her father had told her all about those brutal war years: how he worked at a canteen at the Trawniki camp, serving beer to the soldiers; how he'd secretly tried to *help* the Jews. There was a friendly Jewish boy named David he always mentioned. By his telling, in fact, Trawniki's wartime experience was, as odd as it sounded, a love story of sorts. He told Diane how he wandered into the village for canteen supplies and cigarettes, and there met his beautiful bride-to-be: her mother, Vladislava. He had never even been to Warsaw, he told her, much less murdered Jews in the ghetto. Her father was a gentle man, a devout Catholic, a hardworking man who toiled at a plastics factory outside Worcester, Massachusetts, for thirty-five years. Zajanckauskas was "the best father anybody could have," she told a judge, her native New England accent punctuated by pain. *This* was the man she knew.

The accusations, she said, had wrecked her family. The legal fees were crushing: $200,000 for a couple of well-heeled lawyers an hour away, in Boston. Her parents sold their home to cover the costs, and they moved into a small cottage on Diane's lakeside property nearby. When they had to go to court for hearings, Diane tried to avoid the scornful faces in the courtroom. "Why are they looking at me like a criminal?" her father would ask. At least their supporters — friends, neighbors, church members — knew the truth, no matter what the government said. "Please don't ever lose hope," a neighbor wrote.

With his life in limbo, Vladas Zajanckauskas sat out by the lake and painted nature scenes. The massacres in Warsaw were far from his mind. Sometimes he liked to write. In neat, angular handwriting, he kept a journal of his life story — the *real* story, he insisted, not the government's horrific version — and he scrawled lines from the Bible that he said reflected his journey. "When I sit in darkness the Lord shall be a light to me," he wrote. That was her father, Diane insisted, not the monster they made him out to be.

In New Jersey, Tom Soobzokov's youngest son, Aslan, believed just as fervently in his own father's innocence. The years-long defense of his father became an obsession. He was in high school in Paterson when the stories about his father first circulated. When he walked down the school's hallway, he felt as if everyone's eyes were on him. He was Aslan Soobzokov, "son of the Nazi." At the protests outside his house, with Jewish protesters calling his father a Nazi and worse, he and his Circassian friends would confront the troublemakers. "You've got the wrong guy," he would tell them angrily.

Even after Aslan went off to the Air Force, he was haunted by the thought of his father, Papa Soobzokov, hounded by the ongoing accusations back home in New Jersey. On one blustery day in 1977, Aslan left his air base in northern Michigan and drove four hours to a book signing he had seen advertised at a Jewish Community Center north of Detroit. It was a solitary trek to avenge his father's honor. Howard Blum, author of the best-selling *Wanted!* was there, signing copies of his book, smiling, posing for pictures without a care in the world. Aslan walked up to Blum, handing him a copy of the book with all the vile things it said about his father. He had never met Blum, but he instantly detested him. "My name is Aslan Soobzokov," he said with a mock smile. Blum stiffened up and moved back a pace. He seemed afraid that Aslan, a tall, burly military man, might punch him. "How could you write this about my father!" Aslan finally said, jabbing his finger at the book. "This, this garbage!" He walked away. He had to admit: it felt good to confront one of Papa's accusers.

For Rad Artukovic, the accusations against his own father — Andrija Artukovic, the so-called Butcher of the Balkans — colored his earliest memories. The on-again, off-again effort to deport the elder Artukovic, implicated in the deaths of six hundred thousand Roma, Serbians, and Jews when he served as the interior minister in the Nazi puppet state in Croatia, was one of the longest immigration cases in U.S. history, stretching back three decades to the early 1950s. Rad was just a toddler, three years old, playing with a red fire truck in the back of a Los Angeles courtroom, when his father — his arms in handcuffs raised triumphantly over his head to the cheers of his Yugoslavian supporters — made his very first court appearance in the deportation case in 1951. Whether Rad actually remembered the fire truck, or had simply been told about the scene so many times that he felt he had, was unimportant. What mattered was that he was at his accused father's side every step of the way, every phase of the fight, for the next thirty-five years. He never seriously doubted his father's innocence, no matter what the federal prosecutors said about him. As a boy of eleven, Rad posed with his exuberant father for a newspaper photo after Artukovic won a critical court decision blocking his deportation in 1959. Years later, as

Nazi general Karl Wolff (left) with his boss, SS chief Heinrich Himmler, outside a Nazi train in 1942. Prosecutors at Nuremberg regarded General Wolff as Himmler's "bureaucrat of death," but "Wolffie," a close friend of Hitler's, escaped punishment for war crimes with the help of Allen Dulles (below), the American spy chief in Switzerland during the war.

Dulles (left, with his trademark pipe) said American spies "should be free to talk to the Devil himself" if it would help in the war and believed the United States benefited from working with more "moderate" Nazis like Wolff.

Photos are reproduced courtesy of the United States Department of Justice unless otherwise noted.

Silicon Valley felt touch of ex-Nazi masquerader

Continued from Page 1

Nazi hierarchy, into the CIA and finally to the highest levels of American business.

The list of people he knew, some of whom met him through a California high-technology business venture in 1970, reads like a Who's Who. They include Justice William A. Newsom of the 1st District Court of Appeals in San Francisco; Helene von Damm, President Reagan's personal secretary; Thomas A Fennioli, banker to the Boston Cabot family; Emanuel Pfoenakis, Fairchild Corp. senior vice president; Elmer Bobst, president of Warner-Lambert Pharmaceutical Co.; and Alfred Driscoll, former New Jersey governor and Warner-Lambert's chairman.

"I'm nonplussed," Justice Newsom said. "I thought, if anything, Otto had been pro-American during the war."

As a businessman, von Bolschwing was vague about the war years. He said he had been a Gestapo prisoner and had worked for the CIA in postwar Germany.

In 1969, he was asked about his German past during a job interview with Trans-international Computer Investment Corp., a high-flying investment firm that had founded several companies in the Silicon Valley. Von Bolschwing

a group of Palestinian Germans who lined their pockets by certain extramural intelligence activities, according to Hohne, who wrote that von Bolschwing spied on the Zionist Haganis army.

Ejected by British

Ejected from Palestine by the British for espionage, he surfaced in Romania as a government "oil expert." By his own account, in 1941 he helped the leadership of the Iron Guard, a right-wing movement, escape to Berlin after it had gone on a three-day rampage in which many Jews — the estimates vary considerably — brutally were killed.

The same year, he became a partner in an Amsterdam bank, the Bankvoor Onroerende Zachen. Investigators said they suspect the bank may have played a role in the "Aryanization" — the forced sale of Dutch Jewish farms, businesses, homes and securities.

In August 1941, von Bolschwing was tossed into a Gestapo prison with no formal charges, and in April 1942 he was just as mysteriously released. In 1945, he helped American troops entering Austria catch Nazi officials and SS officers, according to a letter written for von Bolschwing by a colonel in the 71st U.S. infantry.

The war over, von Bolschwing

Otto von Bolschwing (shown here in immigration photos for his 1953 visa and 1959 naturalization) was a Prussian baron who served as a mentor and top advisor to Adolf Eichmann in the Nazi Security Service's Jewish Affairs Office. The CIA used him as a spy in Europe after the war and brought him to America in the mid-1950s. A quarter century later, the Justice Department discovered him (shown here with his lawyer) living quietly at a nursing home near Sacramento.

2 Tues., March 11, 1969   Paterson News   ★

Soobzokov Welcomer For New Americans

Congressman Charles S. Joelson has announced the selection of Tscherim Soobzokov to head his New Americans program. The program is designed to offer advice and service to new citizens who have problems with governmental agencies.

Joelson praised Soobzokov for his willingness to serve on a volunteer basis. "Since Mr. Soobzokov is himself a naturalized citizen who has proved himself in America, it is gratifying to know that he is eager to help others become established in this country," Joelson said.

Soobzokov was born in the Caucasus, and resides at 704 4th Ave., Paterson, with his wife and five children. Keebeclarah, Susanna, Aslan and Sogra. His is a member of the Paterson Zoning Board and is employed by the county of Passaic, as investigator for the

TSCHERIM SOOBZOKOV

Purchasing Department. He is a member of Humboldt Lodge 114, F. and A.M.

gation in New York. The probe reportedly involves Soobzokov's role with the SS in the Caucasus region of the Soviet Union during World War II.

From 7:45 to about 10 p.m., the protesters circled Soobzokov's two-story frame house on 14th Avenue, chanting and carrying signs. In doing so, they defied a court order issued yesterday in Newark by a federal judge. The order forbade the demonstrators to chant and said they were to walk single file.

The order, issued by U.S. District Court Judge Vincent P. Biunno, also allowed Paterson Police to forbid the use of bullhorns on the grounds that the house is in a residential neighborhood

one block from Barnert Memorial Hospital. The demonstrators used no amplifiers.

About 50 policemen, about half the total night shift, surrounded the barricaded block where the demonstrators marched. Deputy Police Chief Robert Mohl, who headed the surveillance, said there were no arrests.

More demonstrations planned

The demonstrators were young and old. Several signs read, "Death to Soobzokov." One read "No free speech for Nazis." A small group stood across 14th Avenue from the house and kept a silent

NEWS BULLETINS

Tscherim "Tom" Soobzokov was considered an immigrant success story in his adopted hometown of Paterson, New Jersey. Secretly, he had been a Nazi Waffen SS officer in Europe before teaming up with the CIA and the FBI after the war. The Justice Department began investigating him in the 1970s, sparking protests in New Jersey.

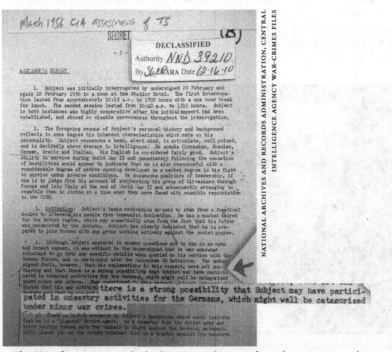

March 1956 CIA assessment of TS

SECRET   (5)

DECLASSIFIED
Authority NND 39210
By SLC RARA Date 12-16-10

ASSESSEE'S REPORT

1. Subject was initially interrogated by undersigned 20 February and again 22 February 1956 in a room at the Statler Hotel. The first interrogation lasted for approximately 10:15 a.m. to 1700 hours with a one hour break for lunch. The second session lasted from 10:40 a.m. to 1315 hours. Subject in both instances was highly cooperative after the initial report had been established, and showed no visable nervousness throughout the interrogation.

2. The foregoing resume of Subject's personal history and background reflects to some degree his inherent characteristics which make up his personality. Subject possesses a keen, alert mind, is articulate, well poised, and is decidedly above average in intelligence. He speaks Circassian, Russian, German, Arabic and Italian. His English is considered fairly good. Subject's ability to survive during World War II and immediately following the cessation of hostilities would appear to indicate that he is also resourceful with a considerable degree of native cunning developed to a marked degree in his fight to survive under adverse conditions. He possesses qualities of leadership, if one is to judge from his account of shepherding his group of Circassians through Europe and into Italy at the end of World War II and subsequently arranging to resettle them in Jordan at a time when they were faced with possible repatriation to the USSR.

3. Motivation: Subject's basic motivation appears to stem from a fanatical desire to liberate his people from Communist domination. He has a marked hatred for the Soviet regime, which may essentially stem from the fact that his father was persecuted by the Soviets. Subject has clearly indicated that he is prepared to join forces with any group working actively against the Soviet regime.

4. Although Subject appeared to answer questions put to him in an open and honest manner, it was evident to the undersigned that he was somewhat reluctant to give any specific details when queried on his service with the German forces, and in particular with the Circassian SS Battalion. The undersigned feels, however, that his explanations in this respect, were not convincing and that there is a strong possibility that Subject may have participated in unsavory activities for the Germans, which might well be categorized under minor war crimes. When questioned in this manner Subject categorically stated that his war activities there is a strong possibility that Subject may have participated in unsavory activities for the Germans, which might well be categorized under minor war crimes.

5. There is nothing evident in Subject's background which would indicate that he is a "planted" Soviet agent. As a deserter from the Soviet Army and later joining forces with the Germans to fight against the Soviets, automatically placed him on the Soviet criminal list as a traitor against his homeland.

The CIA, after interviewing Soobzokov extensively in 1956 for a job as a spy against the Soviets, concluded that he was probably involved in "minor war crimes" with the Nazis, but the agency hired him even so.

As a cabinet minister in the Nazi puppet state of Croatia (left), Andrija Artukovic was implicated in the murders of hundreds of thousands of Serbs, Jews, Roma, and other non-Aryans incarcerated in camps. He lived in Southern California (right) for nearly four decades before he was extradited to Yugoslavia in 1986 and convicted of war crimes.

Jakob Reimer was a Nazi officer (left) and trainer at the Trawniki concentration camp and took part in the brutal liquidation of the Warsaw ghetto. After coming to America (right), he ran a restaurant in New York for years and sold potato chips. He died in 2005 while prosecutors were still trying to deport him.

The prosecution of John Demjanjuk, an auto worker in Ohio, who was mistakenly thought to be the infamous Ivan the Terrible of Treblinka, was the worst black eye in the history of the Justice Department's Nazi unit. Demjanjuk was cleared of the charges linking him to Treblinka, but was found guilty years later in Germany of taking part in the murders of nearly 29,000 Jews as a Nazi guard at another concentration camp. He is shown in his U.S. immigration photo, and standing trial in 1987, viewing a photograph used to identify him.

Wernher von Braun (first row, seventh from right) was the star among dozens of rocket scientists who posed for a photograph at Fort Bliss after coming to America as part of the secret Project Paperclip. Arthur Rudolph, a top deputy to von Braun in producing V-2 rockets at a brutal slave-labor camp in Germany, is shown as well (first row, fourth from left, in light sweater).

Dr. Hubertus Strughold oversaw a clinic in Nazi Germany where brutal human experiments were conducted on children and prisoners. In the United States, he became known as the father of space medicine for his work with the Air Force. When the INS began probing his Nazi ties in the 1970s, powerful congressmen came to his defense.

Arthur Rudolph was the production chief at the V-2 slave-labor rocket factory. Above is his Nazi identification card during the war, with swastikas visible.

PROTEST   PROTEST

AGAINST NAZI WAR CRIMINALS
IN OUR MIDST

HELP GET THEM OUT OF THE U. S. A.

COME AND HEAR ABOUT THESE NAZI MURDERERS WHO
SLAUGHTERED MILLIONS OF JEWS AND OTHER PEOPLE'S,
INNOCENT MEN, WOMEN AND CHILDREN

ONE OF THEM LIVES RIGHT HERE IN BROWNSVILLE!

COME HEAR THE FACTS.....AT A MASS RALLY

WEDNESDAY, MAY 8, 1963 at 8:15 pm
at the
DE LUXE PALACE   Howard and Pitkin Aves.
Admission: FREE

Speakers

● CHARLES R. ALLEN, JR.   ● MRS. THELMA HAMILTON
  Author "Nazi War Criminals Among Us"   Exec. Sec., Parents Workshop In Brooklyn
                                          Negro Leader in Brownsville

● GEDALIA SANDLER   ● RABBI CHAIM RABINOWITZ
  Jewish Leader and Lecturer

You will hear authentic facts, names and descriptions of at least 25 NAZI WAR
CRIMINALS who have found a haven in our country.

We ask: WHY ARE THESE MURDERERS PROTECTED IN OUR LAND?
THEY MUST BE BROUGHT TO JUSTICE!

WE MUST NEVER FORGET AND NEVER FORGIVE THOSE WHO
BELIEVE IN WAR, DESTRUCTION AND MURDER.

Chuck Allen, a left-wing journalist, began investigating suspected Nazis in America in the early 1960s, at a time when few others in the media or the government took any interest. He organized an anti-Nazi protest in Brooklyn and Chicago in 1963. FBI director J. Edgar Hoover (shown below with President Richard Nixon), skeptical that there were any actual Nazis in the United States, secretly designated Allen a national security threat and had agents trailing him for years.

BETTMANN/CORBIS

Eli Rosenbaum (left) and Elizabeth Holtzman (right) leave the Panamanian Embassy in Washington in 1987, along with a representative from a Holocaust survivors' group, after warning the Panamanians of the political damage if Panama gave refuge to Karl Linnas, an ex-Nazi commander who had settled on Long Island and was stripped of his U.S. citizenship. Holtzman spearheaded the creation of the Justice Department's Nazi-hunting office in 1979, while Rosenbaum was a key figure there for nearly three decades.

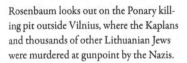

Rosenbaum, in 2012, stands in front of a jail cell in Vilnius, Lithuania, where six-year-old Fruma Kaplan and her mother were ordered jailed in 1941 by a Nazi collaborator, Aleksandras Lileikis, who ran Lithuania's security police during the Nazi occupation.

Lileikis is shown in Lithuania during his time as head of the security police in Vilnius, and in his U.S. immigration photo. After collaborating with the Nazis, Lileikis went on to work for the CIA in Europe and lived quietly in Massachusetts for four decades. Rosenbaum spent more than a decade trying to build a case against Lileikis before he succeeded in prosecuting him at the age of eighty-seven.

Rosenbaum looks out on the Ponary killing pit outside Vilnius, where the Kaplans and thousands of other Lithuanian Jews were murdered at gunpoint by the Nazis.

a young stockbroker in the 1980s, Rad would sneak off the trading floor at the Pacific Stock Exchange and head to the nearby Los Angeles courthouse for dozens of immigration hearings in his father's never-ending case. And after the elder Artukovic was finally extradited to Yugoslavia in 1986 on war crimes charges, Rad made repeated trips to Europe to prepare for a trial he regarded as "a kangaroo court."

Even long after his father died in a Yugoslavian prison while awaiting execution by firing squad, Rad kept up the fight, writing letters, meeting with federal officials, and filling file cabinets in his Southern California home with records on wartime Croatia and his father. Every scrap of paper he found, every official he contacted, he believed, could be the breakthrough he needed to exonerate his father posthumously. His father, he believed, was simply an administrator in the Nazi puppet state, a figurehead with no real authority to send anyone to their death. He wrote once to Allan Ryan, the Justice Department prosecutor, to lay out his case for his father's innocence one more time. Ryan was sympathetic but left no doubt he still considered Rad's father a brutal war criminal. "Unfortunately," Ryan wrote in response to Rad, "in prosecutions of this kind, the family inevitably suffers."

Let it go, friends would tell Rad. But he never would. Bright moments were few in the decades that Rad spent trying to exonerate his father. One came, oddly enough, from one of his father's most ardent accusers. Irv Rubin, the militant leader of the Jewish Defense League in Los Angeles, staged raucous protests at Artukovic's many deportation proceedings, denouncing his defenders as "Nazi pigs," or worse. Artukovic's supporters would sit on one side of the courtroom, Rubin and his accusers on the other, with shouting matches breaking out during recesses and at dueling press conferences staged on the courthouse steps at the end of each day. Rad, a seminary student in high school, pulled Rubin aside and told the militant Jewish leader that he hoped to reach a peace of sorts with his rival, or at least an understanding. Rubin seemed to appreciate the gesture. "You're an honorable son," Rubin told Rad. "I hate your dad, but you're an honorable son, and my faith teaches me that's something to be respected."

In the beginning, Gus von Bolschwing was just like Rad Artukovic and Aslan Soobzokov and Diane Lavoie and all the other children whose fathers were accused of being Nazis. Gus, too, wanted badly to believe his father was an innocent victim, a man wrongly accused, not the monstrous Eichmann aide that prosecutors made him out to be. He wanted to believe that the stories his father told him as a child about fighting Hitler and the Nazis in the underground movement were all true. He wanted to believe that his father was an honest man. Yet the day came when Gus von Bolschwing simply stopped believing.

There was no *aha!* moment for Gus, no deathbed confession or hidden journal that finally revealed his father's true face. Gus could not even say exactly when or why he stopped believing in his father's innocence, but he did.

Maybe it was the lawyerly detachment that Gus tried to bring to his father's case, as he pored over the reams of Nazi SS documents the Justice Department lawyers had accumulated on him. The documents, littered with his father's name and with accounts of his Nazi activities, seemed overwhelming and irrefutable. Some, in fact, were too painful to read. Gus could never quite get through the seventeen-page treatise his father wrote on ridding Germany of "the Jewish problem."

Or maybe Gus stopped believing because, after the Justice Department came after him, his father would never really talk to him about what did or did not happen with the Nazis all those years ago. When Gus would ask, he would get a shrug of the shoulders, or silence, or dissembling. Once, Gus asked his father about a conversation the Justice Department lawyers said he'd had with Eichmann at a German prison. He couldn't make heads or tails of his father's rambling response.

Or maybe he stopped believing in his father simply because father and son had never been terribly close. He'd never idolized Ossie. For five years or so, beginning in the late 1950s, the two weren't even speaking. They quarreled over typical things that a nineteen-year-old and a father quarrel about — money, college, freedom, career plans, promises made, promises broken. Gus, feeling spurned, joined the Army and went to Korea. Looking back, he realized that it was during their estrangement, when the Israelis captured Ossie's old boss Eichmann in 1960, that his father was most in fear of seeing his Nazi past exposed. That was when Ossie figured the Israelis were coming after him next, and he went running back to the CIA for protection. If father and son had been on better terms then, would Ossie have confided in him in his time of fear? Would he have told him the truth, or some rough version of it? Might he have explained to him what had really happened in Germany? Gus could only wonder.

Gus came to a wrenching realization: his father was indeed a Nazi. It was difficult to fathom, but impossible to deny. The realization tore at him. He still found it too hard to believe that his father, a dispassionate man who had never said an anti-Semitic word and married a half-Jewish woman, was driven by pure Aryan ideology and genocidal rage. Instead, Gus came to view his father as a shrewd, amoral opportunist. Whether he was chasing German gold in Palestine, closing a business deal in America, or writing strategy memos for Adolf Eichmann, his father would see an opportunity and run to it. He seemed driven only by personal success. Morality was never a concern. But did motivations matter in understanding his father's past? Gus wasn't sure. Whatever devils drove the old man, he had done what he had done for Hitler. He had become an instrument of pure evil. Even more agonizing for Gus was the question: What did all this say about Gus himself? Was there some genetic flaw passed on from father to son, some DNA strain that made his father so detached and oblivious to the pain of others, and did it live in himself? Am *I* a bad person? Gus wondered.

Gus might never have found out about his father's hidden past had it not been for a random records-check by the Justice Department that led them to a nursing home in Sacramento. The government's Nazi hunters had never even heard of Otto von Bolschwing before 1979. The man they were chasing—the one who led them to von Bolschwing—was Bishop Viorel Trifa, the corrupt partner to von Bolschwing in the 1941 pogroms in Romania that left hundreds of Jews killed, with many skinned and hung from meat hooks. Bishop Trifa was the inspiration for the brutality, giving anti-Semitic speeches about the "kikes" to rally the masses to action. Von Bolschwing was Trifa's Nazi SD patron and protector, giving operational advice and providing a Nazi safe house after the bloodbath to Trifa and his allies in Bucharest.

While von Bolschwing lived anonymously in America after the war, a businessman divorced from his old political life in Europe, Bishop Trifa embraced his past, almost taunting immigration authorities for more than thirty years to come after him. Politically well-connected, Trifa became the national leader of the Romanian Orthodox Church in America. Inside the serenity of his Michigan church compound, he gave an interview in 1973 to the *New York Times*'s Ralph Blumenthal readily admitting that he wore the fascist Iron Guard uniform in Romania and made anti-Semitic speeches leading up to the pogroms. Trifa was so established as a voice of Romanian expatriates in America that Radio Free Europe aired a forty-five-minute interview with him on Romanian affairs, even as the INS was pursuing war crimes charges against him.

In 1979, as the Justice Department was finally pushing ahead with deportation proceedings against Trifa after years of foot-dragging, prosecutors went looking for witnesses who might bolster their case against the cleric. They went to the Germans for help: did they have information on any of the Nazis who may have had knowledge of the Romanian pogroms? One hit came back from the officials in Bonn: a man identified on an SS list only as "von Bolschwing." And there was more: von Bolschwing had left Europe in the mid-1950s, the Germans reported, and he had gone to America.

Even then, Justice Department officials saw this new figure — Otto von Bolschwing — mostly as a witness to the Romanian bloodletting, a man who might be able to help seal the case against Trifa, not as a perpetrator himself. Not until Justice Department lawyers began digging more deeply into the background of von Bolschwing did they realize he was a much bigger cog in the Nazi machinery than they realized. Indeed, he was much bigger than Trifa ever was. Von Bolschwing had lived in the shadows, but he had been a top aide to Eichmann, and his fingerprints were all over Nazi SS documents in Germany, Austria, and Romania. The witness had now become the target.

There was one more list to be checked, and that one belonged to the CIA. Before it moved against von Bolschwing, the Justice Department needed to know whether the spy agency had any connection to him after the war. It wasn't leaving anything to chance. The Justice Department had little reason to think the CIA had any dealings with von Bolschwing, but after the Soobzokov debacle, when the department saw its case implode because of the CIA's involvement with their old Nazi spy, prosecutors weren't willing to assume anything anymore.

A CIA official called Marty Mendelsohn, a senior official in the Nazi unit, to deliver the unwelcome news: yes, in fact, the CIA knew a lot about Otto von Bolschwing. For a decade after the war, he was one of theirs: a CIA spy in Europe. The news was jarring, so jarring that the very next day, Mendelsohn was in a car with one of his lawyers, driving across the Potomac to CIA headquarters to find out exactly what the spies at Langley knew about the Prussian nobleman.

It was another disaster in the making for both the Justice Department and the CIA. For the second time in a matter of months, federal authorities were chasing an ex-Nazi who had worked for the CIA for years as a Cold War spy. But this one was worse. This time the target was a senior SS official much higher in rank than Soobzokov. If the CIA knew enough about Soobzokov's true past with the Nazis to torpedo his deportation case, they knew even more about von Bolschwing's ties to Hitler. Sure enough, his CIA handlers had helped get von Bolschwing into the country in 1954, whitewashing his record to clear his entry. And CIA officials had kept quiet six years later, in 1960, when a panicked von Bolschwing rushed back to them for help after Eichmann's capture. The relationship between the CIA and the former Eichmann aide raised "obvious questions," CIA lawyers said with a bit of understatement, after scrubbing their own files. With the Justice Department now looking to prosecute von Bolschwing, officials at Langley worried about the prospect of their ex-spy "graymailing" them — using the threat of revealing classified information in court to thwart his deportation. The Justice Department, meanwhile, worried that the CIA's own files would show that von Bolschwing, like Soobzokov, had told the CIA all about his Nazi past before he came to America. The Justice Department didn't want to be sandbagged again by the CIA. "Most of our cases are based on a claim that the defendant misrepresented his Nazi background at the time of his entry into the U.S. or at the time of his naturalization," Mausner wrote to the CIA in a letter laying out his concerns. "It is therefore important to know exactly what the INS, State Department, and CIA knew about von Bolschwing at the time of his entry and naturalization."

This was a case that everyone wished would just go away. Certainly Gus von Bolschwing did, as he prepared for a formal interview that the Justice Department wanted to conduct with his father about his wartime activities. Gus was acting as both Otto's son and his lawyer. In the weeks leading up to the scheduled deposition, Gus spent hours on the phone with the prosecutor, Jeff Mausner, at all hours of the night, as they tried to agree on the ground rules. For reasons Gus never quite understood, his father had changed his posture and was now willing to admit to both the Justice Department and to Gus that, yes, he had been a Nazi. His father was willing to confirm his membership in the Nazi Party, the SS, and the SD, but nothing more, Gus told Mausner. No details, no explanations, no follow-up questions from Mausner or anyone else about Otto's connections to Adolf Eichmann, the Romanian pogroms, Nazi atrocities in Austria, the white paper on the "Jewish problem," or any other long-buried Nazi secrets. If the Justice Department wouldn't agree to those terms, von Bolschwing wasn't willing to talk at all. Mausner had a choice to make. He could take what Gus von Bolschwing was offering, or he could spend many months litigating the issue in the hopes of getting the full story. He took the deal.

And so, on an unusually cold February day in Sacramento in 1981, the lawyers met for the deposition at the suburban nursing home where the seventy-one-year-old von Bolschwing had been living for the last year. Doctors determined he was suffering from a rare and incurable brain disease known as progressive supranuclear palsy, which was eating away at his mind and body. One day he would seem fine and lucid; the next, he might not even know where he was. In other investigations, Justice Department lawyers suspected that some of the aging defendants — Rad Artukovic's father, for one — were feigning illness to escape deportation. But in Otto von Bolschwing's case, the Justice Department lawyers were convinced that his debilitating condition was real.

On this day, Ossie seemed lucid enough as he sat down for the interview in a conference room at the nursing home. Among the phalanx of lawyers in the room were two from the CIA. The pair said little, but their purpose was clear: they were there to ensure that neither von Bolschwing nor the Justice Department slipped up and revealed any compromising CIA secrets that could spill onto the public record. The CIA was already exposed enough in its dealings with von Bolschwing. It didn't want to risk further damage.

Officially, this was Otto von Bolschwing's deposition, but it was his son, Gus, who did most of the talking. He had been brooding for weeks over what he would say. Dispensing with a few legal formalities at the outset, he quickly tossed aside his lawyer's hat and began speaking not as an attorney representing his client, but as a son wounded by a father. His words were raw, unscripted, and intensely personal. He was angry, Gus told the government lawyers: angry at the Justice Department for trying to deport his father for war crimes committed so long ago; angry at the CIA for shielding its own duplicitous role in the ugly affair; but mostly, angry at his father for the secrets he had kept for so long.

"I am deeply disturbed by the morality of my father's even belonging to the Nazi Party," Gus began, his Austrian accent still thick after more than a quarter century in America. His father had many relatives in Europe who lived through the war; none that he knew, Gus said, had taken the sordid path his father chose. "I don't know what was in my father's mind when he did what he did when he was a Nazi."

When he was a Nazi. When he had first heard the accusation on that phone call from Mausner the year before, Gus couldn't believe such a thing could be true. Even now, the words were difficult for him to say aloud. "I cannot condemn him," Gus said. "I was not there at the time. I do not know all the facts that were involved in these very unusual times," he said.

"Possibly as he grew older and hopefully wiser, he examined his past," Gus went on. He seemed to be struggling to convince himself as much as anyone. His father sat quietly, but Gus spoke of him only in the third person, as if he were not there. It was difficult to even look at the old man.

Again, Gus mused aloud about how strange it was to consider his father a Nazi: how Gus had never heard him utter an anti-Semitic word; how he had married a half-Jewish woman; how his wife's Jewish relatives in Boston had welcomed the family with open arms after the war. "Never in all that time — they all came from Vienna and Germany, they all had been there — did I ever hear one bad word about my father," Gus said, rambling a bit, still trying to understand it all.

"Although I question my father very seriously," he continued, "I also question the morality and ethics of the United States government in this case." It was the CIA, Gus reminded the lawyers, that had urged Ossie "not to reveal his background, his activities prior to 1945, to anyone." His father's CIA handlers, he believed, had directed the cover-up.

The idea of trying to deport an ailing man for things he had done forty years earlier — things that he had told the CIA about — seemed blatantly unjust, Gus added; it reminded him, he said, of the laws Hitler and the Nazis had imposed in the 1930s to lock up dissidents. "So I wonder as I sit here," Gus said, "does the means justify the end?" Should unjust laws be used to prosecute abhorrent crimes? After so many years, he asked, how could his father be expected "to prove his case, to disprove pieces of paper that are now forty years old? . . . I think we should question ourselves morally. I think it is the height of hypocrisy . . . and I think the time has come to bring an end to such hypocrisy."

Gus finished up his gut-wrenching soliloquy, then announced that his father was ready to answer the narrow set of questions that he and Mausner had agreed upon.

"Mr. von Bolschwing," Mausner asked, "were you ever a member of the Nazi Party?"

"Yes," Ossie answered.

"When were you a member of the Nazi Party?"

Von Bolschwing responded: "1932, I think, through 1945."

And on it went, like a job applicant reciting lines from his resumé.

"When were you a member of the SS?" Mausner asked.

"From 1941 or '42, I don't know."

Gus corrected him: the documents indicated that he had joined the SS in 1940, after passing an examination.

"It's quite possible," the father told his son. "I do not recall the exact dates."

Around that same time, he had joined the SD, the Nazis' political intelligence branch and a sister agency to the SS.

"What was your rank in the SD?" Mausner asked.

"I think *Hauptsturmführer*, which is the equivalent of captain."

They were done. The end, brief as it was, seemed almost anticlimactic. They had stuck to the script. There were just ten questions about his Nazi allegiances and service, most of them answered in just a few terse words. Von Bolschwing had been a Nazi for thirteen years, reaching the rank of captain in the SS, writing strategy memos on purging Germany of the Jews, directing on-the-ground operations in his native Austria, giving safe haven to Bishop Trifa in Romania. All the bloodshed, all the hatred: all of that could be summed up neatly in a few short minutes of questioning. If there was regret, von Bolschwing did not voice it. If there was shame, he did not show it.

A few months after his deposition at the nursing home, word broke publicly about von Bolschwing, as the Justice Department brought charges to strip the Austrian native of his citizenship and deport him. Ossie denied everything. "I never served in the SS or Gestapo or SD," he lied to one AP reporter who called him at the nursing home. Von Bolschwing made another claim, too: he told a few reporters that he had worked for the Americans and the CIA doing intelligence at the end of the war and afterward. Like his Nazi denials, this claim also sounded like an old man's fanciful invention, and few people believed him. An Eichmann aide working for the CIA? Except that this claim was true. Both the CIA and the Justice Department knew that it was true, but they weren't commenting.

For months afterward, von Bolschwing and Gus vowed publicly to fight the denaturalization. Gus reasoned that his father might be able to leverage his spy work for the CIA — and the admissions he had made to them years earlier — to counter the Justice Department's charges that he had lied his way into America. But privately, even as he was plotting a possible defense, Gus was losing the will to fight. The more details he learned of his father's Nazi past, the more difficult it became to represent him. He had already decided, in fact, to stop representing his father entirely and leave it to another Bay Area lawyer. The case was too emotionally laden. Gus wasn't even sure his father would be allowed to put on a full defense, because the Justice Department had secured a gag order preventing his father from saying anything publicly about his CIA work. The CIA knew all along that von Bolschwing was a Nazi, he maintained, but he wasn't allowed to say anything publicly about his dealings with the agency.

So Gus and his father took what his new lawyer called "the easy way out": they cut a deal with Mausner and the Justice Department. Von Bolschwing agreed to give up his American citizenship, which he had held since 1959, and admit to his membership with the Nazis. But in exchange, the Justice Department allowed him to avoid deportation and remain in the United States indefinitely because of his failing health. If a doctor later found his condition was improving, the Justice Department could move again to deport him. No one considered that prospect likely, however.

The deal was attractive not only to von Bolschwing, but to the Justice Department and the CIA. Rockler, the head of the Nazi office, didn't want a public trial with a defendant as frail and occasionally incoherent as von Bolschwing. Rockler called the old man a "wheelchair case"; he could only imagine the sympathy that von Bolschwing, in his condition, would elicit from a judge. A deal would save the years of litigation needed to take away his citizenship. More important, it would avoid the risk of another Soobzokov embarrassment, where von Bolschwing might prove that the CIA knew all about his Nazi history when it helped him into the country.

For the CIA, the deal was even more attractive. The gag order muzzling von Bolschwing would remain in place, and there would be no danger of the agency's decade-long dalliance with a senior Nazi spilling into open court. Any discussion of von Bolschwing's relationship with the CIA would remain, for now, just the fantastic claims of a dying old Nazi trying to save his own skin.

Less than three months after the plea deal was reached, Otto "Ossie" von Bolschwing died. Fifty years after he joined the Nazi Party, von Bolschwing — Prussian nobleman, Nazi SS officer, CIA spy — succumbed at the age of seventy-two to the disease that had ravaged his brain. Mausner, the prosecutor, wasn't sorry to see him go. He had no mercy for a man so despicable. He was just glad he had been able to strip the ex-Nazi of his citizenship first. It was a small victory. He didn't die an American. To Mausner, von Bolschwing died in disgrace. That was something.

Even at the end, Gus von Bolschwing was still struggling to understand his father's dark past. When the local newspaper called to ask him for a comment about his father's death, Gus spoke not from a place of mourning or anger, but of confusion. He was still unable to reconcile the two men he now knew as his father. "I would say," Gus told the reporter, "that in all my lifetime, my father never made an anti-Semitic comment."

In 1989, just as the Justice Department's Nazi team was gaining wide-scale notice, a Hollywood film was released that captured the emotional tumult of the daughter of an accused Nazi. In *Music Box,* a Chicago lawyer played by Jessica Lange defends her father against accusations that he was a Nazi collaborator in Hungary, only to discover photos hidden away in a music box that showed him torturing and killing his Jewish victims.

The film was fiction, written by one of Hollywood's most bankable screenwriters, Joe Eszterhas, who normally veered toward flashier fare like *Basic Instinct* and *Showgirls*. Eszterhas was born in Hungary at the very end of the war, and the film grew out of the shame he felt over his native country's anti-Semitism and complicity in the Holocaust. But as he told interviewers when the film came out, Eszterhas had questioned his parents and other relatives at length about the war years in Hungary and was satisfied that no one in his own family was involved.

The very next year, he discovered the truth. The Justice Department opened a Nazi investigation into his own father. Prosecutors suspected eighty-three-year-old Istvan Eszterhas, the retired editor of a Hungarian-language newspaper in Cleveland, of war crimes. To his shock, Joe Eszterhas learned that during the war his father had written hundreds of anti-Semitic screeds for the pro-Nazi propaganda ministry in Hungary and had penned a book that said of the Jews: "The iron fist of the law must be applied to this parasitic race."

To Joe Eszterhas, the book read like a Hungarian version of *Mein Kampf*. His father hadn't killed anyone with his own hands, at least as far as the prosecutors knew, but he had no doubt inspired hatred and rage in his countrymen through his words of official propaganda. The Justice Department didn't end up prosecuting his father, but Joe Eszterhas cut off contact with him for a time, and their relationship was irreparably damaged by his father's dark past. *Music Box* was supposed to be a made-up story, but the Hollywood screenwriter's own life had come to imitate his art in haunting ways, and the guilt and shame of his father's role with the Nazis were passed from one generation to the next. Like Gus von Bolschwing and others confronted by the sins of their fathers, Eszterhas felt that his father's hidden past had left him with a moral burden of his own. "It's the responsibility of the son to do penance," Eszterhas said, "to correct what the father has done."

10

A Good Party Spoiled

October 13, 1982

SAN JOSE, CALIFORNIA

In the early 1980s, the surge of interest in America's long-hidden war criminals brought a new generation of Nazi hunters to the cause. Two decades
before, Chuck Allen's solitary crusade had met with indifference or even
hostility. But a new band of lawyers, lawmakers, and Jewish activists was
now determined to seize the issue as their own, and the results proved far
different this time.

Eli Rosenbaum was still a third-year law student at Harvard when he
wandered off to the bookstore in Cambridge one autumn day in 1980 and
got his first scent of the hunt. He should have been in the law library studying for his copyright class. Instead, he was thumbing through tomes on
World War II history in the back of the store. This was his guilty pleasure:
he would sneak off to the bookstore and lose himself for hours, usually
in the section dedicated to the war and the Holocaust. That day, he came
across an obscure book on a Nazi concentration camp called Dora, the barbaric place where tens of thousands of slave laborers lived — and died — to
build Hitler's "revenge" missiles.

The book that caught his attention was the English translation of a memoir called *Dora*, written by one of the camp's survivors, a French prisoner of
war named Jean Michel. Its description of the hell that was Dora both cap-
tivated and repulsed Rosenbaum. How was it, he wondered as he skimmed
through the atrocities described in the book, that he knew nothing of the
Dora camp? He considered himself a student of the Holocaust. He had

spent the last summer as an intern working on legal briefs in the Justice Department's new Nazi-hunting office, and he had organized a petition drive at Harvard urging continued war crimes prosecutions in Germany. Yet, like most Americans, he had never even heard of this uniquely perverse place, where prisoners were made to build their jailers' bombs and dig their own graves. Americans knew plenty about the glistening marvels of aviation produced at the camp: the gravity-defying V-2 missiles launched across Europe by Hitler and then imported to America. But they knew virtually nothing about how and where the Nazis had built those missiles, even as books in Europe, like the one in Rosenbaum's hands, were being written on the place. The anonymity of Dora was no accident. General Patton and the military had eagerly publicized America's liberation of Dachau and other concentration camps, but they wanted no such publicity surrounding the secrets of Dora, as America claimed the mountain factory's scientists and its rockets for itself. It was as if the place had never existed.

A few days after he found the French memoir, Rosenbaum went back to the bookstore in search of more information. In the science section, he found a book called *The Rocket Team,* written from a very different perspective. This one, a newly published book by two American scientists, was a glowing account of the technological feats of Wernher von Braun and the Nazi scientists in building the V-2 missiles at Dora's factory, known as Mittelwerk, and its predecessor, Peenemünde. As he skimmed the pages, a photo jumped out at Rosenbaum. It showed Russian prisoners, their heads shaved, working on the machinery. A pleasant caption under the photo read: "Contributing to the manufacture of A4s at Peenemünde were skilled Russian prisoners of war, always under the watchful eyes of German supervisors." Rosenbaum grimaced at the whitewashed account. Prisoners of war "contributing" to the A-4 production under the "watchful eyes" of the Germans? "Slave laborers forced at Nazi gunpoint to build Hitler's missiles" was more like it. Where had this photo even come from? he wondered. He looked in the back for the photo credit: *courtesy of Wernher von Braun.* The father of rocket science himself had apparently kept the photo of the slave laborers as some sort of macabre souvenir. The callousness grated at Rosenbaum. He bought the book and scribbled two large asterisks next to the photo credit, underlining von Braun's name.

A second passage in the book caught his attention, too. A top Nazi scientist under von Braun named Arthur Rudolph, an engineer who was the operations chief at Dora's missile factory, recounted an episode in which he had to rush back to the factory after hours to tend to an unexpected engineering glitch. Remarkably, Rudolph's main concern seemed to be the nuisance it had created for him. It was New Year's Eve, and "I was relaxing at a get-together with a few close associates, enjoying a respite from the horrible pressure of the plant." Rudolph groused about having to put down his champagne and find prisoners to fix the problem. "It was very cold and I cursed at having to leave the party just to get those missiles out," he said.

Rosenbaum shook his head in disbelief. Slave laborers were dying by the day at Rudolph's missile factory from disease and malnutrition, while others were hanged, and this Nazi, a so-called scientist, had the nerve to complain about being forced to put down his champagne to handle an engineering glitch? It was the height of audacity. Rosenbaum wanted to know more about this man Rudolph. When he checked the footnotes in the back of the book to see if he was mentioned, disgust turned to disbelief. The story about the scuttled New Year's Eve party, it turned out, came from an interview the book's authors had done with Dr. Rudolph himself in 1971 — an interview conducted at the military installation in Huntsville, Alabama. It took a moment for the realization to set in. *Arthur Rudolph had come to America. To work for the United States military.*

Like a dog with a bone, Rosenbaum couldn't let go of the idea that a top scientist at a brutal Nazi camp like Dora had come to America — and not just as any ordinary American but, from what he learned, as the top engineer with the Saturn V space program. Rudolph was "Mr. Saturn," a man who helped put America on the moon and received the highest honors from NASA for his work. He had served at the depths of Nazi depravity and the height of American achievement, bookending his life. It was a scandal, Rosenbaum thought. How could this have happened?

Rosenbaum was vaguely aware of Project Paperclip, the secret government program that had brought some sixteen hundred German scientists to America — non-Nazis, he had always heard, or at least not "ardent" ones — but it seemed beyond the pale for the program to have included scientists like Rudolph, a man involved at such a high level in the systematic brutalization of Nazi prisoners. Where was the outrage? And what had happened to this man? Rosenbaum knew that von Braun had died just a few years earlier, in 1977, feted in the United States and around the world as a visionary of space science, with virtually no mention anywhere of his ties to the barbaric conditions at the Dora factory complex. But what about Rudolph?

Rosenbaum was still fixated on Dora months later, when he graduated from Harvard Law School and returned to the Justice Department as part of an honors program to recruit top law school graduates. The young lawyers in the program normally rotated through different sections of the Justice Department, but Rosenbaum, after his internship at the new Nazi-hunting unit the year before, had only one job in mind: he wanted to spend his entire year at the Nazi office. His supervisors were glad to comply; the nascent Nazi section, with a temporary mission and an unclear future, was seen as a dead end, with few lawyers lining up to work there. If this new law school grad wanted to spend all his time chasing Nazi ghosts, the Justice Department was certainly willing to let him have at it.

His first day back at the Justice Department, Rosenbaum sat down with Neal Sher, the top deputy in the Nazi office and a mentor of Rosenbaum's during his internship, who welcomed him back and introduced some of the cases he would be handling. Rosenbaum brought some ideas of his own. He still had a name stuck in his head ever since he'd read about the spoiled New Year's Eve party.

"You ever heard of a guy named Arthur Rudolph?" Rosenbaum asked Sher.

"No," his boss answered, "who's he?"

"He was a scientist who was involved in the German V-2 program."

"Paperclip?" Sher asked.

"Yeah."

Sher could already guess where this was heading, and it didn't sound promising. "Eli, you know those Paperclip cases don't go anywhere."

"Well," Rosenbaum said. "You mind if I look into it?"

Sher gave his new lawyer an indifferent shrug. "Okay," he said finally, "but don't spend a lot of time on it."

With a faint green light from his new boss, Rosenbaum started poking around, gathering up all the information he could find on Rudolph. A phone call to the military arsenal in Alabama revealed that Rudolph was still alive and well and had relocated to a suburb outside San Jose, California, to be near his grown daughter. He was living comfortably in retirement, with dual pensions from both the German government — for his service under the Nazis — and from the United States government for his time in the space program.

Meanwhile, a search of war-era documents connected to the Nuremberg trials confirmed Rudolph's high-level involvement at Dora. Rudolph, von Braun, and General Dornberger, who also came to America under Project Paperclip, were all participants in a secret, high-level Nazi meeting in 1944 to plan for the use of slave laborers to produce a thousand missiles a month for Hitler. A senior SS commander identified Rudolph as one of the twelve men responsible for the actual operations at the slave factory. Mysteriously, the Army listed only eleven of the dozen as "perpetrators" who would face war crimes prosecution. The only name missing: Arthur Rudolph. Someone in the U.S. military seemed anxious to protect Rudolph from the war crimes trials, Rosenbaum suspected.

Those suspicions only deepened when he found a review of the Army's security evaluation for Rudolph in 1945. At the close of the war, the initial Army report characterized Rudolph as "100% Nazi, dangerous type, security threat . . . *suggest internment.*" But rather than being jailed, Rudolph had been brought to the United States in Project Paperclip. By then, the Army had softened its view of him considerably. The official report now declared that Rudolph, rather than being a dangerous, "100% Nazi," posed no security threat to America and "was not a war criminal, not an ardent Nazi."

As Rosenbaum kept digging, a deeper portrait of Rudolph began to emerge.

Rudolph was an early Nazi devotee during the rise of the party, marching proudly down the streets of Berlin, swastika on his arm, and singing the "Horst Wessel Lied," the Nazi anthem. As a promising young engineer in Nazi Germany in the mid-1930s, Rudolph rose steadily in status as he worked to develop rockets for Hitler at a Nazi ordnance factory. One day, he visited a rocket demonstration put on by another team of German scientists. He was confused. How was it, he asked a boyish-looking member of the team, that they were able to gauge the rockets' thrust without actually measuring it with instruments, the way they were always taught? "We don't measure it — we calculate it," the other scientist told him. Shocked at the notion, Rudolph asked his boss afterward who this brash young Nazi scientist was.

"You don't know who that guy is?" his boss answered. "That is Wernher von Braun. He is the brain of that outfit here. Didn't you know that?"

"No," Rudolph answered, "but I know now."

Von Braun was six years his junior, but Rudolph soon went to work for the "boy genius" as a top engineering deputy in the rocket program, beginning a relationship that would span four decades and two continents. When von Braun began developing and building his long-range ballistic missiles for Hitler, Rudolph was one of his key production people. Although Rudolph fancied himself an inventor, he wasn't there for his scientific wizardry; that was von Braun's realm. He was there because he was a competent engineer and a good manager who could make all the intricate pieces fit together precisely the way von Braun wanted.

At the brutal slave-labor factory at Dora, Rudolph was the chief of production for the V-2. He earned a decent salary as von Braun's man at the factory. Sometimes, he would sit in the camp's commandant's office and drink schnapps. He lived in a nearby village in a room with a nice family. Once or twice each day, he would walk through the sprawling labyrinth of tunnels that made up the underground factory at Mittelwerk to oversee missile production, tend to engineering problems, and make sure he had enough *Häftlinge*, or prisoners, to meet Hitler's monthly demand for missiles. He needed five thousand prisoners to build three hundred missiles a month, he told the SS. Where they came from, he didn't much care, as long as the men were strong enough to work. His office in Tunnel 40 sat right next to a giant work crane that the SS used to hang the workers accused of malfeasance. As hundreds of prisoners each month were killed by starvation, disease, overwork, shooting, stabbing, or hanging, Rudolph requested more bodies to replace them. He had to meet his quotas.

With every scrap of paper Rosenbaum turned up, his once-ambivalent boss, Neal Sher, got more and more excited about the prospects for the investigation. After a rocky start in its first few years, the Nazi-hunting unit still had few major victories to claim for itself. The case against Arthur Rudolph was shaping up as a big one.

In the midst of his research, Rosenbaum took a short walk one day down to the Smithsonian National Air and Space Museum in Washington.

He wanted to see something. There among the exhibits was an enormous black-and-white V-2 missile, the fabled rocket that von Braun and Rudolph had produced in Nazi Germany and imported to America. Rosenbaum gazed up at the marvel of engineering, then studied the display below it that described the missile's revolutionary technology. He read the display a second time, just to be sure. It wasn't there: not a single word, Rosenbaum noted, about the brutality of the camps where the rockets were produced. Nothing about the tens of thousands of slave laborers who actually built the Nazis' great missile, or about the estimated twenty thousand prisoners who died in the process. It was as if their deaths had never even occurred.

As he walked away from Hitler's V-2, he was more convinced than ever: Arthur Rudolph did not deserve to call himself an American.

For Rosenbaum, trying to bring ex-Nazis like Rudolph to justice was a personal quest, not just a professional one. His own parents had fled Germany for America in the 1930s before the massacres started, but many extended family members were killed in the Holocaust. Rosenbaum knew, too, that his father, a U.S. Army infantryman, had gone into Dachau the day after the Americans rolled into the death camp in 1945 and discovered its horror. As a boy growing up in a Jewish, middle-class family on Long Island in the 1970s, he had read *The Diary of Anne Frank* with grim fascination. He had heard all-too-brief snippets of Holocaust history in Hebrew school and on the occasional TV show. Yet inside his own home, the topic was not discussed. It was verboten; he knew not to ask. It was simply too painful for his parents to discuss, a horrible void they never dared try to fill. They were typical of their generation, but he was typical of the children of that cohort: he wanted to know. Once, not long after his bar mitzvah, Rosenbaum got up the nerve to finally ask his father about the Holocaust during a long, silent car trip through upstate New York in the midst of a blizzard. What was Dachau like when you got there? What did you see at the camp? The boy yearned to know, to better understand his father's pain and the silent mark it had left on him. Peering straight out at the highway, his father opened his mouth as if to speak. Instead, his eyes welled with tears, his mouth frozen agape. No words came out. He just continued driving in the storm. The boy had never seen his father cry before. He never asked about Dachau again.

With all the evidence Rosenbaum had gathered against Rudolph by the fall of 1982, the Justice Department was finally ready to approach the ex-Nazi scientist himself and see if he would talk. That first contact was always a critical time in any Nazi investigation, filled with both promise and peril. Sometimes the Justice Department lawyers would try what they called a "knock and talk": arrive unannounced at a suspect's home or business and see if they could coax him into discussing what he had really done during the war. Often, the surprised immigrant would tell the lawyers they had the wrong man, or simply slam the door on them. Talk to my lawyer, many would say. But sometimes, if they got lucky, the suspect would open up to them. At one knock and talk, a Lithuanian tailor in Massachusetts — suspected of serving in a Nazi-led mobile killing unit — chatted with Rosenbaum for so long at the front counter of his tailoring shop that the young prosecutor found a parking ticket on his car when he walked back out onto the street. In another unannounced visit, a surprised immigrant in Southern California suspected of Nazi ties invited the Justice Department lawyers into his ornate home — a reflection of his financial success in America — to explain why their suspicions about him were off base. With little sign of trepidation or guilt, the man coolly denied any suggestion of wartime involvement with the Nazis. Days later, however, he killed himself.

With Arthur Rudolph, however, the Justice Department's lawyers didn't think a surprise visit would produce much. He seemed too smart. They opted to send him a formal letter asking to interview him about the war and his immigration to America. "In particular," the letter added, "your activities between 1939 and 1945 in Germany will be the subject of some questions."

Chances seemed slim that Rudolph would agree to talk. But he surprised the Justice Department's investigators. He agreed to sit down for an interview. And no, he said, he didn't need a lawyer. Rosenbaum knew he had caught a break.

A month later, Rosenbaum was in the parking lot outside a Hyatt hotel in suburban San Jose, walking into the biggest interview of his short legal career. It was so big, in fact, that he was joined not only by his boss, Neal Sher, but by his boss's boss, Allan Ryan, as well. The lawyers had been getting ready for this meeting for weeks, preparing questions, going over documents, plotting strategy. Keep Rudolph talking; that was the most important thing. If they hoped to have him deported, they figured they would have to get him to admit not only that he knew about the inhumane treatment of the slave laborers at Dora, but that he was actively involved in carrying it out. That wouldn't be easy. Rudolph wasn't some unschooled Nazi camp guard; he was a noted Nazi scientist. As the lawyers made their way through the parking lot to the hotel, Rosenbaum couldn't help thinking of that old quip used to describe someone of modest intellect: *He's no rocket scientist.* "Think about it," Rosenbaum chuckled to Sher. "Rudolph *is* a rocket scientist."

Inside the Hyatt, the three government lawyers gathered around a long table in a nondescript conference room, a stenographer at their side. Then they waited. The interview was voluntary, and there was no assurance Rudolph would actually show up. But just after 10:00 a.m, the seventy-five-year-old engineer walked in the door. His hands were a bit shaky, but he seemed otherwise steady enough for a man of his age. Slight of frame, he was bald, with a pinkish face and a kindly smile. Rosenbaum peered behind Rudolph as he walked in the door: there was no one else with him — no lawyer, no one at all. Rosenbaum tried to hide a smile. Whether it was arrogance or naiveté that had brought Rudolph there alone, Rosenbaum didn't care. They had their chance now.

In the movies, when an aging Nazi is shown onscreen, there is inevitably that hint of evil: the dark, deathly stare of a Laurence Olivier, or the knowing scowl of a German villain sucking on a cigarette. Rosenbaum saw none of that in Rudolph. He was soft-spoken and grandfatherly as he introduced himself. He seemed utterly and completely normal. Nothing about him suggested his dark past. The "banality of evil," Hannah Arendt famously called this odd phenomenon when writing about Eichmann's trial. Rosenbaum didn't dwell on it. He was happy just to have the old man sitting in front of him after all the time spent tracking him.

The men introduced themselves. The mood was informal, even friendly, despite the gravity of the meeting. Rudolph had even brought along some mementos from the production of the V-2: a small rocket model, some photos from the factory, a packet of letters from the Nazis he had known there, and a few other trinkets. He had saved the items all these years. Like a curator at the Smithsonian displaying a prized invention, he was anxious to show them off. He was clearly proud of what he had accomplished at the missile factory. How it had been accomplished was apparently irrelevant. The macabre nature of the souvenirs did not seem to strike him.

He also brought an honorary letter from a Florida congressman that he received when he retired from the American space program in 1969, the year of the first moon landing, which he'd helped achieve. He wanted the lawyers to have that letter, too. That was his crowning moment: the lunar landing, when his adopted country reached unthinkable heights in no small part due to him, Arthur Rudolph, under his old friend Wernher von Braun. He had a long record of service to America. He wanted the lawyers to know that. They needed to understand everything he'd done for the United States and not just look solely at his Nazi days in Germany.

He hadn't told anyone besides his wife about his interview with the Justice Department. He didn't think he needed any help. If the government lawyers just understood everything that had happened — both during the war and after — he was sure he could erase whatever lingering concerns they may have about him.

The lawyers smiled politely as he pushed all his photos and mementos on the table in front of them and tried to show them off one by one. There would be time for all that later, they told him; for now, they wanted to get on with the interview.

Neal Sher led off the questioning. He wanted to get the legal formalities out of the way. Rudolph understood that the meeting was voluntary and that he could have a lawyer with him if he wanted, correct?

"Ja," Rudolph answered in his clipped German accent.

"I don't see anybody here."

"No, no. I didn't ask for a lawyer."

Rudolph had a question of his own before they went any further. Why exactly was he being questioned? Why was he here?

He wasn't being confrontational. He never raised his voice. He just wanted to understand why Dora and his missile work had come up after all these years.

Sher stuck to the script, revealing little. "Questions have been raised, as we said in our letter, regarding your activities during the Second World War, and because there have been questions raised, we would like to resolve those questions."

"Uh-huh," Rudolph answered. His voice was small and emotionless. It was hard to imagine him as the powerful man who once directed thousands of workers — be they slave laborers or Saturn V technicians — in building the world's most powerful rockets. He once described himself as a choir director at NASA, making all the rocket technicians under him work in concert and sing in harmony. But as he spoke now, his voice so halting and reserved, he sounded almost mute.

Sher began with some questions about Rudolph's modest schooling in Germany and his background in engineering. Soon enough, he turned to the politics of the Third Reich. Sher wanted to know about Rudolph's history with the Nazis. He was an early Nazi, wasn't he, joining the party two years before Hitler's rise to power in 1933?

"Correct, ja," Rudolph said, unflinching.

"In Berlin?"

"In Berlin."

"You weren't forced to join?"

"No, I could say I was talked into it, but . . ." His voice trailed off unconvincingly.

So, Sher wanted to know, was he familiar with *Mein Kampf*?

"Yes, I read it."

Mein Kampf was the book that laid the foundation for Hitler's entire philosophy in Germany, wasn't it?

"It could be," Rudolph said. "I'm, I'm not sure."

"Okay," Sher said. "Did you agree with what Hitler said in *Mein Kampf*, with his theories?"

"No, I didn't agree with everything," he said softly. "But with a lot of things."

Sher paused. Rudolph was obviously a smart man, he said. On which parts of *Mein Kampf* did he actually agree with Hitler?

"Yeah, well, the real thing," Rudolph said, stumbling over his words for the first time, "is that he fought Communism."

But he said more than that in *Mein Kampf*, didn't he? Sher asked. More than just fighting Communism?

"Oh, he said more than that, sure."

"He had certain views regarding the superiority of the races," Sher noted.

"Oh yeah, but you see, there was no such thing — what he called an

Aryan race." The whole notion of a Nordic race — "it's nonsense," Rudolph said. "Far-fetched," he added. Whatever plans Hitler had for a master race, that wasn't why he himself joined with the Nazis, he insisted.

As he sat and listened to the interrogation, Rosenbaum kept waiting for some statement of disavowal, an outright denunciation of Hitler, a clear break with his Nazi past. It never came. Instead, Rudolph hemmed and hawed, finding things here and there that he liked about Hitler, and other things less attractive. The Nazis, to him, were a mixed bag.

The lawyers soon steered Rudolph toward their main reason for being here: his work as a rocket production chief at Dora's mammoth underground factory site at Mittelwerk and the earlier slave-labor factory at Peenemünde, which was bombed out of existence by the Allies in 1943.

As they began talking about the missile production, Rudolph finally got to show off his souvenirs. He had been in America for nearly four decades, but the Nazi rocket factories still clearly held a nostalgic air for him. "You see here?" he said, pointing out a photo in a book. "Here is the whole missile — with no warhead, of course." The early design work at Peenemünde, especially, was good work, he said. Most of the Germans there were good people. After the war, he had even come to the defense of a top SS man at the camp and other Nazis there who were convicted at Nuremberg for Dora atrocities, writing letters vouching for their good character. He laughed when the lawyers showed him some of the old Nazi organizational charts at the factories with his name right near the top. He hadn't seen them in quite a while, but they did bring back memories.

The lawyers weren't there for nostalgia. They wanted to know about the victims. Sher's voice grew stern. Rudolph surely must have known, he asked, that the thousands of laborers he was using to build his missiles were prisoners, slaves of the Nazis?

"That's right," Rudolph said flatly, in that same small voice.

Jews, Frenchmen, Poles — all forced into slavery to build his V-2 missiles, yes?

"Poles and Russians," Rudolph corrected him.

And the conditions were very, very bad, Sher said. People were dying from disease, from starvation, from overwork. "You must have known that," he said.

"Ja," Rudolph said. "I know that people were dying."

Did he review the ghastly SS reports that gave the running tallies on just how many prisoners at the factory lost their lives in the production of his missiles?

Rudolph shrugged. "Ja," he said.

And what happened when he needed more bodies to replace the workers who had died? Would he simply ask the SS for more men?

"Ja, I did," he said.

The lawyers needed to understand how things worked, Rudolph said. He was one of the good ones at the factory, he insisted. He tried to improve the workers' conditions, Rudolph asserted, to the incredulous stares of the lawyers. He tried to shorten their work shifts — to keep them strong for their jobs. "If you put too much pressure on them, the work would be no good," he said. If a prisoner had blisters on his feet, Rudolph said earnestly, he would get him help. The lawyers knew that prisoners were eating gruel out of garbage cans. Yet here was Rudolph, claiming that under his watch, prisoners got as much to eat as the German civilians working at the factory — as much as Rudolph himself ate, in fact.

"But these people were dropping dead of malnutrition," Sher reminded him.

"Oh, not that time, anymore," Rudolph insisted.

"The summer of '44, they were not dropping dead?"

"No," Rudolph said, catching himself. "Well, they still were dropping dead probably from disease, but not malnutrition."

"They were eating well?"

"Ja."

Now Sher wanted to know about all the gruesome hangings he had read about, all the men executed because they were accused of sabotaging the V-2 missile equipment or plotting revolts against their heavily armed SS jailers.

The lawyer brought up one scene he had read about with particular interest in a batch of Nazi documents. "Isn't it true, Mr. Rudolph, that at some point, you yourself actually witnessed the hanging of between six and twelve *Häftlinge*? You were there and you saw it?"

"Ja," Rudolph answered, nodding his head.

The other prisoners were made to watch the spectacle, Sher said. "The purpose was to scare these people to think that if they were involved in sabotage, they too would be hung?" Sher asked. "Wasn't that the purpose of it — to scare them?"

"Ja," Rudolph said, nodding his head again.

And hadn't Rudolph himself ordered a stop to the missile work one day while another group of prisoners were summoned to the assembly tunnel to watch the hangings?

"Ja, I think so," he said.

It was an important moment. Sher now had the scientist on record, acknowledging his role in executions at the factory. But he still couldn't get over Rudolph's claims that the prisoners were well fed and cared for during his time there. He wanted to come back to that. He showed Rudolph a photo of some of the survivors of Dora discovered by Allied troops in May 1945, after the Nazis fled. Their bodies were grotesquely emaciated, their faces gaunt and sickly.

"Do those people look like they're working under good conditions?" he asked.

"No, certainly not," Rudolph said. "Certainly not."

He spoke with that same small, flat voice, that same vacant stare, whether he was telling the lawyers about his daughter's birth in Germany two years before the war started, or the deaths of thousands of slave laborers building his missiles. The absence of any human pathos, of any emotion altogether, was jarring. Sher wanted to try to shake him out of his malaise. "How did you feel when you saw those people working like that, Mr. Rudolph?" Sher asked. "I'd like to know. I'd like to know how you *felt*."

"Awful," the scientist said finally, claiming a flicker of emotion for the first time. "Oh, Mr. Sher, I knew I was in a trap. When I went there, I didn't know what was underground."

"Doesn't it haunt you even today?" the lawyer asked. "Don't you have terrible memories of that?"

"Yes," Rudolph said without elaboration.

And isn't it a bit ironic, Sher continued, to realize that his honored career in the American space program got its start at a place as barbaric as the V-2 factory? This was why U.S. military officials had wanted him and dozens of other space engineers from the V-2 project to come to America: because of what they had accomplished in building Hitler's missiles on the backs of those slave laborers.

"It is sort of ironic, isn't it?" Sher asked.

Rudolph just shrugged his shoulders. He said nothing.

They talked for almost five hours that day, and they still weren't done. Rudolph agreed to meet with the lawyers a second time a few months later, still without a lawyer. Again, he pulled out some photos of his prized missiles, pictures that he forgot to show them at their first meeting. This time, Rosenbaum took the lead in questioning him. There was one thing in particular he was anxious to ask Rudolph — a scene that had gnawed at him ever since he first read about Arthur Rudolph in that bookstore at Harvard nearly three years earlier.

Rosenbaum had read something interesting about a New Year's Eve party at Dora in 1944, he told Rudolph. The scientist apparently had to leave the party early to handle a problem with some missile parts back at the factory?

Ja," Rudolph said. "Correct."

Rudolph laughed. Nearly forty years later, he still remembered the party well, and he was still miffed at being forced to leave it early. Some friends had been celebrating at the home of a fellow Nazi when Rudolph got a call about a problem at the plant, he recalled. Four missiles were supposed to be shipped out soon for bombings, but the straps used to secure them for the move weren't working properly. An SS commander, a Nazi by the name of Sawatzki, summoned him back to the factory immediately to fix it. Rudolph hated Sawatzki. "Since it didn't work, Sawatzki called me and said, 'Rudolph, come here,'" he said. He sounded annoyed even as he retold the story. "I couldn't do a darn thing" to fix the straps, he said. But even so, "I had to be there, because Sawatzki obviously didn't like that I was, you see, at a party." There was no mention of the slave laborers. Even now, as he recounted the scene, Rudolph seemed remarkably indifferent to their plight. He was just peeved to have to leave his party. Now that Rosenbaum had met Rudolph, his first assessment of the Nazi scientist's callousness at the bookstore three years earlier appeared spot-on.

Rudolph had now been going at it with the lawyers for nearly seven hours over two sittings. With each question about Dora, with each photo of the brutalized prisoners, his German accent seemed, oddly, to become thicker. His English, so impeccable at the start of the questioning, became more muddled the more he spoke about those days at Mittelwerk. The stenographer was beginning to have trouble understanding him. "The SS was supposed to get the verd," Rudolph said at one point. The stenographer stopped him. "The verd?" "The verd," he repeated. Rosenbaum broke in: "*W-O-R-D.*"

All his years in America, Rudolph told the lawyers, he had never really worried about being held to account for what happened at Dora. Even as his friends and fellow Nazis at the factory were being prosecuted for war crimes at Nuremberg, none of it fell on him. No one in the United States had ever really asked him about the slave laborers at Dora before, he said. But now, for the first time, he was worried that Dora might have finally caught up with him. He had answered all their questions, but he seemed to realize that he hadn't convinced Sher and Rosenbaum. He made one last push. As the lawyers tried to wrap up their questioning, Rudolph broke in with a final thought — a last, feeble attempt to show that he was not the brutal Nazi they obviously thought him to be.

He began to tell them a story. There was one time at Dora, he said, when the prisoners serving lunch spilt some food on the floor, and Rudolph slipped on the mess, hitting his head. The prisoners apologized profusely. They were worried about getting into trouble. Another Nazi might have disciplined the prisoners. Maybe even beaten them. "I didn't," Rudolph said, as if to demonstrate his righteous character. Then there was another story he wanted to tell: the time he suspected that a young Russian prisoner — the *Häftling* who cleaned his shoes — had stolen a piece of meat from his office. Again, another Nazi might have punished the prisoner, or worse. But not Rudolph. He wasn't that type of man. "So I did nothing," he said.

He did nothing: that was his ultimate defense. He was one of the decent Nazis, one of the good ones.

Rosenbaum was unimpressed. "Do you have anything further you want to say?" he asked Rudolph finally.

"No, no," Rudolph mumbled in that same small, soulless voice.

The lawyers went back to Washington, and Rudolph finally decided to hire a lawyer, an immigration specialist in San Jose. By then it was too late. The evidence of his role in the barbaric abuse of prisoners at Dora — both from his own admissions at the interviews and from the documents that Rosenbaum had unearthed — was overwhelming. Rudolph recognized that, and his lawyer offered Rosenbaum and the Justice Department a deal: Rudolph would agree to leave the United States for good and renounce his American citizenship. The Justice Department would not prosecute him. He would go back to Germany voluntarily, and it would let him keep his U.S. pension and benefits. That was crucial to Rudolph in the deal: he needed to hold on to his pension to support his family. He couldn't risk losing that.

But Rudolph had another demand, too. Keenly aware of his stature as a leading American space scientist, Rudolph didn't want there to be any announcement of the deal when he slipped out of the country. He would agree to a deal only if it were kept secret, Rudolph's lawyer said. Rosenbaum balked at that. "We don't make secret deals with Nazis," he told the lawyer.

The deal was struck, but getting Rudolph back to Germany would require maneuvering around normal diplomatic protocols. The West Germans had made it clear that they didn't want to take back any of America's Nazi war criminals, and so, without Bonn's consent or even its knowledge, the Justice Department secretly arranged months later for Rudolph to return to Germany on his own. Neal Sher met him and his wife at the airport in San Francisco to make sure he got on the plane. Their grown daughter, Marianne, waiting with them at the gate for a tearful goodbye, shot Sher a look of disdain. She still couldn't believe the Justice Department was doing this to her father. He was just doing his job, she said.

Once he arrived in Germany, Rudolph simply walked into a consulate's office and renounced his U.S. citizenship to the surprised American officials, just as Sher and Rosenbaum had arranged it. He was a stateless man now, an American in exile, and he was Germany's problem, whether they wanted him or not.

The Germans were furious about the maneuver, but they grudgingly let Rudolph stay in the country and decided not to bring any war crimes charges against him. The statute of limitations had passed for most of the crimes anyway. He and his wife, Martha, moved into a one-bedroom condominium in Hamburg with a nice view of the city. Still, the Nazi scientist regretted giving up his American citizenship. The decision was "dumb, dumb, dumb," and talking to the Justice Department people without a lawyer was an especially bad move, he said. When old friends from America would come see him in Germany, he would show them the stacks of legal files laid out on his dining room table that he had collected to try to win back his citizenship. He did not deserve to be exiled, he insisted. "It was just bad luck that put me there in that factory," he told one visitor.

Five years after he left, he tried to come back to America for a celebration honoring the twentieth anniversary of the moon landing, but the United States turned him down. He was a bitter man. "They only wanted me for what I could do," he said, "and when it was finished they did not care what happened to me."

A year later, Rosenbaum got a tip at the Justice Department: Rudolph was planning to sneak back into the United States via Canada. The Nazi scientist had arranged to fly into Toronto, then meet up in Niagara Falls with some of his American defenders — he had a number of them, especially among his fellow space scientists — and then cross into the United States to reunite with his daughter. Rosenbaum wasn't about to let that happen. He had forced Rudolph out of the country for his Nazi past, and he was determined not to let him sneak back in. The Justice Department let the Canadians know that the notorious ex-Nazi was coming their way, and they were there at the airport to meet him, blocking his entry and ultimately sending him back to Hamburg unceremoniously after hearing the war crimes charges against him.

Rudolph never made it back into the United States. In 1996, twelve years after he was forced out of the country, he died at the age of eighty-nine as a free man in Germany — in the place he had first made his name as one of Hitler's missile men.

11

"An Innocent Man"

June 1983

"Well," the *New York Times* publisher wanted to know, "was he a Nazi or not?"

Chomping on a cigar at his desk, Punch Sulzberger was upset even to have to ask the question. He was sitting across from Floyd Abrams, his go-to lawyer on big First Amendment cases, and they were talking about Tom Soobzokov. The publisher gazed out his fourteenth-floor window at the newspaper's corporate offices and mulled over the distasteful scenario that was now laid out before him. Soobzokov was suing a book publisher owned by the New York Times Company over what he charged were libelous accusations making him out to be a Nazi. Abrams, grudgingly, was recommending that the company pay Soobzokov $450,000 to settle the case. Neither Abrams nor Sulzberger was happy about the thought. Twelve years earlier, the two men — newspaper titan and star lawyer — had joined together in the *Times*'s landmark First Amendment victory in publishing the Pentagon Papers. Now, Sulzberger and his lawyer found themselves in a much less enviable situation: debating whether to pay off an accused Nazi war criminal to make him go away.

Soobzokov, on his heels for so long, was now on the offensive. Three years earlier, the Justice Department had dropped its deportation case against him after the CIA's last-minute discovery of the records showing he had actually admitted his Waffen SS membership when he came to America. He had won on a technicality. Another man might have taken the win and thankfully dropped out of sight with his American citizenship still intact. Not Soobzokov. He had been a fighter all his life, and he wanted retribution. To pay for all the lawsuits that he was planning to bring to clear his name, he tried to borrow money from his old friends in the royal family in Jordan, who had been so welcoming to him and his refugee clan after the war. Don't bother with lawsuits, a member of King Hussein's entourage told him; leave all the messiness in America behind and come back to live in Jordan. But he was staying. "How can I go back?" he asked his family. "I need to protect my name."

Freed of his legal troubles, Soobzokov mounted a furious public relations and legal campaign to confront his accusers. He demanded that prosecutors investigate four of his original accusers in New Jersey because of what he charged were *their* Nazi ties in the war. He gave his Long Island lawyer the go-ahead to negotiate the rights to "the story of my life" for a book or movie deal. He gave triumphant interviews to some of the same local newspapers that had been describing him for years as an "accused Nazi." And he pressed his libel suit against what he charged was a cabal of critics who aimed to destroy him through the publication of *Wanted!*, the 1977 bestseller published by Quadrangle Books, a division of the New York Times Company. The book's author, Howard Blum; the pit bull investigators Tony DeVito and Reuben Fier; Soobzokov's archrival, Dr. Jawad Idriss — all had conspired "to carry out their false and evil designs" as a personal vendetta against him, Soobzokov thundered.

Two decades before, trying to hold on to his job as a Cold War spy, Soobzokov had admitted to the CIA his role in rounding up Jews and Communists, executing townspeople, and spying on his fellow Russians for the Nazis. Those secret CIA files were still secret, of course. Soobzokov was now declaring publicly, with typical hubris, that he was no Nazi, he had never taken part in any executions, and he had never even been in the villages where the Nazi atrocities occurred. He abhorred the Nazis, he said, and he had worn the Nazi uniform only as a disguise to help his countrymen flee to safety. "I am totally committed to the effort to bring to justice all Nazis and all enemies of our great country, the United States of America," he wrote. He was, he said, "an innocent man."

The New York Times Company was determined to fight the libel suit. Abrams and the company's other lawyers on the case had read through

Blum's notes for *Wanted!* from his interviews with the New Jersey witnesses who placed Soobzokov at the scene of myriad Nazi atrocities in Russia. The notes were solid, the lawyers concluded; they lined up almost line for line with what he wrote in the book. DeVito and Fier were resolute, too: they believed Soobzokov was a brutal Nazi collaborator. The Russians, meanwhile, turned over to the company's lawyers the witness statements taken during the war, in 1943, from Russians who identified Soobzokov by name as a member of a deadly German militia that rounded up locals from their homes as Nazi enemies. One Russian refugee reported that Soobzokov was one of four Nazi collaborators who came to his home around midnight in October 1942 and abducted his son as a supposed "partisan." Two days later, the father found the young man shot to death in the nearby woods.

But while the Russians were opening their files to the libel lawyers in defending the case, American officials were shutting them down. The lawyers put in requests to U.S. intelligence agencies seeking access to reams of secret records on Soobzokov, only to be told that none existed. They approached the Justice Department as well, hoping that the department's files on Soobzokov might corroborate what was printed in *Wanted!* Prosecutors told them they couldn't help. Soobzokov, they said, was too hot to touch. Justice Department prosecutors had spent six years investigating Soobzokov, but now that the deportation case against him had collapsed so spectacularly, they wanted nothing to do with him. The libel lawyers were on their own.

Witnesses began shutting down in New Jersey, too. Immigrants who a few years earlier had given vivid accounts of Soobzokov's wartime role with the Nazis suddenly went silent, or changed their stories altogether, as the libel suit ground on. One witness insisted that Dr. Idriss, Soobzokov's rival in the immigrant enclave, had "brainwashed" him into making his original accusations. Another refugee, Hadgmet Neguch, an electrical worker who came to New Jersey in 1969, had originally recounted that he saw Soobzokov, in full Nazi uniform, take part in the execution of three boys in his town. When his account was published in *Wanted!,* however, his fellow immigrants in New Jersey called him "a liar," he said, and "for this, I got [into] trouble." Soobzokov sued him for libel. When it came time to testify, Neguch changed his story. He never saw Soobzokov in any execution squad, he said. "I don't know nothing for him killing," Neguch said in his fractured English. Yes, he had seen Soobzokov wearing a Nazi uniform, he acknowledged, but he didn't know where he had gotten it. "This uniform—he steal, he buy, it was given to him, this I never asked. Not my business."

So bitter was the libel suit that Tony DeVito ended up in jail because of it. The former INS investigator traveled to the Soviet Union to gather evidence to defend himself, but when Soobzokov's lawyer demanded to know who had paid for the trip, DeVito refused to say. That was confidential, he said, and besides, it was irrelevant. A judge disagreed and held him in contempt of court. DeVito spent ten days in jail, and the episode left him even more embittered over America's frustrating hunt for Nazis. "The hunter goes to jail," he said, "and the Nazis are running around."

With unanswered questions swirling, Abrams saw the New York Times Company's chances of winning the lawsuit as essentially a tossup. *Wanted!* was a solid piece of reporting, he believed, but witnesses were recanting, and Soobzokov himself would no doubt make a compelling witness. He had been telling his sanitized story for many years now. Abrams could only imagine the impact it might have on a jury to hear Soobzokov, forceful and emotional as always, telling of the pain of coming to America as a war refugee only to be unfairly branded a Nazi war criminal. A jury might well buy it.

There was another powerful factor to consider: the insurance company for the Times Company was willing to cover the entire cost of a settlement. With Soobzokov's lawyer hinting that he wanted a settlement in the mid six figures, the insurance company did not want to risk a jury ruling that could total millions. For this reason especially, a reluctant Abrams believed a settlement was the prudent course, and so he scheduled a meeting with Sulzberger.

The publisher didn't normally get involved in legal matters like this, and Abrams had never met with him before to discuss such a case. He knew there would be resistance. The *Times,* as a matter of proud policy, did not settle libel cases; it defended its journalism. On principle, the newspaper itself did not even carry libel insurance. But its book-publishing unit did. This case, if Sulzberger did decide to settle it, would come with an asterisk, since it involved not the newspaper itself but the company's book publisher. But asterisk or not, the idea of the company settling with Soobzokov was still unnerving.

Sitting in Sulzberger's office, Abrams laid out the case and the obstacles — the competing bits of evidence, the recanting witnesses, the stonewalling by the U.S. government — and why he thought it made sense to settle it.

Abrams finished up his summation. Sulzberger, now on his second cigar of the meeting, had one overarching question. "Well," he said, "was he a Nazi or not?" As a businessman, he understood the legal and financial pressures to settle the case, especially with the insurance company willing to cover all the costs. But he was a World War II veteran and a Jew, too, and he was loath to settle if the core accusations against Soobzokov were actually true. "I'm not going to pay money to a Nazi," he said flatly.

Abrams mulled over the publisher's question. Was Soobzokov a Nazi? "I can't know for sure," Abrams said finally. "I believe Blum. He's done fine work, responsible work. I believe his reporting." But once they got into court, Abrams said, anything could happen. Calling someone a Nazi was about as serious a charge as you could make against a man. No matter how strong the evidence, there was no predicting how it might turn out.

Sulzberger was clearly uncomfortable. He wanted some time to think about it.

He called Abrams the next day, an air of resignation in his voice. "Let's go ahead," he said.

They had a deal, with the terms to be sealed from the public. A public announcement would not be good for either Soobzokov or the *New York Times*. There were some last-minute complaints from Soobzokov over how much of the settlement his lawyer would get, but he ultimately agreed to the terms. On June 14, 1983, Soobzokov got a check in his name for $225,000 from a Wall Street bank — his half of the $450,000 settlement, with the other half going to his Long Island lawyer.

Again, the ex–Waffen SS officer had adroitly used the American justice system to take on a powerful institution — first the U.S. Justice Department, now the New York Times Company — and again, Tom Soobzokov had won. Vindication was his.

• • •

Two years later, on a hot summer's night in Paterson, Tom Soobzokov's luck finally began to run out. The first sign that something was amiss came from Soobzokov's German shepherd, Tambo. The dog wasn't barking. Tambo always seemed to be yapping, but on this night, he was just pacing the alleyway in silence. It was almost 3:00 a.m. Back and forth, back and forth, back and forth, the dog walked. Next door, Soobzokov's neighbor, Lidia, a Cuban immigrant in her early fifties, gazed from her second-floor bedroom window down at the dog in the alley that divided Soobzokov's row house and her own home on Fourteenth Street. She couldn't sleep. With no air conditioning in her home, she had the window opened wide. Lidia looked down, mesmerized, as Tambo just kept pacing anxiously. The silence was jarring. She had never seen him quite like this.

It had already been an odd time on Fourteenth Street. The day before, Lidia had noticed a taxi with three passengers driving past her house. At least eight or nine times through the afternoon and evening, the taxi passed by with the three men inside. She lost count as she peered nervously out the front window. The men just looked out; they never stopped. The hardscrabble neighborhood didn't usually get many taxis.

Then came two other men — a tall one and a short one — who knocked on her door and asked her if she was thinking of selling her house. That didn't happen much in her neighborhood either. One of them seemed to be peering at the Soobzokovs' house next door as they spoke. Then there was the episode the night before, when an agitated Soobzokov told Lidia that someone had almost run him over in a station wagon. He had gone to the police to report it.

And now there was Tambo, just pacing in silence in that dark alleyway.

It all seemed very strange, Lidia thought. Maybe she was imagining things. She had grown edgy ever since the Jewish militants had held their protests outside the house years earlier to denounce Soobzokov as a Nazi. During the raucous demonstrations, she used to peer out nervously from behind the curtains. "Qué están diciendo? Que están diciendo?" she would ask her daughter. *What are they saying? What are they saying?* She had never seen demonstrations like this back in Cuba. She was worried for Papa Soobzokov; he was a good man, a helpful neighbor, she thought, and he couldn't have done the terrible things in the war that they said he did.

The Jewish protesters had finally moved on a few years earlier. With the story largely faded from the newspapers after Soobzokov's courthouse victory, the demonstrators didn't come around anymore. Even so, Lidia hadn't really felt at ease in the neighborhood since.

With Tambo still pacing, Lidia finally fell into a restless sleep. An hour or so later, the doorbell awoke her. Someone kept ringing, over and over. Bolting upright in bed, she checked the clock. It was just after 4:00 a.m. She scurried downstairs and peered outside to find a young man at the door motioning wildly toward the street. "Your car's on fire!" he yelled. She opened the door. Sure enough, there was a car ablaze, but it wasn't hers. It was Tom Soobzokov's Buick, parked on the street between their two houses.

She hurried out the door to alert Soobzokov, her own dog following close behind. She ran up the steps of her neighbor's porch — the same porch where she and Papa Soobzokov spent many an evening drinking and laughing with their families; the same porch where he'd sat and watched those angry protesters chanting his name. She pounded on the front door. No one answered. She began rapping on the window. Still no one came. The air conditioner was humming loudly, and she figured Soobzokov and his wife, Katie, were asleep upstairs and couldn't hear her. Louder and louder she banged. The fire was still blazing. A minute passed, then two, then three. She almost gave up. Finally, the commotion woke up the Soobzokovs. Papa Soobzokov hustled downstairs for the door. Don't answer it! Katie yelled as she ran after him. It's the dead of night! Reassured at seeing his friend Lidia, Soobzokov opened the front door. "Tu carro, tu carro!" she yelled, pointing to the street. *Your car, your car!*

Soobzokov's eyes grew big as he glimpsed the flames. He reached for the screen door and began to open it. He turned back toward Katie, who had come downstairs behind him.

An instant later, a thunderous explosion echoed through the night. Blocks away, neighbors were wakened by the blast, their windows shattered. Lidia was blown backward off the porch. Katie was thrust back inside the house and slammed against a wall. Soobzokov himself was thrown in the air amid a hail of wood, glass, blood, and debris, landing motionless in the rubble. He lay silent, barely conscious. Katie screamed for him. She could see that his right leg had been blown off below the knee.

Neighbors from all around streamed out into the dark to see what had happened. Soon, ambulances, fire trucks, and police cars with sirens blaring were everywhere, tending to the victims near the sinkhole that was once Soobzokov's porch. Reporters were not far behind. Tambo was dead. Lidia and Soobzokov's wife were gashed by the flying debris. Inside the house, Soobzokov's grown daughter and his four-year-old grandchild were also hurt. But it was Soobzokov himself who took the brunt of the blast, with the lower half of his body mangled. An ambulance rushed him to a nearby hospital, still alive, for the start of an eight-hour marathon surgery. Somehow, he had survived the bombing.

Local police and FBI agents swarmed the crime scene. There they found yellow wiring, screws, piping, and other remnants of a nine-inch-long pipe bomb. It had been booby-trapped to the screen door with a clothespin. Near the car they found a gas can, used to douse the Buick and fuel the fire that would lure Soobzokov out of the house. Whoever planned this had mapped out every move.

Suspicion focused immediately on the Jewish militant groups that had put Soobzokov in their crosshairs years before. The militants did nothing to deflect the attention. In fact, they reveled in the bombing. "We claim no responsibility, but we applaud the act," Mordechai Levy, a leader of the Jewish Defense Organization — a splinter group of the JDL — said, just hours afterward. "Violence is not a good thing, but sometimes it's a necessary thing." Just a week earlier, Levy had spoken to a Jewish group in Paterson to denounce Soobzokov's Nazi ties, and he was planning to start up the protests at his house again after a long absence.

Now that same house was the scene of a crime that many people in Paterson considered unthinkable.

Neighbors milling around the crime scene talked about what a nice man Soobzokov was. Shocked city leaders condemned the violence. Some locals said they couldn't quite fathom why accusations from the distant past might have led someone to commit such an act of violence. "Nazi Germany died 40 years ago," one college student in the neighborhood said. "If he was involved," another neighbor said of Soobzokov, "he was probably doing what he was ordered, as a regular army officer. He was doing what his country asked of him."

Howard Blum, the author of *Wanted!*, was awakened early that morning by a phone call from a New Jersey reporter. What did he think about the bombing? the reporter wanted to know. What bombing? he asked. Blum knew nothing about it, and he was shaken by the news. This wasn't how it was supposed to end. When he wrote his book eight years earlier, he had wanted to see justice done, but not vigilante justice. Nazis were supposed to be prosecuted and deported, not bombed in their homes.

So, the reporter asked Blum, did he feel responsible for what had happened? No, Blum answered. But part of him really did. Had he set all this in motion? he wondered. Was he the reason Tom Soobzokov was lying in a hospital ER with his leg blown off?

Hours after the bombing, investigators were already at the hospital to interview Lidia as she recovered from the gashes left by the flying shards of glass and debris. They wanted to know about everything, from the bombing itself to the roaming taxi and the strange men looking to buy her house. It was the start of what would prove a long slog for the investigators.

They weren't the only ones anxious to talk to Lidia. As she lay in her hospital bed, a call came through to her room. "You saved him this time," the caller said, "but next time he won't be so lucky."

It took a week before Soobzokov, badly injured and heavily drugged, was well enough for investigators to talk to him at the hospital. Even then, doctors would let him answer only yes-or-no questions because he was so weak. Did he know who had done this to him? Soobzokov nodded yes. Did he think it was the JDL? Again, he nodded yes. He knew more, he indicated to investigators with a silent nod of the head, but that would have to wait for another day.

His family was at his bedside at the hospital for weeks. Through all the investigations, all the accusations, all the protests, his wife and children had always stood by him, no matter what, and they surely weren't going to abandon him now. "I guess I won't be able to do the tango anymore," he told Katie with a wan smile, motioning to his amputated leg. He grew serious as he turned to his son, Aslan, who had rushed back from the Middle East to be with his father as soon as he learned of the bombing. "I can't believe they did this to me," Soobzokov said finally.

Not long after, Soobzokov came down with pneumonia. Already weak, he fell in and out of consciousness and soon lapsed into a coma. Twenty-two days after the bombing, on September 6, 1985, at 9:21 a.m., Tom Soobzokov died. The cause of death was listed as "multiple traumatic injuries." He was sixty-one.

Soobzokov had always been a survivor. For more than four decades, he had found protection from the many threats that came his way. The Nazis had protected him. The CIA and the FBI had protected him. His political friends in New Jersey had protected him. Even the American justice system had protected him. But no one could protect him from the vengeance of a vigilante with a pipe bomb.

Less than five hours before Soobzokov died, sixty miles north on Long Island, a drummer in a rock band who was returning from an early-morning gig stopped at a 7-Eleven around 4:30 a.m. and noticed flames in front of a nearby house. He rushed over and banged on the door to alert the residents. Inside, a Latvian immigrant named Elmars Sprogis, a seventy-year-old retired construction worker who had also been accused of collaborating with the Nazis, heard the banging and went to see what was happening. When he opened the door, a huge explosion rocked the neighborhood. This time, it was the Good Samaritan outside the door who took the force of the blow, losing his right leg in the blast. Sprogis himself was not hurt.

"Listen carefully," an anonymous caller told the local newspaper minutes later. "Jewish Defense League. Nazi War Criminal. Bomb. Never again." Once more, Jewish militants publicly denied responsibility, but once more, they praised the bombing as "a righteous act . . . It was a brave and noble act."

The parallels in the two bombings were undeniable. Sprogis, like Soobzokov, had faced deportation after the Justice Department accused him of complicity with the Nazis in Eastern Europe. Like Soobzokov, Sprogis admitted to some involvement with the Nazis; he acknowledged that as a deputy police chief in Latvia, he had arrested Jews, confiscated their property, and turned them over to the Nazis, who he knew would likely kill them. Like Soobzokov, he won his case anyway; an appeals court found that "Sprogis seems only to have passively accommodated the Nazis," rather than actively persecuted anyone. In the court's view, that wasn't enough to deport him.

Just as in Soobzokov's case, the dismissal of the court case against Sprogis enraged Jewish groups. Just like Soobzokov, someone went after Sprogis with a bomb tripwired at his front door, with a fire lit in the street as a diversion sometime after 4:00 a.m. And as they did with Soobzokov, Jewish militants cheered the ugly vigilante justice, declaring that violence had begot violence.

If there was any doubt the two bombings were connected, the FBI soon settled the question. Forensics testing established that the materials used in the Long Island bombing at Sprogis's home were practically identical to remants of the bomb left sixty miles away at Tom Soobzokov's home in New Jersey. This was no copycat crime. The FBI had a serial bomber on its hands. Someone was trying to kill accused Nazi war criminals.

12

Backlash

April 15, 1987

WASHINGTON, D.C.

Ignored for decades, Nazis in America had suddenly become a political flash point by the time Ronald Reagan was in the White House, with anger fomenting on all sides. The vigilantes leaving bombs on the doorsteps of ex-Nazis were only part of the firestorm. Many conservative Cold Warriors were furious, too, but for very different reasons. While the Jewish militants were angry that the American justice system hadn't gone far enough to track down ex-Nazis, the conservatives were upset that it had gone *too* far, playing right into the hands of the Communists, they charged. Inside the gates of the White House, the conservative critics found a fierce ally in President Reagan's own firebrand advisor, Pat Buchanan.

Buchanan, a former Nixon aide with a rapier tongue and a pugnacious personality, didn't mask his disdain for what he called the "revenge-obsessed" and "hairy-chested Nazi hunters" at the Justice Department. He believed that the entire Nazi-hunting team should be abolished, and from his prominent perch in Washington — as a top aide to Reagan at the White House, in his nationally syndicated newspaper columns, and in his frequent cable-TV appearances — he launched what amounted to a one-man PR assault through the 1980s. The Justice Department had better things to do than "running down seventy-year-old camp guards," Buchanan wrote, or "wallowing in the atrocities of a dead regime."

Like J. Edgar Hoover and Allen Dulles before him, Buchanan saw the Nazi issue as a reflection of the Cold War. The Soviets, Buchanan charged, were peddling manufactured evidence to American prosecutors to villify anti-Communists as supposed Nazis. "Totally innocent" men like Tom Soobzokov, he charged, were being wrongly accused, and even killed, because of the Justice Department's misguided pursuits, he declared. In actuality, little convincing evidence had ever emerged to show that the Soviets were doctoring evidence of Nazi ties against American suspects, but Buchanan and his supporters were unbowed. Even as many Jewish leaders accused him of anti-Semitism, Buchanan fired back. He couldn't understand, Buchanan wrote, "how a handful of American Jews can routinely slander as 'Nazi sympathizers' their fellow Americans simply because we do not wish to collaborate with a brutalitarian and anti-Semitic regime that is Hitler's surviving partner from World War II."

The political maelstrom swirling around America's Nazis came to a dramatic climax one spring morning in 1987 at the Justice Department in the elegantly appointed waiting room outside the attorney general's office. Inside, Reagan's oft-embattled attorney general, Ed Meese, was huddling with his top advisors to determine the fate of Karl Linnas, one of the worst Nazi collaborators ever to call America his home. Outside the attorney general's office, in the anteroom, Justice Department prosecutor Neal Sher was pacing — and seething. Sher was the aggressive young chief of the Nazi-hunting unit at the Justice Department, but despite the impressive-sounding title, he was not invited to the attorney general's meeting; the question of what to do with Linnas, a sixty-seven-year-old retired land surveyor on Long Island, was a political decision that was being made on high within the Reagan administration. Sher, camped outside the attorney general's office as he waited anxiously to find out what was happening inside, was an outsider looking in.

Just the night before, as he was about to head out of his office, Sher was stunned to find out from a colleague that top Reagan administration officials had come up with a surprise eleventh-hour plan to deport Linnas — not to Russia, where the courts and everyone else expected the onetime Nazi to be sent to face war crimes charges, but to Panama. The American courts had already stripped Linnas of his citizenship for running a Nazi concentration camp in Estonia, and he had been held in custody in New York for a year while U.S. officials figured out what to do with him. The Soviets had been all set to put Linnas on trial on charges that he ordered the murders of thousands of Jewish women and children at the Nazi camp. But now, Sher had learned, higher-ups in the Reagan administration had decided that Linnas would instead be getting on a 4:30 p.m. flight out of JFK bound for Panama in just a few hours, courtesy of the American government. Meese and his aides were meeting at this very moment inside his office, on the other side of those imposing wooden doors, to finalize the plans. And Sher had not been invited. Meese's aides could guess what Sher thought of the plan, anyway. The thought of sending Linnas to Panama turned Sher's stomach. For Nazis facing deportation, South America was seen as less a punishment than a destination. Sher could almost picture a smiling Linnas relaxing under the palm trees on the beaches of Panama, living out his days as some sort of bon vivant in exile.

Sher had fought like hell to get approval for Linnas to be deported to Russia. With the mass murders at the Nazi camp committed in what was now part of the Soviet Union, and with no other country except Russia willing to take Linnas, it only made sense, Sher believed, to send him back there. The State Department had already signed off on Linnas's deportation to the Soviet Union. Two U.S. courts had upheld the deportation plan. Five months earlier, in December of 1986, the Supreme Court had declined to stop it. All the boxes were checked. Everything was set. Karl Linnas was going to Russia.

But Linnas's fate had now become a Cold War quagmire for the White House, with Pat Buchanan fueling the conservative backlash. The idea of sending an American citizen back to the Soviet Union, a place that Reagan had dubbed "the evil empire" just a few years earlier, was "Orwellian and Kafkaesque," Buchanan said. "Soviet justice is an oxymoron," he said. It was an odd and polarizing situation: a senior aide in the White House publicly attacking his own Justice Department's legal position and lobbying to undermine it. A presidential aspirant, Buchanan was a skilled politician and noted wordsmith, and he knew how to make his case. On White House letterhead, he told Meese that Russia did not have the "moral authority" to try war criminals. As support, Buchanan pointed to some fifteen thousand postcards, letters, and calls that he said he had received from people sharing his concerns.

For all the heated political rhetoric, there was legitimate reason to question whether Linnas or anyone else could get a fair trial in Soviet Russia.

The Soviets had already put Linnas on trial once before, in absentia, a quarter century earlier, and the Soviet press reported at that time that he was sentenced to death even *before* the supposed trial took place. Even some people inside the Nazi-hunting unit, normally insulated from outside politics, were upset over the idea of sending Linnas to the Soviet Union. One Justice Department historian in Sher's office quit in protest over the plan. As a Nazi war criminal, Linnas deserved to be deported, the historian wrote to Sher in his letter of resignation, "yet I cannot help but feel that no person should be deported to a dictatorship which ... has no moral right to try anyone, least of all, for crimes against humanity."

Until now, Panama had never even been mentioned as a possible home for Linnas. Yet the Panamanians, in this last-minute deal of mysterious origins, were agreeing to take him off the Americans' hands on "humanitarian" grounds. It wasn't clear if the Panamanians even realized who Linnas was, or what the American courts concluded he had done in that Nazi concentration camp so long ago. Sher knew there was almost no chance Linnas would be put on trial in Panama. In the hours since he found out about the plan, in fact, Sher had already decided to quit the Justice Department in protest if the decision stood. Congress had created his office to bring Nazi war criminals to justice, but now, after Linnas's case had wound through the Justice Department and the courts for eight years, its very mission was being undermined by Pat Buchanan and Cold War politics. The Panama plan, as Sher saw it, didn't just provide a sanctuary for Linnas; it threatened the very existence of his office and its ability to bring future cases. If the decision stood, the government's Nazi hunters would become paper tigers.

It didn't help matters that President Reagan's own record on the Nazis was already suspect — and not just because of Pat Buchanan's vitriolic attacks on Sher's office. Holocaust survivors had been aghast five years earlier, in 1982, when the White House defended Reagan's presidential appointment of an industrialist who had employed a convicted Nazi war criminal from Germany's IG Farben as a chemical consultant. Then there was Bitburg, the infamous German cemetery that Reagan visited two years earlier. Plans for Reagan's trip became an international spectacle when it was revealed that the president was going to be visiting the cemetery where some four dozen Waffen SS officers were buried. It was Buchanan, not surprisingly, who had pushed hardest for Reagan to go ahead with the visit even in the face of Jewish pressure, and it was Buchanan who was blamed as the behind-the-scenes source of the single most damaging element of the whole Bitburg affair: Reagan's jaw-dropping, public insistence that the German SS officers and soldiers buried at the cemetery were "victims" of the Nazis "just as surely as the victims in the concentration camps."

And now, Reagan and his administration were ready to give one of America's worst Nazi collaborators a free pass to Panama, with Pat Buchanan paving the way. As he waited for the meeting to break up, Sher had no real idea what to do, but he knew that if he didn't do something, Linnas would be on his way to Panama in just a few hours. He needed help — from outside the Reagan administration. On an impulse, he picked up the phone in the anteroom, got an outside line, and dialed the first person who came to mind — Elizabeth Holtzman, the onetime congresswoman who had spearheaded the creation of the Nazi office. She was in a meeting, Holtzman's secretary at the district attorney's office in Brooklyn said. Was it important? "It couldn't be more important," Sher said. Holtzman got on the line. "The Justice Department is planning to send Linnas to Panama today," Sher told her. He was practically shouting. He wanted Meese's secretary, within earshot across the waiting room, to be able to hear him. He was going to make sure that word got back to the attorney general that the head of his own Nazi-hunting team was not going to stay quiet while the government sent Karl Linnas, a Nazi mass murderer, to Panama. He wanted Meese to know that he was pissed. "They've worked out an arrangement for the Panamanian government to take him," he told Holtzman.

Holtzman was almost as incredulous as Sher over the news. Nazis in America had remained a sacred cause for her even after leaving Congress, and she, too, wanted to see Linnas deported to the Soviet Union to stand trial. What time was he supposed to leave? she wanted to know. He had a 4:30 flight, Sher said. That didn't leave much time. Holtzman would see what she could do, she promised.

Sher left the attorney general's suite and went back to his own office to start drafting his letter of resignation. He wanted his protest on record. He hunted for a copy of a court ruling — an opinion issued a year earlier by an appeals court giving its legal blessing to Linnas's deportation to the Soviet Union. The twenty-one-page decision laid out what the judge called "overwhelming" evidence: how Linnas had served as the chief of the Nazi concentration camp in Tartu, Estonia; how he ordered Jewish women and children to be led to the edge of a death pit in their underwear, their hands tied, and then shot dead; how one witness remembered him personally leading a Jewish schoolgirl from a bus and then, after she was killed, placing the doll she was carrying in a ghastly pile of the victims' belongings; how he lied to the INS when he came to America and claimed to have been a university student during the war, not the commandant of a Nazi concentration camp. Linnas had never really challenged the accusations against him, even as he fought his deportation. One particularly powerful section of the court's ruling had always stuck with Sher, and he had practically memorized it. It was the judges' rejoinder to Linnas's pleas for the court's decency and compassion. "Noble words such as 'decency' and 'compassion' ring hollow when spoken by a man who ordered the extermination of innocent men, women and children kneeling at the edge of a mass grave," the ruling read. "Karl Linnas' appeal to humanity, a humanity which he has grossly, callously and monstrously offended, truly offends this court's sense of decency."

Court ruling in hand, Sher headed to the Panamanian Embassy in Washington and hand-delivered it to the ambassador's staffer. He wanted to be sure the Panamanians knew exactly what kind of man they were welcoming into their country. Holtzman and her aides, meanwhile, were working the phones. It was Passover, and she knew that many of the Jewish advocates who had been pushing so hard for Linnas's removal to Russia would be busy preparing for the holiday. She didn't think that this was by accident: the Reagan administration, she suspected, was looking to sneak Linnas out of the country just when the people who cared most weren't looking. She called Eli Rosenbaum. The young lawyer had left the Justice Department's Nazi unit and was now general counsel at the World Jewish Congress and had pushed to deport Linnas to Russia. Rosenbaum, in turn, tipped off reporters at major newspapers to what the Reagan administration was about to do. Meanwhile, Holtzman and Rosenbaum got on a plane from New York to Washington for a hastily scheduled meeting that same afternoon at the Panamanian Embassy. She intended to give the Panamanians an earful.

By the time she arrived at the embassy with Rosenbaum and another lawyer from a Holocaust survivors' group, a thicket of tipped-off reporters and photographers was already camped outside. The outlines of a diplomatic brouhaha were taking shape: Panama, a refuge for the deposed shah of Iran in 1980, was now about to accept a top Nazi collaborator onto its shores. The press wanted to be there for the fireworks, and the Panamanians seemed blindsided by the sudden interest in their affairs. It was the most attention the embassy had gotten since the United States agreed to return the Panama Canal ten years earlier, the bewildered ambassador admitted to his visitors.

With court files stuffed in his briefcase, Rosenbaum came ready with a presentation for the ambassador about Linnas's war crimes and the damage Panama was risking to its world standing if it took him in. But soon after the meeting started, it became clear that the big lobbying push was unnecessary. Rosenbaum didn't need to make his pitch, because Panama was already caving in. The embassy had been hearing from reporters all day with questions about Linnas. Meanwhile, a senior Reagan administration official — equally upset about the idea of sending Linnas to the beaches of Panama — had already called the ambassador with his own concerns. "We would like to make sure that you know precisely who this person is and what you're getting into," the official told the ambassador with a note of warning. The Panamanians got the message. Their government had already decided, the ambassador told a surprised Rosenbaum and Holtzman as they sat before him, that it would withdraw its hasty offer to take Linnas off the Americans' hands. The deal was off.

Almost simultaneously, the embassy put out a statement for the many reporters still asking unpleasant questions about Linnas. Panama joined with "important sectors of the Hebrew community and the rest of the world," the embassy said, in condemning "the crimes committed by fascism."

The first thing Rosenbaum did as he left the embassy was to look for a pay phone on the street. He needed to call Neal Sher, his old mentor and frequent cohort at the Justice Department, to make sure he'd heard the news. The Panama plan was dead. Karl Linnas wouldn't be spending his days sunning himself in the Caribbean after all.

Five days later, with his last appeals to the Supreme Court rebuffed, a handcuffed Linnas was shoved into a police car at JFK and driven up to the tarmac where a Czechoslovakian airliner awaited. He tried jumping out of the police car on the way. "What they're doing right now is just murder and kidnapping!" an agitated Linnas shouted to the crowd of reporters gathered at the airport to watch him leave. Then, as if in final salute to his thirty-six years as an ex-Nazi living a life of comfort in the United States, he yelled: "God bless America!"

By the time Karl Linnas was flown off to Russia in the spring of 1987, Sher and his band of once-obscure lawyers, investigators, and historians had established themselves as a force to be feared. They no longer had to explain to outsiders who they were or what the Office of Special Investigations did. People already knew.

Since its creation eight years earlier, the Nazi office had investigated many hundreds of leads and brought more than fifty cases against Americans suspected of links to the Third Reich, from anonymous camp guards at Auschwitz to major figures like rocket scientist Arthur Rudolph, Eichmann aide Otto von Bolschwing, and Croatian minister Andrija Artukovic. In cities up and down the Eastern Seaboard, in immigrant neighborhoods throughout the Midwest, and along the beaches of Southern California, it was big news whenever the Nazi hunters at the Justice Department came calling to accuse an unknown, elderly man in the area — always a decent individual, stunned neighbors would inevitably say; always a hard worker — of having secretly helped Hitler decades before. "Former Nazi Death Camp Guard Relieved from School Job," read a typical headline in Chicago in 1984 after the Justice Department came after a well-liked school janitor who had been an SS guard at a death camp in Poland.

The reach of the Office of Special Investigations extended beyond American borders. The Nazi unit was roiling international waters, too. In 1983, after former Gestapo chief Klaus "the Butcher of Lyon" Barbie was arrested in Bolivia and sent back to France to stand trial for war crimes, the United States took the extraordinary step of formally apologizing to France for its longtime complicity with Barbie. The apology grew out of a scathing Nazi office investigation that Allan Ryan conducted into the American military's protection of a man who was notorious for using an acetylene torch to torture his prisoners during the war. Over the course of more than three decades, Ryan revealed, American officials had coddled Barbie as an anti-Soviet operative, paid him for Russian intelligence, spirited him away to safety in South America, lied to the French about his whereabouts, obstructed the search for him, and covered up his crimes. America's protection of such a notorious war criminal was illegal and unjustifiable, Ryan concluded. As one newspaper put it after Ryan's 218-page report made headlines around the world, "the obsession to oppose communism at any cost led six U.S. Army officials to make a pact with the devil— Klaus Barbie."

America, it seemed, was finally starting to come to terms with its own past as a safe haven for the Nazis.

The Nazi investigators were making headlines in Austria, as well. But this time, there were no mea culpas, and the United States played the part not of guilty collaborator, but of brash accuser. In 1986, Eli Rosenbaum got a tip at the World Jewish Congress suggesting that Austria's Kurt Waldheim — a well-known presidential candidate at the time who had been the secretary-general of the United Nations for ten years — had covered up his wartime service with the Nazis. Rosenbaum learned that Waldheim had secretly been an intelligence officer with a German unit in the Balkans that took civilian hostages, shot prisoners, burned homes, and deported Jews.

These were damning accusations, especially in a country with as tortured a Nazi history as Austria. As he would often do, Rosenbaum passed on what he had learned to his friend Neal Sher, who soon began collecting wartime documents himself at the Justice Department. Convinced that Waldheim was a Nazi collaborator, Sher proposed to his bosses what amounted to diplomatic hari-kari. The United States, he wrote, should bar Waldheim from the country under a provision that denied entry to Nazi persecutors. When his first recommendation got him nowhere, Sher wrote another memo, then another. New evidence from Yugoslavian archives pointed to Waldheim's role in personally processing Nazi prisoners for deportation and execution. Sher kept up the pressure. Finally, Attorney General Meese decided to look at the Nazi roster himself. Waldheim's name was on it. What struck Meese as much as anything were Waldheim's many contortions over the years in covering up his Nazi service; the diplomat had always maintained that he had been a law student in Vienna for most of the war, but the Nazi roster clearly showed otherwise. As the evidence against him mounted, Waldheim tried to explain it all away, but his shifting stories were starting to "sound like the 'I just worked there and followed orders' explanation," a senior aide to Meese remarked.

In the spring of 1987, just a week after sending Karl Linnas to Russia, Meese signed off on an order barring Waldheim, the newly elected president of Austria, from coming into the United States. It was an astonishing moment: America was branding a foreign head of state as a Nazi. It was an audacious step unlike anything the United States had ever done before. Furious, Austria pulled back its ambassador to the United States in protest for a time. Later, Austria barred Sher himself from coming to Vienna to interview an Austrian witness in a Justice Department investigation. Meanwhile, Waldheim and the Austrians lobbied in vain to get his name taken off the "banned" list. The embarrassed Austrian president wasn't even allowed to come to New York City to attend anniversary celebrations at the United Nations — the organization he had proudly led for a decade. In 1989 Waldheim sent a handwritten note to President George H. W. Bush, pleading that his diplomatic privileges be restored. The White House turned him down flat.

The Nazi hunters at the Justice Department were now at the height of their power, shining a harsh light onto places that had remained dark for decades. But with the newfound prominence came a wave of counterattacks — not just from foreign allies like Austria, but from anti-Soviet hawks in Washington, rocket scientists in Alabama, Eastern European immigrants around the country, and even from some Jews. Their particular agendas differed, but the opponents shared one overriding theme in their blistering attacks on the Justice Department: this long after the war, the "zealots" in the Nazi-hunting office were going too far.

For Sher and his deputies, power made them a target. Besieged Justice Department lawyers didn't realize just how far their opponents were willing to go to ruin them. In the midst of several particularly sensitive investigations, Justice Department officials began to suspect a leak. Verbatim accounts of confidential internal documents prepared by the Nazi team's investigators were mysteriously showing up in the pages of newspapers and on the desks of defense lawyers. Officials figured that there must be a mole inside the Nazi office who was exposing its secrets. They were so alarmed that they brought in the FBI to investigate the leaks.

The truth proved to be more embarrassing. There was no mole. Instead, FBI investigators discovered that, almost every workday for two years beginning in 1985, a group of immigrants opposed to the Nazi team was secretly collecting all the office trash from a dumpster behind the building; poring over the thousands of pages of discarded leads, memos, and case reviews; and doling out copies to lawyers and relatives of the accused who were equally upset about what the Justice Department was doing. The rogue trash-collection operation was all perfectly legal. Belatedly, the Nazi team began burning its trash.

Baltic immigrant groups with inspiring names like Americans for Due Process and Latvian Truth Fund began sprouting up around the country in opposition to what they charged were biased and unjustified inquisitions targeting entire ethnic communities. An investigation into a camp guard from Ukraine or Lithuania was seen as a slur against his whole ethnic enclave. That Sher and a number of his top people were Jewish did not go unnoticed. In a letter to the Reagan administration demanding the Nazi office be shut down, one ethnic leader in New York railed against the "Jewish Zionist special interest groups," charging that officials in the Justice Department's Nazi office had "greater loyalty" to Israel than to America. Sher and his people were regarded as the enemy. Ethnic newspapers posted the names of "known employees" of the Justice Department team and warned their readers not to say anything if they came calling at their door asking questions about the war years. "Let us chase these interviewers from our homes," urged one Lithuanian-language newspaper in Cleveland.

Doors were shutting in Huntsville, Alabama, too. Arthur Rudolph's expulsion to West Germany in 1984 had angered his fellow rocket scientists at the NASA flight center there — and triggered fears among the German scientists that the Justice Department might be coming after them as well. A number of the scientists who had come to America with Rudolph through Project Paperclip retained a prominent Huntsville attorney to represent them in case the Justice Department came calling. They had seen the mistake that Rudolph had made in that hotel room in San Jose in answering hours' worth of questions from Sher and Rosenbaum — all without a lawyer. He had been too trusting. The Saturn V legend had admitted what he did about the horrific conditions at the slave factory at Dora only under duress from the Nazi prosecutors, his friends in Alabama insisted, and they were determined not to make the same mistake.

They had reason for concern. Fresh off their success in expelling Rudolph, the Justice Department lawyers had created a secret "Paperclip" team in Washington to investigate more than a dozen German rocket scientists and doctors in connection with evidence that they, too, had engaged in atrocities. If von Braun hadn't died a decade earlier, prosecutors would almost certainly have opened a war crimes file on him, they said amongst themselves. The Justice Department lawyers approached several of the key surviving Huntsville scientists to see if they might sit down voluntarily to discuss what they had done in the war years. No thanks, they were told. The Justice Department could contact their lawyer. The scientists weren't talking.

The prime suspect from the start — the target of what the Justice Department lawyers called a "promising investigation"— was Dr. Hubertus Strughold, the Air Force's renowned space medicine researcher. His Texas congressman had helped quash the INS's investigation after Strughold's name surfaced publicly in 1974, but with its congressional mandate, the Nazi unit at the Justice Department had begun looking anew at Strughold and his role in the Nazis' infamous 1942 "cold conference" at Nuremberg. The lawyers examined not only his role in subjecting prisoners to extreme cold and high pressure, but a new avenue as well: his possible involvement in experimenting on human guinea pigs at the camps with live explosives and chemical weapons. Investigators had information that Strughold and two other Paperclip scientists now in America "participated in chemical experiments forcibly conducted on human beings during the Second World War." Some lawyers on the Paperclip team believed they had enough evidence to finally confront Strughold directly. He was in his mideighties, in failing health, and they wanted to try to interview him before he died. There seemed little chance of actually deporting Strughold at his age, but the lawyers believed that, if nothing else, his legacy should not go unchallenged.

This time, however, Sher, usually so aggressive, was ambivalent about going after the doctor. While there was plenty of evidence showing that Strughold knew about the horrific human experiments conducted by the Nazis on camp prisoners, it would be more difficult to prove his active participation. Sher wanted to make sure they had the goods on him before they confronted an ailing, elderly doctor so esteemed that in 1985 the Texas Senate had declared a "Dr. Hubertus Strughold Day."

It all came to naught. Strughold died in Texas in 1986 at the age of eighty-eight, still an American citizen after four decades in the country, still remembered as a medical legend. As Rosenbaum often liked to say when chasing elderly Nazi suspects, "We're always in a race with the grim reaper."

The Justice Department lawyers could take some small solace, though. A medical library at Strughold's old air base in San Antonio had been named after him years before, and his image, alongside the likes of Hippocrates and Marie Curie, adorned a stained glass mural at Ohio State depicting medical heroes in history. After Strughold's death, prosecutors forwarded what they'd found to officials in Texas and Ohio and helped get Strughold's name stricken from the library and his image removed from the mural. Strughold, the so-called father of space medicine, may never have been deported as a war criminal during his life, but his legacy, like his image on the stained glass mural, was irreparably shattered after his death.

With the Paperclip scientists in Alabama finding themselves in the crosshairs of the Justice Department, they looked to the Reagan administration for help. Pat Buchanan, as always, offered a sympathetic ear. He agreed to meet with two leaders in the Alabama space community at the White House in the summer of 1985. A Paperclip rocket scientist and an aerospace writer were upset about rocket scientist Arthur Rudolph's expulsion the year before. Rudolph had been wrongly thrown out of the country, his enormous contributions to American science shunted aside, and the Paperclip scientists en masse were being unfairly targeted as well, Buchanan's visitors told him as they pleaded their case. They didn't have to plead very hard. He, too, believed the Justice Department had strayed too far from its mission in going after a much-admired scientist like Rudolph, he told his visitors. What Rudolph had done for American space exploration had earned him a right to stay in America. He would help them if he could, Buchanan promised.

Buchanan was a natural ally for the Alabama scientists, with his public attacks on the Nazi office filling the opinion pages of newspapers nationwide. The Nazi hunters and Soviet intelligence officials had reached "a devil's bargain" to go after wrongly accused men, he charged, and the Americans they accused were left "undefended" and presumed guilty. Testimony from witnesses who survived the Nazis was deeply suspect, with "a

Holocaust survivor syndrome" leading to "group fantasies of martyrdom and heroics," he said. Carbon monoxide from diesel engines at the concentration camps could not have actually killed prisoners in the way that historians said. And Hitler himself, for all his faults, was "an individual of great courage," Buchanan wrote.

To Buchanan's opponents, his attacks on the Justice Department smacked of Holocaust revisionism and anti-Semitism. "Why is Pat Buchanan so in love with Nazi war criminals?" Allan Ryan asked. The *New York Post,* one of the biggest outlets for Buchanan's opinion pieces, questioned its star columnist's "attitude toward Jews as a group," and said his writing "betrays an all-too-familiar hostility" toward Jews. But for Buchanan, the attacks only seemed to energize him.

At the height of the tensions, Sher, an occasional target of Buchanan's barbs, was attending an engagement party thrown by talk show host Larry King at a famous Washington eatery when he saw that Buchanan was also among the guests. Sher's boss, Mark Richard, sensed trouble brewing. "Stay away from Buchanan," he advised. His mother would have said the same thing, Sher decided. Then he thought about what his late father would have told him: *Go tell the sonofabitch off.* So he did.

Sher walked across the room and introduced himself to the man who had so often denounced the "hairy-chested Nazi hunters" at the Justice Department. "We've never met," he said, "but you've written about me." The things that Buchanan had been saying about the government's Nazi investigations were unfair, misguided, and damaging, Sher charged. "I don't understand you people," Buchanan retorted. "Why don't you want to debate these things?" Back and forth they went, discussing long-ago Nazis and current-day Americans. Sher tried to hold his temper. But when Buchanan began arguing that Treblinka was not in fact a death camp, but a "transit camp" used as a pass-through point for prisoners, Sher had heard enough. Some nine hundred thousand Jews had died at Treblinka, but to Pat Buchanan, Holocaust revisionist, it was only a deportation point, Sher thought to himself. "You're kidding me!" he yelled. Then he walked away. He knew he would never persuade Buchanan, but at least he'd had his say. His father would have approved.

· · ·

As divisive as many of the Justice Department's Nazi investigations had become, none would raise quite so many vexing moral questions as the case of Jacob Tannenbaum, a Brooklyn man who was both a Jewish survivor of the Holocaust and, in Sher's view, one of its perpetrators.

In many ways, the horror of Jacob Tannenbaum's life story read no differently than those of hundreds of thousands of other survivors. Born in Poland, Tannenbaum lost virtually his entire family to the Nazis. His wife, their six-month-old daughter, and five of his siblings were all killed. Tannenbaum himself was imprisoned in a string of concentration camps and wound up at the Görlitz camp in eastern Germany.

At Görlitz, however, Tannenbaum's path veered away from that of the typical survivor. He was made the chief *kapo,* or overseer, taking charge of other Jewish prisoners as they were forced to build military parts and machinery for the Nazis. He got the job, he said, because he was "tall and presentable," and he spoke a little German; the SS looked for men like him — and even some women — to help run the camps. As chief kapo, Tannenbaum had his own room, he got to wear a civilian jacket instead of the prisoner uniform, and he was allowed to go into town on his own for supplies.

The SS entrusted hundreds of functionaries like Tannenbaum with keeping order over the other camp prisoners. But Tannenbaum was not like other kapos, his fellow survivors said. He was brutal — more brutal, in fact, than even the SS officers who ran the camp at Görlitz, they said. He was not a man of mercy, but of rage. Tannenbaum was notorious for beating prisoners even when the SS officers weren't watching, and he seemed to thrive on the power the Nazis had given him. Stories about his collaboration with the Nazis were legion. Once, he reported two hungry prisoners to the SS after he caught them rifling through a pigsty in search of food. They were quickly executed.

Tannenbaum came to America in 1950 and settled in Brooklyn, starting a second family and working in the dairy industry inspecting eggs. He mentioned nothing to U.S. immigration officials about serving as a kapo in the war. But decades later, a Holocaust survivor in Brooklyn recognized him as the brutal henchman of Görlitz and reported him to the INS.

The case, like so many others, sat dormant for years. Prosecutors were reluctant to touch it. Walter Rockler, the former Nuremberg prosecutor who led the Justice Department's new Nazi-hunting unit at its inception in 1979, inherited the investigation and thought the idea of prosecuting a Jewish kapo was pure insanity; the kapos might not have been the most likable people, but they were prisoners and victims themselves, he believed, and they did what they had to do to stay alive. They were the last group that Rockler wanted his Justice Department lawyers to be targeting.

But when Sher became chief of the Nazi office four years later, he took a very different view of Tannenbaum. He was particularly swayed by the testimony of more than three dozen survivors who knew of Tannenbaum's particularly cruel brand of camp administration. Virtually every survivor contacted by the Justice Department about Tannenbaum wanted to see him prosecuted and deported. Their emotions were still raw four decades later. Some said they still had nightmares about him. "He's still alive?" one survivor asked. "Give me his address, and you won't have to worry about him." He was no better than the Nazis themselves, several said. What set Tannenbaum apart from the other kapos, Sher believed, was the testimony that he routinely beat Jewish prisoners even when the SS officers were *not* watching. He was not simply saving his own skin or following orders, and the whippings were not just for show to satisfy those in charge. He was a sadist, Sher believed.

Sher knew that the prosecution of a Jewish kapo would be controversial, so he decided to handle the case himself. The investigation was a secret even within the office, in fact. If there was fallout, Sher wanted it to land on him. He interviewed Tannenbaum personally. Sher was an intense interrogator. Once, he was so confrontational in questioning an immigrant in New York accused of helping to wipe out the Warsaw ghetto — "You must really think we're stupid," Sher told him angrily when the man denied involvement — that the judge threw out much of the testimony. Sher was not going to go easy on Tannenbaum. Over three days of interviews, the two sparred over what Tannenbaum was forced to do at the concentration camp, and what he *chose* to do. He had served as kapo only to save his own life, Tannenbaum insisted, and he had spared the lives of prisoners who were destined to be killed otherwise. Sher wasn't buying it, and he let Tannenbaum know it. The interrogation was so contentious that, at the start of the third day, Tannenbaum slumped down in his chair and had to be taken to the hospital, where he remained for nearly three weeks being treated for heart problems.

When word surfaced in May 1987 that the Justice Department was bringing a denaturalization case against Tannenbaum, a Holocaust survivor and Jewish kapo, it proved polarizing from the start. Tannenbaum cut a sympathetic figure in many ways. At seventy-two, he was a man who had worked hard in America and never caused any trouble, his friends and neighbors all said. He had lost his family to the Nazis and survived the Holocaust. He was a deeply religious man, an Orthodox Jew who regularly helped make up the minyan of ten men needed to begin prayer at his Brighton Beach synagogue. He had lit a candle at a Holocaust remembrance ceremony, and he gave money to the Simon Wiesenthal Center. Was this really the kind of man the Justice Department was going to throw out of the country?

Rockler, the former director of the Nazi office, was so incensed that he offered to defend Tannenbaum pro bono. He wrote in protest to Sher, a lawyer he'd always liked when he was his boss at the Justice Department. "I regard such a suit as more than a little dubious as a matter of law," Rockler wrote to Sher, "and improper, if not outrageous, as a matter of policy."

Sher pressed on anyway. Ultimately, he and Tannenbaum's lawyers reached a deal: the ex-kapo agreed to give up his American citizenship and admitted to "brutalizing and physically abusing prisoners outside the presence of German SS personnel." The admission of brutality and abuse was pivotal to Sher; he wanted it made clear that Tannenbaum was no "ordinary" kapo. In exchange for his admissions, the Justice Department allowed Tannenbaum to stay in the United States indefinitely because of his poor health. It was a compromise that left people on both sides of the case wrestling with their own notions of right and wrong. Even the judge, a war veteran who had been at Dachau after its liberation, was torn by the ethical complexities. "I dreaded the day when this case was to come to trial," he said. "I have often wondered how much moral and physical courage we have a right to demand or expect of somebody in the position of Mr. Tannenbaum . . . I sometimes wonder whether I might have passed that test."

For the survivors of Görlitz, the claims of moral dilemmas rang false.

To them, there was nothing complicated about Tannenbaum's situation: he was a brutal Nazi collaborator, no matter what God he claimed, and he was lucky to get off with the deal that he did, they said. They wanted vengeance for Tannenbaum, not compassion or understanding. "Is this all he is getting, for what he did?" one former prisoner at Görlitz asked. Declared another survivor: "I would have hanged him with my own hands."

13

Ivan the Terrible

November 17, 1993

SIXTH CIRCUIT COURT OF APPEALS, CINCINNATI, OHIO

For all the attacks that Pat Buchanan waged against them, the most damaging blow the Nazi hunters at the Justice Department would ever suffer was self-inflicted. The deep wounds it left would remain raw for years, after an ex-Nazi camp guard living outside Cleveland was nearly executed in 1993 for another man's barbaric war crimes.

It all began with a seeming stroke of luck sixteen years earlier, in 1977, with a photo lineup at a warehouse outside Tel Aviv. An Israeli war crimes investigator was showing a Holocaust survivor named Eliyahu Rosenberg a photo album filled with snapshots of middle-aged men in suits and ties. Rosenberg, a warehouse manager, had escaped from the death camp at Treblinka thirty-four years earlier; the ghastly images of the place still haunted him. American prosecutors were hoping Rosenberg might be able to pick out the photo of a Connecticut factory worker, Feodor Fedorenko, who they knew had worked as a low-level Nazi guard at Treblinka. They knew that a solid eyewitness identification from a Treblinka survivor could make their case.

The warehouse manager leafed through the pages of the album. There were seventeen photos in all. Did he recognize anyone, the investigator asked? On the third page, Rosenberg stopped at the very last photo. Yes, that man looks very familiar, Rosenberg said. He didn't remember his name, but he was a guard at Treblinka, he said. Just as prosecutors had hoped, the photo he picked was Feodor Fedorenko's.

Then Rosenberg's gaze turned back to the photo just before Fedoren-ko's — photo 16. It was an intimidating-looking man with short hair, large ears, and a steely gaze. Rosenberg seemed paralyzed by the image staring back at him from the page. This man had been at Treblinka, too, Rosenberg told the interviewer, his tone disbelieving. His name was Ivan, and he was not just any guard. He worked the gas chamber. He was a monster, Rosenberg said; a man so feared and reviled he had acquired his own grim sobriquet. This was the man, Rosenberg said. *This was Ivan the Terrible.*

There must be a mistake, the interviewer told him. Investigators thought the man in photo 16 might have been at another camp in Poland — at So-bibor — but not Treblinka. This man had never worked there, the inter-viewer said.

No, it was him, Rosenberg repeated. The man in the photo was Ivan the Terrible. Rosenberg was made to work every day just a few yards from him at the gas chamber, he said. He could never forget that face.

So began a torturous, thirty-five-year legal odyssey that would set off bitter battles in the United States, Israel, and Germany, call into question the ethics and competence of the Justice Department's Nazi hunters, and threaten their very mission.

The man in the photograph that Rosenberg picked out was a fifty-six-year-old car mechanic at a Ford auto plant outside Cleveland. He was a Ukrainian immigrant who came to America seven years after the war. He lived with his wife and three children in a tidy suburban rambler, with a well-tended lawn and colorful flowerbeds. He was a regular at the local Ukrainian church. His name was John Demjanjuk.

Two other Treblinka survivors in Israel picked Demjanjuk's photo out of the same album. Like Rosenberg, they identified him, with obvious ag-itation, as the man known in the camp as Ivan the Terrible. A muscular Ukrainian in his early twenties, Ivan was a man of almost mythic monstros-ity, the survivors recounted: He would wield a sword and a lead pipe as he herded the prisoners to the gas chamber, cutting off men's ears and slashing women's breasts along the way. Sometimes he would force the prisoners, adults and children alike, to perform sex acts on each other before he and his partner, Nikolai, shoved them inside the gas chamber. Then he would walk down a flight of stairs to an engine room known as Ivan's Area, where he would crank the diesel engine and pump the gas into the chamber until the prisoners' screams turned deadly silent.

Demjanjuk (pronounced dem-YAHN-yuk) was no one of any great significance to American prosecutors before the Israeli survivors picked him out of the photo lineup. His name had surfaced in a book about the Nazi camps and on a list of reputed guards prepared by a Ukrainian immigrant in New York. But those accounts placed him not at Treblinka, where nearly nine hundred thousand people were killed, but at Sobibor, as a faceless Nazi guard of no particular note. American authorities were not actively investigating him. He was just one more mug shot in a photo album filled with Ukrainian immigrants who, based on random leads, might or might not have ties to the Nazis.

With eyewitnesses identifying him as a particularly notorious Nazi, however, Demjanjuk was now a much bigger target. American prosecutors had reason to suspect that he was not just a cog in the machine, but one of its most sadistic operators. The more evidence they gathered, the more confident they became. In all, eighteen Treblinka survivors, in addition to a German worker at the camp, ultimately picked out Demjanjuk's photo as the man they knew as Ivan the Terrible. Another key piece of evidence came from the Soviets: a Nazi identification card with Demjanjuk's name on it, beneath what looked like a photograph of him as a young man. The card placed him at the camps at Trawniki and at Sobibor, not at Treblinka, but at the very least, it seemed to confirm that this Cleveland autoworker had been a card-carrying Nazi guard.

Then there was the name itself. Demjanjuk had changed his first name to John when he came to the United States. His given name, investigators learned, was Ivan. Some of the Treblinka witnesses remembered the brutal Treblinka guard's real last name as "Marchenko"; indeed, an Ivan Marchenko was listed as a guard at Treblinka in a document provided by Polish authorities. The investigators learned that Demjanjuk, in filling out his visa application to come to America, had listed his mother's maiden name. It was Marchenko.

To American authorities, the connections seemed too overwhelming to be written off as coincidence. Prosecutors at the Justice Department were convinced: John Demjanjuk and Ivan the Terrible were one and the same. "Prosecuting him, for all of us, became an obsession," one prosecutor said.

On August 26, 1977, the Justice Department brought charges in Cleveland against John Demjanjuk alleging that he was Ivan the Terrible of Treblinka and seeking to strip him of his citizenship for war crimes. That evening, Demjanjuk returned to his home in suburban Cleveland and found a local newspaper reporter, Walt Bogdanich, waiting for him outside with a photographer. Demjanjuk's daughters, one a teenager, the other in her midtwenties, were there too. Bogdanich asked to speak with Demjanjuk in private; this might not be easy for his children to hear, he explained. They could hear whatever he had to say, Demjanjuk insisted. Bogdanich told him that the Justice Department was trying to revoke his citizenship because of his reputed role as a Nazi guard at Treblinka. "I don't know anything—what do you mean?" Demjanjuk asked in a voice of quiet alarm. Bogdanich began to explain what exactly the Justice Department was saying about him. His daughters were in tears as they listened to the reporter's account. Their father was being labeled a Nazi — and not just any Nazi, but a particularly sadistic one known as Ivan the Terrible.

Demjanjuk finally interrupted the reporter. He had heard enough. "People say things. I don't know anything," he said. The photographer started to snap his picture. Demjanjuk stuck his hand out in front of the camera — striking the familiar pose of an accused man trying to avoid the spotlight.

The next day, desperate to clear his name, Demjanjuk agreed to speak with a Cleveland television crew at his home. He was a German prisoner of war, not a camp guard, he insisted in his fractured English. His wife, Vera, sitting next to him on the living room couch, broke in to declare his innocence as well. "Is not true! Is not true! Is not true!" she screamed at the camera. Then she slumped silently against her husband's shoulder. She had fainted. The interview was cut short and an ambulance was called.

Demjanjuk was suddenly big news, not just in Cleveland, but around the country. "Ohioan Is Called Nazi War Criminal," read the headline in the *New York Times*. Just as prosecutors were beginning to move more aggressively against suspected Nazis after decades of indifference, they now had in their sights a man of monstrous savagery who seemed to put a bald and bespectacled face on Nazi evil. If Adolf Eichmann was the brutally efficient architect of Hitler's Final Solution, then Ivan the Terrible, living in Cleveland, Ohio, was the barbaric executioner, a sadist who corralled women and children in the gas chamber, beating and torturing them as they went.

With Demjanjuk's visibility now so high, prosecutors faced intense political pressures not to repeat the kind of legal missteps that had riddled Nazi prosecutions for years. On the House immigration committee, Congressman Joshua Eilberg made clear that he wanted the Justice Department to throw everything it had at deporting Demjanjuk. "We cannot afford the risk of losing another decision," he wrote to the attorney general regarding Demjanjuk.

With the Justice Department's aggressive new Nazi office grabbing hold of the case, prosecutors were confident that there would be no slip-ups. Allan Ryan, for his part, had no doubts. As the case moved toward a trial in 1980, he laid Demjanjuk's Nazi identification card side by side with the photo a decade later from Demjanjuk's U.S. visa application. The similarities were striking. Beyond the photos, prosecutors had eyewitnesses — Holocaust survivors — who were ready to place Demjanjuk at Treblinka, running the gas chamber where hundreds of thousands were killed. They would no doubt make sympathetic witnesses. The case appeared airtight.

You son of a bitch, Ryan thought to himself as he studied the photos. *We've got you.*

But doubts about the case were already beginning to emerge, even within the Justice Department.

One of the prosecutors on the case, George Parker, couldn't get past one nagging question: How could Demjanjuk have been in two places at once? The Nazi identification card from the Soviets showed Demjanjuk as a nondescript, rank-and-file guard at Sobibor beginning in 1942, but the eyewitness accounts from the survivors identifying him as Ivan the Terrible placed him about a hundred miles away at Treblinka during essentially that same time period. One or the other could be true, Parker believed, but not both. "Demjanjuk could not have been Ivan the Terrible at Treblinka as well as the Demjanjuk known to [another witness] at Sobibor," he wrote to his bosses, Ryan and Rockler, in a long memo.

Parker had "gnawing doubts" about the veracity of the case against Demjanjuk and about the ethical cloud hovering over prosecutors if they moved ahead anyway, he wrote. No one doubted the sincerity of the Israeli survivors in picking out Demjanjuk's photo, but they were being asked to remember traumatic events nearly forty years earlier, and eyewitnesses to Nazi crimes had been wrong before. Parker believed that Demjanjuk probably *was* a Nazi guard at a death camp — just not the infamous guard the prosecutors thought he was, and not at the same camp where they thought he worked. In a line that would prove prophetic, Parker warned his supervisors that "we may have the right man for the wrong act."

Parker proposed "radical surgery" to salvage the prosecution. Instead, the Justice Department went ahead with the case largely unchanged, tinkering with a few elements but holding steady on the central claim that Demjanjuk was Ivan the Terrible. Parker quit the Justice Department in frustration. He was now convinced that Demjanjuk was not the larger-than-life murderer that the Justice Department thought he was, and he did not want to put his own legal career at risk.

A year later, Demjanjuk went on trial in Cleveland. Five survivors from Treblinka were flown in from Israel to testify. One of them was Eliyahu Rosenberg, the man who had first identified Demjanjuk's photo for the war crimes investigators at his warehouse outside Tel Aviv four years earlier.

Testifying in Hebrew through a translator, Rosenberg explained to the dead-quiet courtroom how he was forced to watch Ivan's savagery every day. The Nazis had stationed Rosenberg outside the gas chamber to remove the corpses of the victims once Ivan was done with them, he said. Ivan would always have a weapon of some sort as he and his partner, Nikolai, herded prisoners into the gas chamber, Rosenberg testified. "He had a pipe, a sword, a whip, and he tortured the victims with this before they entered the gas chambers, especially the women. He cut pieces between their legs. I saw this with my very eyes." Such acts of brutality, he said, "happened every day."

Rosenberg couldn't go on. He broke into sobs, with his head bowed and his body shaking as he sat silently on the witness stand. The memory of that place was too much for him. After a minute, he lifted his head, took a deep breath, and somehow kept going. The prosecutor showed him a batch of photographs and asked if he recognized the accused. Just as he had done four years earlier in Tel Aviv, he picked out one man from the group and identified him as "Iwan," the Ukrainian derivation of "Ivan." "Iwan was there, younger, he was thinner, the way he was in Treblinka," Rosenberg said, pointing to the photo. It was John Demjanjuk's visa photo from 1951.

Rosenberg was shown a second batch of photos and picked out one of the men as Ivan. It was Demjanjuk's Nazi identification card from 1942. He was certain: it was Ivan.

Four months later, a judge stripped Demjanjuk of his citizenship, concluding that he had concealed his service with the Nazis when he came to America three decades earlier.

But there was still the task of deporting Demjanjuk and finding a country that would take him. Earlier cases had taught prosecutors a painful lesson: as difficult as it was to take away suspected Nazis' citizenship, it was only half the battle. Finding someplace to send them — preferably someplace that would try them for war crimes — took years. Many convicted Nazis died in America, stripped of their U.S. citizenship, before authorities could find a willing state to take them in. The Germans, despite their historic complicity, had made clear that they had no interest in accepting deported Nazis back on their soil. As one German official asked Allan Ryan ruefully, "Who would want to take back America's Nazi war criminals?"

Ironically, the Israelis hadn't been terribly helpful either. Israel had not put any Nazi suspects on trial in two decades, since Eichmann's stunning capture in 1960 and the historic trial that followed, and it had never been willing to seek the extradition of a Nazi suspect in America. Some Israeli law enforcement officials believed that holding war crimes trials for lesser Nazis would dilute the impact of the Eichmann trial as a seminal moment in history. But there were signs of a thaw. Younger generations had forgotten the Holocaust, the new thinking went, and another major trial was needed to galvanize world attention.

In early 1982, just months after Demjanjuk was stripped of his American citizenship, Neal Sher, Eli Rosenbaum, and a third Justice Department prosecutor traveled to Jerusalem to talk with their Israeli counterparts about extraditing Nazi war criminals. The Israelis were willing, for the first time, to consider putting an American Nazi on trial. That would be a huge step. But they would not accept just anyone. If the Israelis were going to stage their first Nazi war crimes trial since Eichmann, they wanted to make a bold statement. They wanted someone who would be representative of the horrors of the Holocaust. It had to be a Nazi perpetrator who was accused of personally murdering Jews, and it had to be someone who would have to sit face to face in a courtroom with a Holocaust survivor in

Israel testifying to his crimes, the Israelis told their American visitors. Some might call it a show trial. The Israelis called it justice.

Sher went over the American "candidates" with the Israelis. Colonel Menachem Russek of the Israeli national police, a Holocaust survivor himself, mulled over the Americans' list of the accused. Finally, Russek settled on the one from Treblinka. "I think this fellow Demjanjuk would be a proper case," he said. After two decades, the Israelis were finally ready to put another Nazi on trial for war crimes, and they wanted Ivan the Terrible.

Demjanjuk's lawyers in Cleveland tried to block his extradition. One of the appeals court judges who had to consider whether to send Demjanjuk to Israel was Judge Gilbert S. Merritt, in Tennessee. The judge was troubled by the case. He thought the evidence was weak; it relied largely on eyewitness testimony from Treblinka survivors who picked out Demjanjuk as Ivan the Terrible. Could those eyewitness accounts really be reliable? "We know that eyewitness testimony, even when it's immediate, is very suspect," he said to one of his clerks as he debated what to do. "And this was years ago." Judge Merritt wanted his clerk to do more research: Were there grounds to block the extradition? The answer came back no. The appeals court didn't have much discretion in a case like this, Merritt concluded. Grudgingly, he voted to uphold Demjanjuk's extradition. He would come to regret that decision perhaps more than any he ever made on the bench.

Demjanjuk was sent to Israel and jailed almost immediately. His eleven-month trial in Jerusalem was largely a redux of his trial in Ohio, but on an even bigger stage, with Israeli prosecutors and Holocaust survivors reliving the horrors of Treblinka and painting a picture of a brute of a man named Ivan with no regard for human life. Just as he had done in Cleveland, Eliyahu Rosenberg, the sixty-five-year-old Treblinka survivor, testified against Demjanjuk, and again he was asked if he could identify the man he remembered as Ivan the Terrible. This time he was looking not at a photo album, but at the accused himself, an elderly man sitting in the courtroom before him. Rosenberg walked toward Demjanjuk; he wanted to look into his eyes, he said. Demjanjuk removed his eyeglasses and reached out as if to shake hands with Rosenberg. "Shalom," a smiling Demjanjuk said in Hebrew. Rosenberg recoiled. "Ivan!" he shouted to a stunned courtroom. "I have no shadow of a hesitation or a doubt. It is Ivan from Treblinka, from the gas chambers — the man that I am looking at this very moment. I saw the eyes, the murderous eyes and the face. And how dare you give me a hand, you murderer!"

Demjanjuk insisted they had the wrong man: he was a German prisoner of war, not Ivan the Terrible. He had never worked in a concentration camp, he insisted; Rosenberg and the other survivors were liars. The Israeli judges did not believe him. In the spring of 1988, the court found him guilty of crimes against humanity; the reading of the verdict aloud from the bench took ten full hours. A week later, the court sentenced him to death by hanging. "What punishment must be given this Ivan the Terrible?" one judge asked. "A man who killed both tens of thousands and individuals, who tortured and treated sadistically those taken to death in their last hour, what is his sentence? A thousand deaths cannot compensate for what happened, but at least we have judged one of the angels of death. The human hand is unable to measure a punishment equal to the charges." Israelis gathered around TVs at restaurants to listen, erupting in songs and cheers in the streets when the sentence came down.

Twelve years after he first identified Demjanjuk from the photo lineup at his warehouse, Eliyahu Rosenberg choked back tears when he heard the verdict. There was a measure of satisfaction in seeing Demjanjuk sentenced to death, he said, but "there is no verdict that can erase the crimes and murders he committed."

The story could have ended there, with the man known as Ivan the Terrible — a living symbol of Nazi brutality — doomed to death in a moment of retribution for Israel and the world. America's long tolerance of Nazis in its midst would have been rectified, on a triumphant note, with one of history's worst killers finally receiving the ultimate punishment after living a quiet life in Cleveland for a quarter century. Eliyahu Rosenberg would have been vindicated, and justice would finally have been served.

But the story did not end there. Because John Demjanjuk was not Ivan the Terrible.

Just as Justice Department prosecutor George Parker had warned eight years earlier, Demjanjuk had never even been at Treblinka. The evidence was clear that he was a Nazi guard at other German camps — at Sobibor, at Flossenbürg, and at Majdanek — but not at Treblinka. Just as Parker had foreshadowed, prosecutors had "the right man for the wrong crime." Demjanjuk was indeed a small cog in the Nazis' killing machine, but not its savage operator.

That such a grievous mistake was acknowledged at all was an unlikely testament to the ebbing of the Cold War. With relations between Russia and the West thawing under glasnost, Israeli lawyers were allowed to travel to Moscow to look at archival war records, even as Demjanjuk appealed his death sentence. There, the KGB turned over some eighty files that had been found in the basement of a secret police building in Kiev, including interviews the Russians conducted immediately after the war with more than thirty Nazi guards at Treblinka. The testimony from the guards — many of them later executed by the Russians for war crimes — identified the brutal gas-chamber operator known as Ivan the Terrible as a Ukrainian named Ivan Marchenko, the same name that had surfaced years earlier in the case. American prosecutors had always thought that Ivan Marchenko and John "Ivan" Demjanjuk were the same man; Demjanjuk, after all, had even listed his mother's maiden name as Marchenko. But the KGB files provided all sorts of details on this Ivan Marchenko that did not match Demjanjuk — his hometown, his birthdate, his military record, his family life, and more. The files even included a photo of this Ivan Marchenko; there was some resemblance in the photo to Demjanjuk, but Marchenko had a scar on his cheek, and darker hair. This man, last seen by his fellow Nazis leaving a brothel in Croatia months before the war ended in 1945, was clearly not John Demjanjuk.

Handed the new evidence, the Israeli judges saw no choice. Demjanjuk was not Ivan the Terrible, they concluded. He did appear to have served as an anonymous Nazi guard at other camps — an "accomplice to the Holocaust," the judges called him — but there was no real indication of what he had done at any of the camps, and the court was not about to keep him in prison for it. That was not why he had been put on trial, the judges said. The United States had extradited him, and Israel had put him on death row, because he was thought to be Ivan the Terrible.

And so, in the summer of 1993, the Israeli Supreme Court threw out his conviction and declared John Demjanjuk a free man. He would soon be on his way home to Cleveland after nearly eight years in prison, much of it in isolation in a barren cell in Jerusalem.

• • •

Few could have predicted an ending like this, with one ironic turn after another. It was, after all, the Soviets — accused by Pat Buchanan of forging Demjanjuk's Nazi identification card to implicate Demjanjuk — who had produced the long-buried documents that ultimately cleared him. It was the Israelis, so anxious to bring another big war crimes case, who had ultimately set Demjanjuk free after his own country declared him Ivan the Terrible. And it was the Americans, sluggish for so long in pursuing suspected Nazis, who were shown to have gone after this one too aggressively.

In the United States, Neal Sher and prosecutors in his Nazi office were smarting from the setback, but still unwilling to let the case go. They were determined to see if Demjanjuk could be prosecuted for serving as a guard at Sobibor and other Nazi camps. But first, they had to deal with the fall-out from the collapse of the Israeli case. The postmortems into what went wrong began even before Israel sent Demjanjuk back to America. Judge Merritt and his fellow judges on the Sixth Circuit Court of Appeals in Cincinnati ordered a full investigation into whether the Justice Department's Nazi office had misled the courts in stripping Demjanjuk of his citizenship. Six separate ethics investigations into the prosecutors' conduct were opened. A jubilant Buchanan took aim at the Nazi hunters at the Justice Department, who he said "were desperate to prove [Demjanjuk] was 'Ivan the Terrible'" and "are responsible for the destruction of this man's life and career."

George Parker's 1980 memo figured prominently in assessing the wreckage of the case. It suggested that higher-ups had ignored early warning signs that Demjanjuk might not be Ivan the Terrible. Then there were clues found in the trash that the Justice Department's adversaries pilfered years earlier from the dumpster behind the building. At the trial, one key piece of evidence came from the positive identification of a German worker, who reportedly said "that is him" with confidence when shown a photo of Demjanjuk. But the raw notes taken during the photo lineup — retrieved from the trash — indicated that the witness was not nearly so certain as prosecutors made him out to be, and actually seemed unable to pick out Demjanjuk the first time as a guard at Treblinka.

A federal judge in Tennessee, Thomas Wiseman Jr., spent six months reviewing hundreds of pieces of evidence in the case and interviewing witnesses to determine what had gone so wrong. The ultimate findings were damning for the Justice Department. Judge Wiseman concluded that prosecutors played "hardball" in keeping evidence from Demjanjuk's lawyers and "were blinded to what we may now perceive to be the truth" — not willfully so, he said, but blind nonetheless.

At the appeals court in Cincinnati, Judge Merritt and the two other judges who reviewed Wiseman's findings were far less forgiving. They concluded that Justice Department prosecutors "acted with reckless disregard for the truth" by assuming Demjanjuk's guilt even in the face of evidence that pointed to another man as Ivan the Terrible. The government's failure to turn over evidence that might have exonerated Demjanjuk, the judges concluded, amounted to "fraud on the court."

Even worse for the Justice Department, the judges said in their blistering ruling that they believed political pressure from Jewish groups and others was partly to blame for the department's "reckless" prosecution. As evidence, the judges cited a memo that Allan Ryan had written about how his Nazi office had secured "support from Jewish organizations," and they also pointed to a ten-day trip Ryan had taken to Israel for a lecture tour paid for by the Anti-Defamation League, a prominent Jewish group. "It is obvious from the record," the appeals court said, "that the prevailing mindset at [the Nazi office] was that the office must try to please and maintain very close relationships with various interest groups because their continued existence depended upon it." Privately, Judge Merritt was appalled. He had never seen a prosecution that, in his view, was so tainted by outside politics. When Neal Sher left the Nazi office the very next year to become executive director of the American Israel Public Affairs Committee, one of Washington's most influential lobbying groups, the move only confirmed in the judge's mind that the Justice Department had indeed become too close to Jewish groups.

The court's suggestion of undue political influence by Jewish groups hit prosecutors in their most vulnerable spot. Justice Department officials had always been acutely aware of the perception in some quarters — unjust though they thought it was — that they were essentially an arm of Jewish advocacy groups, with a common agenda and a revolving door between them. Now here was a federal appeals court charging not only that prosecutors had botched the landmark case, but that they had done so recklessly because of Jewish pressure. Prosecutors were furious over the charge. The ruling, Jewish leaders said, perpetuated hurtful stereotypes about Jewish influence and "offered fodder to the anti-Semites among us." So raw were the emotions that Sher would go on to accuse Judge Merritt of "an obsession with Jews"; the court's comments on Jewish pressure, Sher charged, reflected ideas usually heard only among "hate mongerers and neo-Nazis." In the midst of the Demjanjuk fallout, the Clinton administration floated Judge Merritt's name as a possible Supreme Court nominee. Jewish groups howled, in no small part because of his handling of the Demjanjuk case, and the idea stalled. Things had indeed gotten personal. What had started years earlier as the high-profile prosecution of a Nazi guard had now become something much different: an ugly battle over dueling charges of zealotry at the Justice Department and anti-Semitism at the courts.

Allan Ryan, for his part, had left the Justice Department a decade earlier and was now working at Harvard, but he was still furious over the appeals court's findings, particularly the reference to his paid trip to Israel. "What the fuck are they talking about!" Ryan yelled when he read the line. He had gone on the trip four years *after* he left the government; he was a private citizen, and the trip had nothing to do with what had happened in the case, he seethed. He demanded that Judge Merritt and the court correct the record over what he saw as an unfair attack on his character. They never did.

It was a dark time indeed for the once high-flying Nazi hunters. Before this, Eli Rosenbaum, the second-ranking official at the time, had always been proud to tell people that he was a lawyer for the Justice Department's Nazi-hunting team. For him, it was a righteous cause. He had worked to expel Nazi rocket scientist Arthur Rudolph from the country. He had sat with Holocaust survivors in Israel and heard their poignant stories. He had even kept a piece of Joseph Mengele's scalp locked in his desk drawer to try to determine if the "Angel of Death" had really died in Brazil in 1979. (He had.) Rosenbaum had always reveled in the job. Now, however, when he told people outside the Justice Department that he worked for the Office of Special Investigations, he was often met with a look of discomfort. "Oh, Demjanjuk?" people would ask, if they could pronounce the name. Or simply, "Ivan the Terrible?" Sometimes it was a look of sympathy, as one might reserve for the victim of a terrible accident. Other times it was a look of scorn over a case that had become so notorious. Rosenbaum was quick to tell people that he had nothing to do with the Demjanjuk prosecution himself. But the reputation of the office that he now helped lead was, by his own admission, "in the toilet." Dozens of successful Nazi investigations had been overshadowed by a single, massive failure. Now, when people asked Rosenbaum what he did for a living, he no longer mentioned the Nazi team. He would simply say that he worked for the Justice Department. He didn't want to get into the rest of it.

14

The Road to Ponary

September 1993

VILNIUS, LITHUANIA

The bastard must have signed his name somewhere. A scrap of paper, a
death warrant, an order rounding up the Jews — there must have been
something with that name scrawled at the bottom: *Aleksandras Lileikis.*
But if it was there, Mike MacQueen wasn't finding it. MacQueen, a racecar
driver turned historian for the Justice Department's Nazi team, had spent
days rummaging through the dog-eared war files at the archives in Lithuania, but he was coming up empty.

This was the fourth trip to Lithuania in the last few years for MacQueen,
who had taught himself Lithuanian just for the job. The secrets held in the
Vilnius archives, opened up to American researchers after the fall of the
Soviet Union two years earlier, had turned up plenty of grim, eye-popping
details about the Nazi massacres in the Baltics, but nothing on the man
MacQueen most wanted to nail: Lileikis, the onetime chief of Lithuania's
security police and a proud Massachusetts resident for the last thirty-five
years.

The old man had practically dared the Justice Department's Nazi hunters to find something on him when Eli Rosenbaum had first come knocking on his door in Boston years earlier. Sure, his men in Vilnius might have
rounded up Jews, Lileikis had scoffed, but that didn't mean he had ordered
it. He knew nothing about any executions, he told Rosenbaum. "Show me
something that I signed," he had said in that cool, defiant manner of his. He
was taunting them. He knew if the prosecutors couldn't find evidence that

he played some active role in the massacres in Lithuania all those years ago, they had no case. MacQueen figured that unless he could find something on him, Lileikis would live out his days in America.

As he scoured the records, MacQueen was growing frustrated. In Vilnius, the Nazis had wiped out one of the great meccas of Jewish civilization in all of Europe, machine-gunning to death nearly all of the city's sixty thousand Jewish men, women, and children at a notorious pit outside town. It was inconceivable to him that the chief of the special security police — the dreaded Saugumas force — wasn't involved. Could there really be nothing with his John Hancock on it? Impossible, MacQueen thought. The Nazis wrote down everything, a macabre testament to their own brutality. He knew that the Germans had burned many of their records as they fled Vilnius, but still, there must be *something* that survived with Lileikis's stamp of approval on it.

That's when MacQueen realized that he had been going at his search backwards. Instead of looking for the files on the murderers, he began looking for the files on their victims. He searched the records for a prison in Vilnius where he knew many Jews were jailed before they were killed. In the prison records, he discovered a canvas-bound book with the names of nearly twenty-nine hundred wartime prisoners typed in Russian. He pulled the files on the ones with Jewish-sounding names. There were hundreds. Some of the documents were lightly singed; it looked like the Nazis had started burning the records on their way out of town, but ran out of time.

In the batch, after some digging, he found a red file with the records for a young Jewish man named Rachmiel Alperovicius, who was arrested by Lithuanian security police on September 4, 1941, and executed just two weeks later. Like farmers advertising their livestock, the security police described the young Jew's physical attributes: big, flattened ears; strong body; broad shoulders; small teeth. And there at the bottom of the page, in thick, black ink, was the signature MacQueen had been struggling to find for more than three years now: *Aleksandras Lileikis, chief of the security police in Vilnius.*

Soon, MacQueen found the records for another Jewish prisoner with Lileikis's signature at the bottom, then another, then another. Suddenly, Lileikis's long-elusive name was everywhere. MacQueen worked through lunch, taking photos of the documents and typing notes on his laptop as he dug deeper into the files. He had been at the Justice Department for five years since he first answered an ad for a war historian on the Nazi team. Nothing topped this moment.

That night, MacQueen returned to the Radisson Hotel in Vilnius. The place was a dive, but at least he could get an international phone line. He needed to call Washington. He reached Eli Rosenbaum, his boss at the Justice Department, who had been struggling off and on for a decade to build a case against the former Vilnius police chief, ever since meeting the Lithuanian immigrant at his home in Boston.

"Remember we needed a document signed by Lileikis?" MacQueen asked Rosenbaum.

"Yeah?" his boss answered.

"How would you like about twenty?"

Rosenbaum was so excited that he would have gotten on the next plane for the Baltics himself if he could. The Justice Department had been getting pummeled for months over the collapse of the Ivan the Terrible case. Any bit of good news was welcome in Washington. MacQueen had now delivered it, signed and sealed.

A handwriting expert compared the signatures to another one on file for Lileikis in Germany. It was a match. To MacQueen, the signatures were a smoking gun— evidence that Lileikis had ordered Jews in town to be rounded up and turned over to the Gestapo for certain death. Lileikis, he was convinced, was a *Schreibtischtäter* — a desk murderer. He gave the orders. He hadn't roused any of Vilnius's Jews from their homes himself. He wasn't the one who pinned the Stars of David on their shirts or herded them into ghettos surrounded by barbed wire and armed guards. He hadn't trucked them to a death pit outside town, stripped them down to their underwear with his own hands, or machine-gunned to death all but five thousand of the local Jews. He never even wore a Nazi uniform. But MacQueen was convinced that Lileikis was in control. He had directed the carnage in concert with the Gestapo. The distinguished-looking gentleman from Boston, he believed, had been the Nazis' henchman in Vilnius, a man with the blood of many thousands on his hands.

MacQueen studied the names of the victims, reading the stories of their unmourned murders in the long-buried files: Beila Levinson, Danielius-Antanas Konas, Chaja Lapyda. Two names stood out from the rest: Gitta

Kaplan and her daughter, Fruma. The girl was six years old. She and her mother had fled the Jewish ghetto and gone into hiding at the nearby home of a Catholic family that had tried to protect them. Lileikis's men discovered them there. Lileikis was the one who signed an order imprisoning mother and daughter on November 28, 1941. The two shared a cell in the Lithuanian prison — cell 17, the order noted matter-of-factly.

Three weeks later, the Nazis took them, along with the others in their death shift, to an excavation site six miles outside town. The pit was at a wooded hamlet called Ponary. In the Jewish ghetto, the mothers had a dark song that they sang to one another about the place. *All roads lead to Ponary, but no roads lead back.* The Nazis would line the Jews up ten at a time at the edge of the crevice and shoot them, their bodies falling backward into a mass morgue in the pit below. A small few, wounded but not killed, hid among the dead in the pit and lived to tell of the horrors of the place. Legend had it that the executions were so unsettling even to the brutal Nazi gunmen that they began lining up the victims with their backs to their executioners so as to avoid their terrified gaze.

The Nazis kept typed "execution cards" for each of their victims, with a slash mark in red or blue pencil confirming that the fatal deed was done. Fruma had a card of her own. *Kaplan, Fruma Juedin. geb. 1935.* "Kaplan, Fruma: Jew. Born 1935," it said. Below that was the same ice-cold euphemism that was typed on the cards of thousands of other victims at Ponary to confirm their fate: *Befehlsgemass behandelt.* "Treated according to orders."

Mike MacQueen would never forget Fruma's name. After all he had learned as a student of the Holocaust in Eastern Europe, it was still difficult to fathom such cruelty: a little girl imprisoned and killed at the age of six, all because she was Jewish. On his bulletin board, MacQueen put a copy of Fruma's execution card; he vowed to keep it there until Lileikis was prosecuted.

It proved a long road. MacQueen had to travel more than forty-five hundred miles from Washington to Lithuania to gather evidence on Lileikis and his role in the massacres at Ponary. He had no inkling that evidence of the Boston man's crimes had been gathering dust much closer to home. It sat dormant for four decades right across the river from the Justice Department, in Langley, Virginia — in the secret files of the CIA.

The CIA had a file on Lileikis because the former Nazi collaborator was one of their own. Like Tom Soobzokov in Paterson, New Jersey; like Otto von Bolschwing in San Jose; like Edgars Laipenieks in San Diego, and like dozens of others with Nazi ties on their resumés, Aleksandras Lileikis, too, had worked for the CIA as a Cold War spy targeting the Soviets.

The CIA first recruited Lileikis when he was living in Munich in 1952, seven years after the war had ended. The United States was recruiting ex-Nazis en masse in Europe, and Lileikis fit the bill. As the saying went, no one hated the Soviets more than the Nazis. The agency thought he might be of use in getting information from Lithuanian nationals working for the Communists in East Germany. He had no particular skills in spying, the CIA admitted in assessing him, but he appeared committed to working with "any western anti-Soviet power," and he needed a job to support his family.

His Nazi ties were not a secret to the agency. His CIA file noted that Lileikis "was the chief of the political Lithuanian Security Police in Vilna during the German occupation and that he was possibly connected with the shooting of Jews in Vilna." The file also noted that just two years earlier, Lileikis had been unanimously rejected for entry into America because he was "under the control of the Gestapo." In fact, he had been investigated as a war criminal, his CIA file noted. As the CIA's own notes made clear, Lileikis and people like him in power in Lithuania during the German occupation "were generally there because of their known Nazi sympathies."

Lileikis's history with the Nazis might have been enough to keep him out of the United States, but it was not enough to keep him out of the CIA. Despite all the evidence in its filings cataloging Lileikis's ties to the Nazis, the CIA concluded that there was "no derogatory information" on him. The agency gave him a security clearance and hired him as a spy — at a salary of about $1,700 a year, plus twenty-one pounds of coffee and two cartons of cigarettes each month to feed his habits. He met secretly with fellow Lithuanians in East Germany, did some surveillance and interrogation work, helped with a bit of translating, and fed the CIA's insatiable appetite for intelligence on the Russians.

Lileikis worked for the CIA for five years in Europe. Then, in 1955, he applied anew for entry to the United States, just six years after he had been unanimously rejected. He had always hoped his work with the CIA in Europe might allow him to whitewash his record and get into the United States, and it did. On his second try, without explanation, his visa was approved. The CIA denied any role in his sudden reversal of fortune, but the agency did keep an eye on its Nazi spy after he immigrated. In 1956, after Lileikis had moved to central Massachusetts near old friends from Lithuania, CIA officials learned that investigators from the immigration service were asking questions about his past. Concerned, the CIA demanded to know what was behind the inquiries. The agency told the INS that it had a continued "interest" in Lileikis. In other words: Stay away from him. It was a false alarm. INS officials assured the CIA that they were asking questions about Lileikis not because of any possible immigration problems, but because they, too, hoped to use him as an informant. The INS thought the ex-Nazi loyalist could provide the agency with intelligence on fellow Lithuanian immigrants. Lileikis was a man in high demand.

Lileikis had company from the old country. His second-in-command on the brutal Vilnius security force, a Lithuanian named Kazys Gimzauskas, also came to America — and like his boss, he had help from the CIA. In Nazi-occupied Vilnius, Gimzauskas was the man in charge of "interrogating" the Jews. By one account in the CIA's files, he also took part in shooting to death "hundreds" of Polish academics, lawyers, political leaders, and others in the region during the Nazi siege. The CIA brought him on its team after the war anyway, making him a part of the huge anti-Soviet intelligence network in Europe led by ex-Nazi general Reinhard Gehlen. Like his old boss, Lileikis, he longed to come to America soon after the war. The State Department rejected Gimzauskas and his wife for entry at first because of his obvious Nazi ties in Lithuania. But his employers at the CIA helped grease the skids for the couple because of the spy work he had done for the agency. In a 1955 memo, the CIA said the agency "still feels a moral obligation to aid them in speedy resettlement to the U.S." Soon, Gimzauskas and his wife were on their way to St. Petersburg, Florida, where he worked for years as a machinist among a close-knit community of Lithuanian immigrants.

Two lower-ranking men on Lileikis's security force, both implicated in rounding up Jewish children in Vilnius, also wound up settling in St. Petersburg, and a third became a real estate agent in Ohio. In all, at least three dozen Lithuanian immigrants with ties to the Nazi massacres there found sanctuary in the United States beginning in the 1950s, clustered in Florida, Massachusetts, and Illinois. With U.S. immigration policies wide open to immigrants from the Nazi-occupied "captive nations" in the Baltics, these men had little difficulty getting into America, hiding themselves among thousands of legitimate war refugees from the region. More than a dozen of them came from a single Nazi-controlled battalion in Lithuania that carried out a string of massacres in the region that were considered brutal even by Third Reich standards. Resettled in America, these Nazi collaborators from Lithuania were now American success stories: leaders of their churches, pillars of their communities, exemplars for other U.S. immigrants.

Aleksandras Lileikis, for his part, lived an unremarkable life in Massachusetts for a quarter century. He belonged to the Lithuanian social club in the Boston suburb of Norwood, he attended a Lithuanian Catholic church, and he worked for a Lithuanian encyclopedia company, painting houses on the side. Lithuanian maps and artwork lined the walls of his home. While his English was decent enough, he would sometimes insist on speaking only in Lithuanian. He clung to the ways of his old country even as he lived comfortably in his new one.

He rarely mentioned the war. Not until Lileikis was in his midseventies, in fact, would he have any reason to fear that his Nazi ties might finally be exposed.

But then, twice in the same week in the fall of 1982, his name surfaced at the Justice Department as a possible war criminal. First came a cable to Washington from Berlin saying that a man named Lileikis was "listed as head of Lithuanian Security Police in Wilna [Vilnius]" and may have been connected to Einsatzkommando 3, one of the Nazis' infamous mobile killing teams. He was last known to be living in Massachusetts, the cable added. Next, by chance, came an interview with a Lithuanian in the United States in the course of another investigation. At the end of the interview, the Justice Department lawyer asked, almost as an aside, whether the man knew of any other Lithuanians in America who had collaborated with the Nazis. Yes, the man said, he did know of one: a man from Vilnius named Aleksandras Lileikis.

Two mentions in a span of days was enough to get Eli Rosenbaum's at-

tention. The prosecutor began collecting what few documents were available on Lileikis's war years. Months later, he and an investigator headed to
an address in the suburbs of Boston for one of his surprise "knock and talk"
visits. This was the address Rosenbaum had found for Aleksandras Lileikis
— the same Aleksandras Lileikis, he was certain, who was mentioned in
that tantalizing cable from Berlin months earlier. This could be big. If the
leads were right, Lileikis wasn't just some low-level guard; he was a senior
Nazi collaborator who issued orders in one of the Holocaust's most notorious massacres — a Nazi killing field where at least fifty-five thousand Jews
were murdered, along with tens of thousands of Poles, Russians, and others.

Rosenbaum knocked on the door of a pretty yellow house on Sumner Street in a tree-lined, middle-class neighborhood. A housekeeper answered. He and his investigator had come from the Justice Department to
speak with a Mr. Lileikis, Rosenbaum explained to her. The housekeeper
let them in and sat them down on the sofa in the living room. Lileikis, tall
and distinguished-looking, with slicked-back white hair and glasses, joined
them.

Rosenbaum gave Lileikis his standard opening line: the Justice Department had some questions about his immigration status. Lileikis gave no
hint of alarm. In Vilnius during the war, Rosenbaum asked him, had he run
the security force known as the Saugumas? Yes, Lileikis answered; that was
him. Rosenbaum suppressed a smile. They had the right man. And what
were his duties there? Routine stuff, Lileikis answered; basic security work.
Rosenbaum, however, knew there was nothing routine about the activities
of the Saugumas. These were the plainclothes officers who did political intelligence work in Vilnius, and they were aligned with the Nazis.

Rosenbaum began pressing Lileikis. Certainly he was aware, Rosenbaum said, that the Nazis had rounded up tens of thousands of Jews and
killed them in the death pit at Ponary?

For the first time, Lileikis seemed agitated. He had heard rumors about
the killings, he said, but only rumors. He himself was not involved. "How
could I know? I was in the office," he said. But he was the chief of the special intelligence police force, Rosenbaum said. His men were the political
arm of the Vilnius police. They must have cooperated with the Germans,
Rosenbaum said. "No, no, the Germans did that on their own," Lileikis
said. Rosenbaum pressed him again: his men on the force must have had

some involvement, he said. "Absolutely not," Lileikis repeated. "That was all the Germans."

Rosenbaum reached into his briefcase and took out a document with a list of fifty-two names typed down the side. This was going to be his gotcha moment.

"Then how do you explain this?" Rosenbaum asked, handing Lileikis the paper.

Lileikis studied the document for a minute. It was an order dated August 22, 1941, and it listed the names of fifty-two imprisoned Jewish men, women, and children who were to be handed over to the Nazis. "I request that you turn over the Jews listed below, currently held at my disposition, to the custody of the Commander of the Ypatingas Burys" — a Nazi execution force operating in Lithuania. At the bottom, typed out, was his last name and title: "Lileikis, District Chief."

"I've never seen this before," Lileikis said finally, handing the order back. He did not seem flustered.

"Are you saying it's a forgery?" Rosenbaum asked. This was the typical defense in such cases — the Soviets had faked the evidence — and Rosenbaum expected nothing less now. But Lileikis surprised him. "I don't know," he said. "It may be real, it may be not. I'm not saying it's not real. It could be that my men did things under my name without telling me."

Then Lileikis spoke the words that Rosenbaum would remember like the sound of nails on a chalkboard for years to come. "Show me something that I signed," he said.

Was that a slight smile that Rosenbaum thought he saw? The old man sounded smug, almost as if he were daring the Justice Department: *Show me something that I signed.* Lileikis had studied law in Lithuania, and he appeared to have learned it well. He wasn't admitting anything. Rosenbaum knew he would need more than just Lileikis's name typed on a prison form if he wanted to deport him. Too many cases had fallen apart in the last few years over less. He would need a signature, an eyewitness, an admission. He needed proof that Lileikis really had been a "desk murderer." Rosenbaum knew he didn't have it. He left the pretty yellow house on Sumner Street and headed back to Washington empty-handed.

The investigation stalled. Rosenbaum couldn't find anything else to link Lileikis to the brutal crimes. Ten long years passed. The Berlin Wall came down. The Baltic republics became free nations. And finally, Mike MacQueen found the canvas-bound notebook in the long-hidden archives. During those ten years, Lileikis lived quietly in Boston, hearing nothing from the Justice Department.

The case had languished for so long that Rosenbaum, a junior lawyer on the Nazi team when he first knocked on Lileikis's door, was now running the office. The documents unearthed by MacQueen, Rosenbaum believed, were enough to finally move ahead in trying to deport Lileikis. A nervousness pervaded the Nazi unit in the wake of the Ivan the Terrible fiasco. The Justice Department couldn't afford any more big mistakes. But to Rosenbaum, the case now seemed rock-solid.

Just one thing bothered him as he prepared to request approval from the higher-ups at the Justice Department: Lileikis was now eighty-seven years old. The Nazi team had never prosecuted anyone that old before. Even with accused Nazis in their sixties or seventies, critics inevitably howled over the defendant's age: Why, they asked, was the Justice Department hounding old men who belonged in a nursing home, not a courtroom? They should be left alone. Even some Holocaust survivors in America thought the time for punishment had passed. "These criminals must now be in their eighties and on their way out," one Auschwitz survivor wrote to the Justice Department when he was asked to testify in a case. "Let God deal with them, if he hasn't already."

Rosenbaum disagreed. The refrain that these men were too old to be prosecuted was heard so often that he had a stock response he delivered to anyone who raised it: There was no statute of limitations for the monstrous crimes that had made these men unworthy to call themselves Americans. Holocaust survivors shouldn't have to live alongside men who took part in genocide. And the United States needed to send a message, he said, to anyone else who might be looking for a haven to escape their past crimes: They were not welcome here, no matter how old they were. So long as these men were fit enough to stand trial, Rosenbaum wanted to go after them. He just prayed that they stayed alive long enough to be sent away in disgrace.

At the Justice Department, he laid out the evidence against Lileikis for Mark Richard, the senior official who had to sign off on bringing the case in court. "You should know," Rosenbaum said, "that he's eighty-seven." He paused, waiting for the pushback. Just in case, he had even put together what he impolitely called his "geezer file," filled with prosecutions of other elderly defendants accused of standard crimes much less appalling than rounding up Jews or delivering them to execution squads. "This is easily the oldest person we've ever recommended," Rosenbaum continued, "but I think when you read the file, you'll see why. He caused these people to be delivered to their murderers." Rosenbaum waited, but there was no objection from his boss. He didn't even need to bring out his geezer list. Richard made clear that he didn't care how old Lileikis was, so long as the evidence against him was solid. Go ahead and file the case, he told Rosenbaum.

Everything was a go. But just as he was readying the final charges that fall of 1994, Rosenbaum got a call. "Eli, you can't file this case," the caller said. It was a lawyer for the CIA. Officials at Langley had learned the Justice Department was about to bring Nazi charges against their onetime spy, Lileikis, and they were not happy. The CIA did not want to risk seeing classified records on Lileikis's spy work spilling into public view, the lawyer told Rosenbaum. "We can't guarantee you'll be able to produce the documents in court," the lawyer said. "You can't file this case," he repeated.

Rosenbaum was startled by the demand. Unknown to him, the CIA had used much the same tactic years earlier to muddy a number of budding Justice Department investigations into Nazis-turned-CIA spies like Otto von Bolschwing in California and Tom Soobzokov in New Jersey. But for Rosenbaum, still new to the director's job at the Nazi-hunting unit, this was a first. He had never confronted a demand like this himself. He wasn't sure what to say. The CIA had no formal authority to shut down a Justice Department investigation, he knew, but he couldn't just ignore the CIA's claims that they were protecting national secrets. "Look, I tell you what," Rosenbaum said finally, grasping for a compromise. "If we have to produce his records in court and you tell us we can't release them, well, then, we will dismiss the case." It was an unusual arrangement for both sides, but his CIA counterpart seemed satisifed. "Okay," he said. The agency stood down. Its secret connections to Lileikis were still safe.

Days later, in the fall of 1994, prosecutors filed their case at the federal courthouse in Boston, calling Lileikis one of the most important Nazi collaborators ever targeted by the United States. In announcing the prosecution, Rosenbaum made sure to mention Fruma and Gitta Kaplan. Like Mike MacQueen, he too had been touched by their story. This was not just about faceless victims, but real people. "Fifty-three years ago, on a day in late December 1941, a little girl, just six years old, was removed from a cell at the dreaded Vilnius Hard Labor Prison," Rosenbaum told reporters. "She was taken, with her mother, to a heavily wooded site a few miles from the city." This was Ponary, he said, "a place from which, as all of the terrorized Jews of Vilna knew, there was no return."

Reporters rushed to Lileikis's neighborhood afterward to try to interview the eighty-seven-year-old man who had been unmasked just hours before as the security police chief in Nazi-occupied Lithuania. "No comment," he said as he slammed the door.

Sixteen months later, after a long bout of legal wrangling, Lileikis showed up at a third-floor conference room at the federal courthouse in Boston to face questions from federal prosecutors at a sworn deposition. His lawyer and his priest from his Lithuanian church sat with him at the long conference table, as prosecutors questioned him for three hours. He was scared, he admitted to his lawyer, but he hid his fears behind a wall of silence. He had no interest in answering the Justice Department's questions, even as the lawyers showed him one arrest order after another with his signature on them.

"Did anyone order you to turn Gitta and Fruma Kaplan over to the German security police?" the prosecutor asked as he showed Lileikis the prison record with their names.

"Fifth Amendment," Lileikis said tersely. He was not going to incriminate himself by answering.

"What ultimately happened to Gitta and Fruma Kaplan?" the prosecutor continued.

"Fifth Amendment," he repeated.

"You knew, did you not, that most or all of the people who you turned over to the German security police would be killed?" the lawyer asked.

"Fifth Amendment," Lileikis said again.

"Did you ever personally participate in the interrogation or torture of prisoners?" he was asked. Once more, Lileikis pleaded the Fifth.

Again and again, the prosecutors asked Lileikis about his role in rounding up Jews for slaughter, and again and again, he refused to answer, with no hint of regret. The prosecutors could ask him whatever questions they wanted about Vilnius; he wasn't talking.

His silence did not help him in court. A federal judge in Boston concluded that his refusal to answer such damning questions about his role in the war amounted to an admission of his complicity. Nor was the judge sympathetic to Lileikis's claims that he was essentially just an administrator in Vilnius with no real power — "a disembodied signer of orders," as Lileikis's own lawyers characterized it. At Nuremberg, the accused Nazis had claimed they were just following orders. Now, the judge scoffed, "Lileikis is attempting to stand the classic Nuremberg defense on its head by arguing that 'I was only *issuing* orders.'" Unimpressed, the judge stripped Lileikis of his American citizenship, saying he never should have been allowed in the country in the first place.

The decision was a much-needed win for the Justice Department's Nazi hunters. After botching the Ivan the Terrible case, the prosecutors had succeeded in deporting another significant perpetrator of the Holocaust. Yet at the CIA, the prosecution was an unwanted reminder of the agency's old ties to Lileikis. Once a valuable anti-Soviet asset, Lileikis was now nothing but a liability. With the Justice Department identifying him publicly as a Nazi collaborator, the CIA moved to distance itself from him as quickly as it could. In the spring of 1995, CIA officials wrote to their overseers at the House intelligence committee with a glossed-over account of the agency's involvement with Lileikis years earlier. "Although Lileikis was a CIA asset from 1952 to 1957," the CIA said in a classified letter to the intelligence committee, "there is no evidence that this Agency was aware of his wartime activities." The account was a gross distortion of what the CIA knew about Lileikis. In fact, there was plenty of evidence that the CIA was aware of his wartime activities. In the agency's own files was evidence that Lileikis "was possibly connected with the shooting of Jews in Vilna," that he worked "under the control of the Gestapo," and that his Nazi ties got him rejected the first time he tried to come to America. None of that was mentioned in the letter.

It had been four decades since Lileikis worked for the CIA in Europe. The Cold War was now over, Lileikis would soon be headed back to Lithuania to face war crimes charges, and the CIA agents who hired him as an American spy were long gone from the agency. Yet even in 1995, the CIA was still covering up what it knew about the Lithuanian immigrant's ties to the Nazis and his role in the brutal massacres at Ponary. For years, the

CIA had joined with Lileikis and dozens of other Nazi war criminals in a Faustian bargain against their common Soviet enemy. As the CIA's Allen Dulles said after meeting with Himmler's chief of staff, General Wolff, over a bottle of Scotch, American spies "should be free to talk with the Devil himself" if it would help win the Cold War. But its own complicity in working with someone like Aleksandras Lileikis was still too damaging for the CIA to admit, even in 1995.

Deported to Lithuania in 1996, Lileikis died four years later, at the age of ninety-three, still awaiting a verdict in a courtroom in Vilnius on charges that he took part in the Nazi genocide there. Until the end, he denied any role in the massacres. He was the victim in all this, he insisted.

Twelve years later, in the winter of 2012, Eli Rosenbaum traveled from Washington to Lithuania. He was there to try to get the Lithuanians to take back another Nazi collaborator in Massachusetts, this one an ex-SS officer in Warsaw. But Fruma Kaplan was still on his mind.

During a break in the talks one morning, in the middle of a snowstorm, he arranged for a side trip to a nearby prison. A guard walked him down a long, cold cellblock. They stopped at a green metal door with the number 17 written in white at the top. This was Fruma's cell. The place had been modernized and now served as a maximum-security prison — not for Jews, but for convicted criminals. But the cell was still there, seventy years later. Rosenbaum asked to look inside. The guard opened the door to reveal another door lined with metal bars — and a young man standing inside. The prisoner seemed happy to have company. He smiled broadly and waved at the visitor in the trench coat.

The young man had no idea of the cell's history, but Rosenbaum did. He knew that Fruma Kaplan and her mother, Gitta, had spent three long weeks there in cell 17 in December of 1941 at the Lukiski "hard labor" prison after they had been discovered in hiding. He knew that Aleksandras Lileikis, with a swipe of his pen, had put them there — and that his next swipe of the pen sent them to their deaths.

Rosenbaum stood at the cell door in silence for a few minutes. When he had brought the case against Lileikis eighteen years earlier, his own daughter was six years old. He wondered what those three weeks must have been like for Fruma, sleeping in that godforsaken cell while Lileikis was in his office signing her death warrant. It must have been cold and dark on the concrete floor. He wondered if she knew the fate that awaited her. Had she ever heard the foreboding song sung in the ghetto? *All roads lead to Ponary, but no roads lead back.* At least Fruma and Gitta were together. They had each other.

Rosenbaum had another stop to make. He wanted to follow Fruma's path. He wanted to go to Ponary. An oversize black SUV from the American Embassy in Vilnius took him and three American colleagues on a snow-packed road, six miles outside the city. It was a comfortable drive; nothing like the hellish trek that Fruma and Gitta would have endured en route from the prison. The Nazis had probably marched them on foot through the snow, with dozens of others, in a grim processional that cold December day. Or maybe, if they were lucky, mother and daughter avoided the march and rode in a Nazi truck packed with other hungry, filthy prisoners. Either way, they would have ended up at the edge of that horrible pit — the same one that Rosenbaum was now tramping through the deep snow to reach.

No one else was there, and the place was eerily quiet. The clearing was blanketed in a sea of white, with a row of tall, arching pine trees giving way to a gentle slope. It was bucolic. In another place, this might have been the perfect setting for a little girl to go sledding. But here, the slope led down to a cavernous ring about twenty-five yards wide. Before the war it had been a petroleum excavation site. The ditch itself was now filled with snow, but the outer rim was still visible to the eye: a marker of horror. A stone memorial with a Star of David and a menorah carved on it marked the site. It was the closest thing to a gravestone that Fruma would ever have. Rosenbaum could almost picture what it must have been like for her and the many thousands of victims brought here: stripped down, lined up, shot dead. He hoped the end was short for Fruma. Maybe she was still together with her mother, as they had been for those three weeks in cell 17.

Standing at the edge of the ditch, Rosenbaum thought of Aleksandras Lileikis's smugness in 1983. *Show me something that I signed.* It had taken a long time, too long, but the Justice Department had finally shown him something. They finally got him. That held special importance to Rosenbaum. To outsiders who hadn't seen the things he had seen, Lileikis might have seemed like just another Nazi who made it into America, but it was more than that for Rosenbaum. He had taken down Lileikis for Fruma's memory. The bastard who signed her death warrant had died in disgrace, haunted by his past.

Rosenbaum had been at this for nearly thirty years. What started as a summer internship in an office that was supposed to be around for only a few years had instead turned into a career spent chasing Nazis. He knew what some people called him: a zealot, a man too emotional about his job to see things through the sober lens of law enforcement. He always winced at the word, but if being a zealot meant he was passionate about chasing Nazis, so be it. That much he would admit. In his time there, the Justice Department had brought more than one hundred successful denaturalization and deportation cases against Americans with Nazi ties. It was justice delayed, but it was something. How many others had gotten away? How many other Eichmann aides and SS officers and Sobibor guards and Nazi collaborators in America had lived out their lives undiscovered? Hundreds, certainly, Rosenbaum knew. Thousands, probably. Perhaps even more than ten thousand, as another Justice Department prosecutor had once estimated. The truth was that no one really knew, because the United States had made it so easy for them to fade seamlessly into the fabric of the country. America's disinterest in Nazis after the war was so prolonged, its obsession with the Cold War so acute, its immigration policies so porous, that Hitler's minions had little reason to fear they would be discovered. How many Nazis had lived and died quietly as free men in their adopted country, with their death notices silent about their horrific crimes? Too many, Rosenbaum knew. That was the only real answer. However many Nazis had called America their home after the war, it was too many.

Rosenbaum peered one last time at the snow-covered pit. It now looked so deceptively peaceful, nothing like the godforsaken place it must have been seven decades earlier. He trudged through the deep snow, making his way back down the hill, back down the road from Ponary that the Jews in the ghetto used to sing about as they awaited their certain deaths. They never had the chance to take the road back out of Ponary, but Rosenbaum did. He got back in the SUV. He still had a few more Nazis left to chase.

EPILOGUE

In 2010, a secret internal history of the government's decades-long hunt for war criminals concluded that the United States became a refuge for the Nazis after World War II. "America, which prided itself on being a safe haven for the persecuted, became — in some small measure — a safe haven for persecutors as well," the Justice Department report acknowledged.

Sixty-five years after the war, it was the first time the U.S. government had made such a stark admission.

In 2011, a German court convicted John Demjanjuk, the onetime Ohio autoworker, of taking part in the murders of twenty-eight thousand prisoners as a guard at Sobibor. The ninety-one-year-old Demjanjuk lay motionless in a cot set up for him in the courtroom as the verdict was read. In a case that had proven such a black eye for the U.S. Justice Department for decades, prosecutors maintained that justice had finally been achieved.

Demjanjuk died the next year, claiming innocence until the end.

In 2012, with Tom Soobzokov's murder still unsolved after more than a quarter century, his son pressed authorities to reopen the investigation. Internal FBI documents showed that agents in the 1980s tracked several Jewish militants in the United States and Israel who were suspected in the bombing at Soobzokov's New Jersey home and in three other pipe-bombings linked to it. Soobzokov's son, Aslan, charged as part of a lawsuit that prosecutors failed to bring charges against anyone because of his father's notoriety as a Nazi.

The lawsuit was ultimately tossed out, and the Supreme Court refused to hear the case. The bombings remain unsolved.

In 2013, pressure from its own scientists led the Space Medicine Association to stop giving out its annual Strughold Award, named for "the father of space medicine," Dr. Hubertus Strughold, one of the first Nazi scientists brought to America in Project Paperclip. While Dr. Strughold's name had been dropped years earlier from a number of other tributes, the space association had been the final holdout. It finally bowed to complaints from scientists who were uncomfortable with the idea of honoring a man implicated in gruesome Nazi medical experiments.

Prosecutors continued investigating some of the surviving Paperclip scientists into the twenty-first century. Among them was Wernher von Braun's brother, Magnus, a rocket engineer in the V-2 slave-labor camp at Dora who also came to America under Paperclip. Prior to his death in Arizona in 2003, prosecutors were still scrutinizing Magnus von Braun's wartime role with the Nazis. Only one Nazi scientist — von Braun's deputy, Arthur Rudolph, the engineer forced out of the United States in 1984 — was ever prosecuted in America for his work with the Nazis.

In 2014, authorities arrested one of America's last surviving Nazis — eighty-nine-year-old Johann Breyer — at his red brick townhouse in Philadelphia. He was charged with taking part in the gassings of 216,000 Jews at Auschwitz as a Nazi "Death's Head" guard at the concentration camp. Breyer, who volunteered for the SS at age seventeen in his native Czechoslovakia, admitted being a guard at Auschwitz, but insisted he had nothing to do with the notorious killing operations. Prosecutors did not believe him, and a judge in July ordered him sent back to Germany to face war crimes charges. Seven decades had not dulled his involvement in "Nazi atrocities against humanity," the judge said. "No statute of limitations offers a safe haven for murder," he wrote.

But for the onetime Auschwitz guard and thousands of Nazis like him,

America had proven to be exactly that: a safe haven for Hitler's men, a place where unthinkable war crimes were easily concealed and quickly forgotten.

On the very day he was ordered back to Germany, Johann Breyer died in a Philadelphia hospital. The retired toolmaker had lived freely in his adopted country for sixty-two years. "He's been hiding in plain sight," said the daughter of two Holocaust survivors in Philadelphia, "and, well, he got away with it. He lived a long life."

In the spring of 2015, auditors tallied up all the Social Security benefits that the U.S. government had paid out to Nazis in America over the past half century. The numbers were startling: beginning in the 1960s, when the wartime refugees started retiring, the U.S. government had paid out more than $20 million in benefits to at least 133 immigrants tied to Nazi atrocities — people like Arthur Rudolph, the Nazi slave-labor rocketeer. The actual total over the years was probably far higher. Indeed, a handful of elderly Nazis who had fled the United States to return to Europe were still receiving Social Security checks as of late 2014 — before Congress learned about the payments in the newspapers and belatedly cut them off amid the public uproar. The millions in retirement checks were yet another sobering confirmation of just how easily the Nazis had managed to settle into the fabric of America and call the place their home—with all the many benefits that came with it.

That same spring, one of the final postwar Nazi trials began in the northern German town of Lüneburg, as a ninety-three-year-old ex-SS officer known as the "accountant of Auschwitz" went on trial as an accomplice to mass murder. Oskar Gröning, an eager Nazi loyalist who volunteered for SS duty at the age of nineteen, was a bookkeeper at the concentration camp who collected all the cash, bank notes, and personal belongings from the trainloads of incoming prisoners before they were led away to the gas chambers. As he watched the Jews sent to their deaths, he felt nothing at a sight he regarded as routine, he admitted. His job was to count up the Nazi loot and send it on to Berlin, he said, and he did his job well.

After the war, Gröning lived a quiet, comfortable middle-class life in Germany with his wife, two sons, and their dachshund, collecting stamps and working as an accountant at a small factory. He spoke little of the war. After his secret was finally exposed, he stood contrite before a German court in April 2015 — seven decades after Hitler's defeat — and begged for forgiveness. The judges would have to decide, he told them, whether what he had done at Auschwitz made him guilty in the eyes of the law or not. Regardless, he said, "for me, there's no question that I share moral guilt." His pleas for mercy did little to sway the German judges. The onetime Nazi SS sergeant had gone unpunished for seventy years for "an unfathomable crime," the chief judge said that summer as he sentenced Gröning — now stooped and white-haired at age ninety-four — to four years in prison. "What you consider to be 'moral guilt' and what you depict as being a cog in the wheel," the judge told him, "is exactly what lawmakers view as being an accessory to murder."

Circle size indicates
number of cases

- 1
- 5
- 10
- 20

Where cases were prosecuted in district or immigration
court, the location is shown. In cases where the suspect fled
the country, died, or the case was otherwise unresolved,
the last known residence is used.

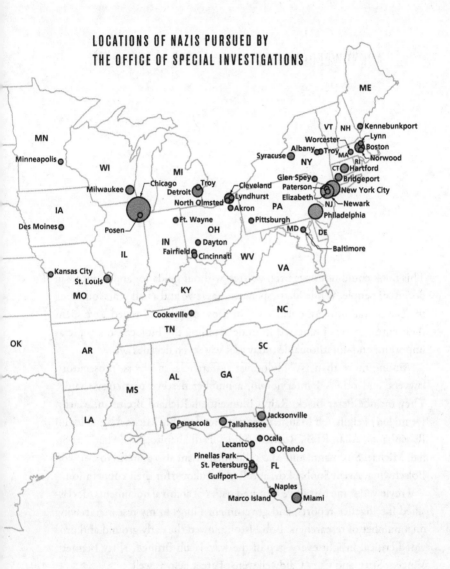

LOCATIONS OF NAZIS PURSUED BY
THE OFFICE OF SPECIAL INVESTIGATIONS

ME

MN

Minneapolis

WI
MI
Milwaukee   Chicago   Troy   Cleveland
                             Detroit   Lyndhurst
IA   North Olmsted   Akron
Des Moines   Ft. Wayne   PA
                             Posen   OH   Pittsburgh
                             IN   Dayton
                             Fairfield Cincinnati
IL   WV
Kansas City
St. Louis   KY
MO
                             Cookeville
                             TN   NC

OK
            AR   SC
                             AL   GA
            MS
            LA   Jacksonville
                             Pensacola Tallahassee
                                        Ocala
                             Lecanto   Orlando
                             Pinellas Park
                             St. Petersburg   FL
                             Gulfport
                                  Naples
                             Marco Island Miami

VT   NH   Kennebunkport
Worcester   Lynn
      Albany Troy MA   Boston
Syracuse   NY   RI   Norwood
            Glen Spey   CT   Hartford
            Paterson   Bridgeport
            Elizabeth   New York City
                  NJ   Newark
                        Philadelphia
                  MD
                        DE
                  Baltimore

VA

ACKNOWLEDGMENTS

This book could not have been written without guidance and input from dozens of people. While I have spent the past two and a half years following the Nazis' trail into America, many of those on whom I relied have spent their entire careers immersed in understanding the Holocaust, a topic as important and unfathomable today as it was seven decades ago.

Among more than 150 Holocaust researchers, survivors, prosecutors, lawyers, and others I interviewed, a number deserve particular thanks. They include Peter Black, Ralph Blumenthal, Richard Breitman, Martin Dean, Judy Feigin, Jeff Mausner, Martin Mendelsohn, Michael Neufeld, Eli Rosenbaum, Allan Ryan, Rochelle Saidel, Paul Shapiro, Neal Sher, Art Sinai, Michael Sussmann, and Mark Talisman. I am also grateful to Gus von Bolschwing, Aslan Soobzokov, and Rad Artukovic for their cooperation.

I reviewed some forty-five hundred pages of archival documents, declassified intelligence reports, and government filings in my research, relying on a number of researchers. Bob Elston plowed the early ground and provided critical insight every step of the way. Jacob Brunell, Kitty Bennett, Vincent Slatt, and Cary Caldwell were of great help as well.

Two works were invaluable. An internal Justice Department report, *The Office of Special Investigations: Striving for Accountability in the Aftermath of the Holocaust,* by Judy Feigin, which I first wrote about in the *New York Times* in 2010, provided the impetus for this book and proved an exhaustive resource. *U.S. Intelligence and the Nazis,* by Richard Breitman, Norman J. W. Goda, Timothy Naftali, and Robert Wolfe, was indispensable as well.

I am also indebted to friends and colleagues who took the time to read rough drafts. Lenny Bernstein, Bob Elston, Kevin Johnson, Marc Lacey, and Scott Shane helped shape the manuscript from something barely readable to its current form. Martin Kanovsky and Ellen Teller, Anita Lichtblau and Richard Brunell, Matt Lait, Jennifer Maisel, Cathy and Len Unger, and Nancy and Harold Zirkin offered important feedback as well. Our children — Matthew, Andrew, Annabel, and Harold — provided constant inspiration through their questions and curiosity, and left me confident that future generations will not forget the Holocaust. And my wife, Leslie, read through countless late-night revisions, when she would no doubt rather have been sleeping. She provided a font of ideas and somehow kept things together at home all the while.

My literary agent, Ronald Goldfarb, saw the potential in this project from the very beginning, while Bruce Nichols, my editor at Houghton Mifflin Harcourt, shepherded the project through its various fits and starts with a keen eye and a gentle touch. My copyeditor, Melissa Dobson, put it all in final shape.

Lastly, the *New York Times* and executive editor Dean Baquet gave me the time and support to complete this project, while my 2013 fellowship at the Jack, Joseph and Morton Mandel Center for Advanced Holocaust Studies, part of the United States Holocaust Memorial Museum, provided critical access to its vast archives and top-notch researchers. The museum's mantra — "Never Again" — was a constant reminder of why this still matters.

NOTES

Prologue

page

xi *He was in trouble:* "Tscherim Soobzokov" file, Nazi War Crimes Interagency Working Group, Declassified Records of the Central Intelligence Agency (Record Group 263), National Archives and Records Administration. Some of the Soobzokov documents remain classified today.

long-ago friend John Grunz: In a number of letters to Soobzokov, his CIA handler identified himself as "John Grunz." This was almost certainly an alias. (See, for instance, letter to Soobzokov of February 14, 1956: "Looking forward to seeing you, I am. Yours Sincerely, John Grunz"; CIA Soobzokov file.)

secret psychological workups: CIA Soobzokov file, including internal memos referencing security reviews and polygraphing of Soobzokov on February 20–22, 1956.

xii *don't give him:* Internal CIA memo dated July 12, 1974, CIA Soobzokov file. The congressman was Representative Robert Roe of New Jersey, a friend of Soobzokov's.

xiii Führer of the North Caucasus: Accounts from fellow immigrants, including handwritten note from Isa Hoket, of Paterson, New Jersey, dated March 30, 1969; CIA Soobzokov file.

xiv *in the* New York Times!: Internal CIA memo of July 8, 1974, "Memorandum for the Record: Subject: Abd-Al-Karim Subzikov"; CIA Soobzokov files.

"ashamed to work for a Jew": Internal CIA memo on "Telephone call from SOOBZOKOV," August 11, 1958; CIA Soobzokov file.

xv *facing a "significant flap":* Internal CIA memo of July 12, 1974, on Soobzokov and public reports about his Nazi ties, CIA Soobzokov files.

xvi *J. Edgar Hoover had:* FBI letter, June 25, 1958, from Hoover to Dulles, director of CIA, regarding Dulles's "suggestion" in a letter nine days earlier that the FBI consider using Soobzokov as an informant; CIA Soobzokov files.

1. Liberation

1   *"human garbage"*: Jacob Biber, *Risen from the Ashes: A Story of Jewish Displaced Persons in the Aftermath of World War II* (San Bernardino, CA: Borgo, 1990).

2   *only forty thousand people:* Elmer B. Staats, Comptroller General of the United States, *Widespread Conspiracy to Obstruct Probes of Alleged Nazi War Criminals Not Supported by Available Evidence; Controversy May Continue,* report prepared for House Committee on the Judiciary, Subcommittee on Immigration, Citizenship, and International Law, released May 16, 1978.

    men like Jakob Reimer: United States v. Reimer, 2002, archived collection of Justice Department Office of Special Investigations records on file at United States Holocaust Memorial Museum; Reimer file.

    "He was never entitled": Ibid.

3   *they were bunked:* Mark Wyman, *DPs: Europe's Displaced Persons, 1945–1951* (Ithaca, NY: Cornell University Press, 1998), 134.

5   *"we do not exterminate them":* Earl G. Harrison, *The Plight of the Displaced Jews in Europe: A Report to President Truman* (New York: Reprinted by United Jewish Appeal for Refugees, Overseas Needs and Palestine on behalf of Joint Distribution Committee, United Palestine Appeal, National Refugee Service, 1945).

    "Harrison and his ilk": Personal journal of General George S. Patton, including entry for September 15, 1945; excerpts on file at United States Holocaust Memorial and Museum.

    "kikes" and "Jew boys": Michael Beschloss, *The Conquerors: Roosevelt, Truman, and the Destruction of Hitler's Germany, 1941–1945* (New York: Simon and Schuster, 2002), 200.

    "the Jews have no place to go": Michael Beschloss, *Presidential Courage: Brave Leaders and How They Changed America, 1789–1989* (New York: Simon & Schuster, 2007), 200.

6   Who can answer me?: Author interview with Miriam Isaacs, former fellow in residence at the Center for Advanced Holocaust Studies. Isaacs's research focused on music and oral culture of Holocaust survivors in Nazi camps and ghettos.

    "A general malaise was growing": Biber, *Risen from the Ashes.*

7   *Dmytro Sawchuk got a visa:* Justice Department case file on Sawchuk.

    "Asks for help": International Tracing Service search of Soobzokov records, United States Holocaust Memorial Museum.

    "Did We Beat the Nazis": Gerald Steinacher, *Nazis on the Run: How Hitler's Henchmen Fled Justice* (New York: Oxford University Press, 2011), 173.

8   *secret cable on the Nazis' flight:* Ralph Blumenthal and E. J. Dionne Jr., "Vatican Is Reported to Have Furnished Aid to Fleeing Nazis," *New York Times,* January 26, 1984.

10 *"living royally in a ski hotel":* Daniel Lang, "A Romantic Urge," *New Yorker,* April 21, 1951.

11 *"don't put that in the papers":* Reimer file, United States Holocaust Memorial Museum.

12   *"a thousand little Führers"*: Opening statement by Jackson at Nuremberg trial, November 21, 1945; video on file at United States Holocaust Memorial Museum.

13   *"It is all forgotten"*: Reimer file, United States Holocaust Memorial Museum.

2. The Good Nazis

14   *they sat by a crackling fire*: Allen W. Dulles, *The Secret Surrender: The Classic Insider's Account of the Secret Plot to Surrender Northern Italy During WWII* (Guilford, CT: Lyons, 2006), 96.

15   *persuaded their Latin American neighbors*: Max Paul Friedman, *Nazis and Good Neighbors: The United States Campaign Against the Germans of Latin America in World War II* (New York: Cambridge University Press, 2003), 2–6.
      "heart had not really been in the Nazi cause": Petronella Wyatt, "The Quality of Mercy," *Spectator,* February 1, 2003, p. 48, quoting Ned Putzell, former intelligence official under William Donovan for the Office of Strategic Services at the Nuremberg trials.

16   *included remarkably little*: Neal H. Petersen, ed., *From Hitler's Doorstep: The Wartime Intelligence Reports of Allen Dulles, 1942–1945* (University Park: Pennsylvania State University Press, 1996), 50. Petersen describes Dulles's intelligence reports to Washington on the topic of the Holocaust as "inexplicably meager."
      "I do not see much": Dulles cables to OSS headquarters in Washington in 1943; cited in ibid., 63–64, 188–90.
      simply enjoyed a stroll: Photos on file at United States Holocaust Memorial Museum of Himmler and Wolff together, including photo no. 60466 of the two men taking a walk on Himmler's birthday in 1941; and Jochen von Lang, *Top Nazi: SS General Karl Wolff; the Man Between Hitler and Himmler* (New York: Enigma, 2005), 45–46.

17   *"it was an honor"*: Ibid., 358.
      "bureaucrat of death": Michael Salter, *Nazi War Crimes, U.S. Intelligence, and Selective Prosecution at Nuremberg: Controversies Regarding the Role of the Office of Strategic Services* (New York: Routledge-Cavendish, 2007).
      "wholesale slaughter of populations": Office of Strategic Services, Research and Analysis Branch, *Principal Nazi Organizations Involved in the Commission of War Crimes: The Nazi Party,* R & A report no. 3133.7, September 10, 1945.
      "save their skins": Salter, *Nazi War Crimes,* 113.

18   *"free to talk to the Devil himself"*: Dulles, *The Secret Surrender,* 87.
      a list of character references: Ibid., 93.
      more moderate element in Waffen SS: Cable from Dulles to Washington after meeting with General Wolff on March 8, 1945, reprinted in Petersen, *From Hitler's Doorstep.*
      "no ogre": Dulles, *The Secret Surrender,* 61.

19   *"He was good-looking"*: Ibid., 71.
      "protect certificates from being sent to Germany": Secret cable from Allen Dulles to OSS headquarters in Washington, March 12, 1945. It is not clear what happened to the

stock certificates or whether General Wolff was able to hold on to them with Dulles's help. The certificates were likely looted from Jews who had been killed or imprisoned on Wolff's orders.

A grateful Wolff thanked: Dulles, *The Secret Surrender,* 190–91.

"If after my death": Ibid., 157.

Germans and Italians: Richard Breitman, *Analysis of the Name File of Guido Zimmer,* Nazi War Crimes Interagency Working Group, Declassified Records of the Central Intelligence Agency (Record Group 263), National Archives and Records Administration.

20 *"such distrust, such lack of faith":* Secret diplomatic cable from FDR to Stalin, April 3, 1945, as cited in Petersen, *From Hitler's Doorstep,* 637.

even went yachting: Gaston Cobentz and Seymour Freidin, "Strange Story of an SS General," *New York Herald Tribune,* January 23, 1962; and Kerstin von Lingen, "Conspiracy of Silence: How the 'Old Boys' of American Intelligence Shielded SS General Karl Wolff from Prosecution," *Holocaust and Genocide Studies* 22, no. 1 (Spring 2008), 74–109.

allies "owe some moral obligation": Christopher Simpson, *Blowback: America's Recruitment of Nazis and Its Effects on the Cold War* (New York: Weidenfeld & Nicolson, 1988), 92; and Richard Breitman et al., *U.S. Intelligence and the Nazis* (New York: Cambridge University Press, 2005), 317–29.

21 *"It is thanks to Mr. Dulles":* Von Lingen, "Conspiracy of Silence," 90.

"much more inhumane": Von Lang, *Top Nazi,* 318.

"lost more than his shirt": Von Lingen, "Conspiracy of Silence," 93, citing letter from Dulles to a Swiss intelligence officer on June 12, 1950, after Wolff complained publicly about his treatment. While Dulles helped Wolff escape prosecution at Nuremberg after the war, the West Germans took a new look at his case two decades later, and the Nazi general was imprisoned for five years for complicity in genocide. As he faced his belated jailing in 1963, Wolff again reached out to Dulles for help. But Dulles, fired as CIA director two years earlier, declined to come to his aid this time.

22 *"if you need these men":* Raymond Daniell, "Denazification Hit by U.S. Officers," *New York Times,* September 21, 1945.

"I could not have done it": Transcript of interview with Dr. Hubertus Strughold, U.S. Air Force Oral History Project, Office of Air Force History, conducted November 25, 1974, p. 14. Obtained under Freedom of Information Act.

23 *"I was transported":* André Sellier, *A History of the Dora Camp,* translated by Stephen Wright and Susan Taponier (Chicago: I. R. Dee, 2003), 77.

24 *prevent German chemists:* Tom Bower, *The Paperclip Conspiracy: The Hunt for the Nazi Scientists* (Boston: Little, Brown and Company, 1987), 121.

25 *"little scientific acumen":* Linda Hunt, *Secret Agenda: The United States Government, Nazi Scientists, and Project Paperclip, 1945 to 1990* (New York: St. Martin's, 1991), 91.

26 *"'beating a dead Nazi horse'":* March 1948 letter from Navy to State Department; Declassified CIA war crimes files, National Archives and Records Administration, "Paperclip" collection.

27   *The military said it was "cognizant":* Hunt, *Secret Agenda,* 100–101.

     "Memo to would-be war criminal": Joachim Joesten, "This Brain for Hire," *Nation,* January 11, 1947.

28   *an article charging:* Drew Pearson, "Air Force Hires Nazi Doctor Linked to Ghastly Experiments," *Washington Merry-Go-Round,* syndicated column, July 14, 1952.

29   *"no longer refer to them as Germans":* Transcript of interview with Colonel Paul C. Campbell, MD, U.S. Air Force Oral History Project, Office of Air Force History, November 22, 1974, and June 10–11, 1976, p. 36. Obtained through Freedom of Information Act.

30   *"We knew what we were doing":* Simpson, *Blowback,* 159.

     "The West is fighting": GAO Report on Nazi War Criminals in the United States, Oversight Hearing Before the Subcommittee on Immigration, Refugees, and International Law of the Committee on the Judiciary, House of Representatives, 99th Congress, 1st sess., 1985 (Washington, DC: Government Printing Office, 1986), 37.

     wouldn't work for them: Richard Breitman and Norman J. W. Goda, *Hitler's Shadow: Nazi War Criminals, U.S. Intelligence, and the Cold War* (Washington, DC: National Archives and Records Administration, 2010), 41.

     executed 277 German: Thomas Alan Schwartz, "John J. McCloy and the Landsberg Cases," in *American Policy and the Reconstruction of West Germany, 1945–55,* edited by Jeffry M. Diefendorf, Axel Frohn, and Hermann-Josef Rupieper (Washington, DC: German Historical Institute; Cambridge: Cambridge University Press, 1993).

31   *McCloy in 1944 had rejected:* Richard Breitman and Allan J. Lichtman, *FDR and the Jews* (Boston: The Belknap Press of Harvard University Press, 2013) 283–4; and other sources.

     "Now that the Americans have Korea": Ibid.

32   *"inestimable value":* Breitman et al., *U.S. Intelligence and the Nazis,* 253.

     Gustav Hilger: "Gustav Hilger" file, Nazi War Crimes Interagency Working Group, Declassified Records of the Central Intelligence Agency (Record Group 263), National Archives and Records Administration.

     "I feel no need": Gustav Hilger and Alfred G. Meyer, *Incompatible Allies: A Memoir-History of German-Soviet Relations, 1918–1941* (New York: Macmillan, 1953), 272.

33   *Barbie seemed like:* Allan A. Ryan, *Klaus Barbie and the United States Government: A Report to the Attorney General of the United States* (Washington, DC: U.S. Department of Justice, Criminal Division, 1983).

     "Now was the ideal time": Breitman et al., *U.S. Intelligence and the Nazis,* 380.

     at least a hundred, by one count: Ibid., 377. Dozens of Gestapo and SD members served in the Gehlen spy organization — on the American payroll. With four thousand operatives in the Gehlen group at its peak in the early 1950s, the actual number of Nazi war criminals among them was likely much higher than one hundred.

34   *They were untouchable:* Gehlen amassed enormous influence in postwar Germany with the backing of the Americans and led West Germany's intelligence service, the BND, for more than a decade after its creation in 1956.

     "He is convinced": Breitman et al., *U.S. Intelligence and the Nazis,* 356.

35   *as "insurance" against something:* Ibid., 357.
      "He is a Nazi": U.S. intelligence memo, April 17, 1945; "Wilhelm Hoettl" file, Nazi
      War Crimes Interagency Working Group, Declassified Records of the Central Intel-
      ligence Agency (Record Group 263), National Archives and Records Administration.
36   *Dulles agreed:* Ibid.
      "incomprehensible to all decent Germans": Breitman et al., *U.S. Intelligence and the Na-
      zis,* 274.
38   *"no subtantiation of the allegations":* Ibid., 229.
      Hoover didn't want the president ambushed: Ibid.
39   *pogroms in Bucharest:* Allan A. Ryan Jr., *Quiet Neighbors: Prosecuting Nazi War Crim-
      inals in America* (San Diego: Harcourt Brace Jovanovich, 1984), 228.
40   *"need men like J. Edgar Hoover":* Breitman et al., *U.S. Intelligence and the Nazis,* 243.

3. "Minor War Crimes"

41   *A former Nazi SS officer:* CIA Soobzokov files.
43   *"sparkling and vivacious":* CIA Soobzokov files, including internal CIA memos from
      security reviews and polygraphing of Soobzokov on February 20–22, 1956.
      "we are not at all interested": Memo of October 8, 1952, written by Kermit Roosevelt,
      the CIA's station chief in the region; CIA Soobzokov file. A grandson of President
      Theodore Roosevelt, Kermit Roosevelt engineered the 1953 overthrow of the Iranian
      government.
46   *"somewhat reluctant":* CIA internal security report on polygraph examinations of Feb-
      ruary 20 and 22, 1956, CIA Soobzokov files.
      "minor war crimes": Ibid.
      "regarding war crimes": Internal memo of March 9, 1953; CIA Soobzokov files.
48   *"awful to watch":* Quoted in Irmgard von Zur Mühlen and Bengt von Zur Mühlen,
      The Trial of Krasnodar, 1943 ([Germany]: Chronos Film, 1987), VHS, 55 min.
49   *"You see before you":* Ibid.
52   *"ashamed to work for a Jew":* CIA internal memo on "Telephone call from SOOBZO-
      KOV," August 11, 1958, CIA Soobzokov files.

4. Echoes from Argentina

66   *got off a ramshackle bus:* Peter Z. Malkin and Harry Stein, *Eichmann in My Hands:
      A Compelling First-Person Account by the Israeli Agent Who Captured Hitler's Chief
      Executioner* (New York: Warner, 1990).
      a well-appointed apartment: Author interview with Gus von Bolschwing, son of Otto
      von Bolschwing.
67   *von Bolschwing feared:* "Otto von Bolschwing" file, Nazi War Crimes Interagency
      Working Group, Declassified Records of the Central Intelligence Agency (Re-

cord Group 263), National Archives and Records Administration. Some of the von Bolschwing documents remain classified today.

"*A largely anti-Jewish atmosphere*": Breitman et al., *U.S. Intelligence and the Nazis;* and Judy Feigin, *The Office of Special Investigations: Striving for Accountability in the Aftermath of the Holocaust*, ed. Mark M. Richard (draft report of United States Justice Department, December 2008), 259–61.

68 "*Heil Hitler*": Feigin, *The Office of Special Investigations*, 270.

"*the least of all evils*": Testimony in Adolf Eichmann trial, July 10, 1961.

69 "*loyalty to the United States*": CIA internal memo of February 2, 1961, CIA von Bolschwing files.

70 *$20,000 a year:* Ibid.

"*rests almost entirely*": Ibid.

71 "*Consider it essential*": Ibid., and Breitman et al., *U.S. Intelligence and the Nazis.* The author of the CIA memo urging protection for von Bolschwing was Richard Helms, who went on to become director of the CIA.

72 *Warner-Lambert and the Cabot Corporation:* Author interview with Gus von Bolschwing, son of Otto von Bolschwing.

Not until the Israelis: Scott Shane, "C.I.A. Knew Where Eichmann Was Hiding, Documents Show," *New York Times,* June 7, 2006; and Breitman and Goda, *Hitler's Shadow,* 13–14.

73 "*failed to advise us*": February 1961 memo, CIA von Bolschwing files.

74 "*The purpose of the meeting*": Internal memo recapping von Bolschwing's meeting with two CIA officers on May 15, 1961; CIA von Bolschwing files.

5. Tilting at Swastikas

77 *packed into a meeting hall:* Personal papers and unpublished memoir of Charles E. Allen, archived at the YIVO Institute for Jewish Research, New York; and *Chicago Sentinel,* May 30, 1963.

78 "*forbidden all clergy to aid Jews*": Charles Allen, "Nazi War Criminals Among Us," *Jewish Currents,* April 1963, 37.

79 "*doing combat against these wahoos*": Rochelle G. Saidel, *The Outraged Conscience: Seekers of Justice for Nazi War Criminals in America* (Albany: State University of New York Press, 1984), 59.

fell for a Jewish refugee: Ibid., 70.

80 "*Listen, mister*": Allen, "Nazi War Criminals Among Us," 11.

81 "*We were very glad*": Quoted in "Barbie Called One of Many Nazis Aided by U.S.," Reuters, February 20, 1983.

82 *let loose ten white mice:* Allen personal papers.

"*one of the cute tricks*": *Chicago Sentinel,* May 30, 1963.

had used the same tactic: Ben Urwand, "The Chilling History of How Hollywood Helped Hitler," *Hollywood Reporter,* August 9, 2013.

83   *Allen jotted down:* Allen personal papers.

      he "is potentially dangerous": FBI national security memo signed by J. Edgar Hoover, February 12, 1968; copy among Allen personal papers.

84   *Hoover secured from FDR:* Sanford J. Ungar, *FBI: An Uncensored Look Behind the Walls* (Boston: Little, Brown, 1975), 101.

      The FBI had plenty of help: Allen personal papers.

      "Will ascertain subject's plans": Internal FBI security memo on Charles R. Allen Jr., 1965; copy among Allen personal papers.

85   *"in a front group":* Under the Freedom of Information Act, Allen secured thousands of pages of documents that the FBI, CIA, and other intelligence agencies had compiled on him. He sued the government over what he charged was an illegal years-long surveillance and ultimately won an unusual $1,000 settlement from the CIA as a result.

      Allen wrote to the Justice Department: Allen personal papers.

      DeLoach, in an internal memo: Memo from FBI to Justice Department on Allen inquiries, January 10, 1963; copy among Allen personal papers.

      "Dear Mr. Allen": Allen personal papers.

86   *a chance conversation:* Simon Wiesenthal, *Justice Not Vengeance* (London: Mandarin, 1990), 163.

87   *whipped the child:* Ibid., 164.

      Wiesenthal went first: Allen Levy, *Nazi Hunter: The Wiesenthal File* (London: Robinson, 2002), 388.

88   *under the headline:* Clyde A. Farnsworth, "Sleuth with 6 Million Clients," *New York Times Magazine,* February 2, 1964, p. 11.

      named Joe Lelyveld: Lelyveld, a young reporter when he wrote the Braunsteiner Ryan story, later became the top editor at the *New York Times.*

      He got lucky: Joseph Lelyveld, "Breaking Away," *New York Times Magazine,* March 6, 2005.

      "a Housewife in Queens": Joseph Lelyveld, "Former Nazi Camp Guard Is Now a Housewife in Queens," *New York Times,* July 14, 1964.

6. In the Pursuit of Science

90   *"Does 'Hubertus Strughold' mean anything to you?":* Allen personal papers on Strughold; and Charles R. Allen Jr., "Hubertus Strughold, Nazi in USA," *Jewish Currents,* December 1974.

      a former INS investigator named Tony DeVito: Allen did not identify DeVito by name in his 1974 article in *Jewish Currents,* describing him only as an investigator with the INS.

92   *"Go tell it to your congressman!":* Author interview with Bruno Manz, German soldier and scientist who came to America as part of Project Paperclip and worked with von Braun.

      Disney happened to be aboard: Strughold interview, Air Force Oral History Project.

93   *von Braun clutched: Walt Disney Treasures — Tomorrow Land: Disney in Space and Beyond* (Los Angeles: Disney Inc., 1959), video.

94   *a dozen tours von Braun had taken:* Transcript of 1969 deposition of von Braun in New Orleans; translated from German by Martin Dean, scholar at United States Holocaust Memorial Museum.
      a "new Napoleon": Michael J. Neufeld, *Von Braun: Dreamer of Space, Engineer of War* (New York: Vintage Books, 2008), 64.

95   *"We used to have thousands of Russian prisoners of war":* Lang, "A Romantic Urge."
      "that damned Nazi": Neufeld, *Von Braun,* 368.
      he was worried: Ibid., 428.

96   *"I never saw a dead person":* 1969 deposition of von Braun.
      "fortunately I have heard nothing more": Neufeld, *Von Braun,* 429.

97   *official Air Force biography:* Air Force biography for Strughold, 1958.
      he liked America so much: Strughold interview, Air Force Oral History Project.

98   *The Humane Society blocked him:* Ibid., 4.
      "I doubt that Lyndon Johnson": Ibid.

99   *"I had no affiliations with the Nazi Party":* Ibid., 15.

100   *featured some of the most graphic testimony:* Karl Brandt "Medical Case" files from Nuremberg War Crimes Trial, 1946–47, against twenty-three Nazi doctors (*United States of America v. Karl Brandt et al.*); file no. 2-3606, United States Holocaust Memorial Museum.

101   *"honorable, conscientious and self sacrificing" doctor:* Hunt, *Secret Agenda,* 88, describing Nazi doctor Oskar Schröder.
      "one of the first men": Colonel Campbell interview, Air Force Oral History Project.

102   *There at the conference:* Internal Justice Department investigative reports, 1980–86, on Strughold and Nuremberg "cold conference." Obtained by author under Freedom of Information Act.

103   *"He was the director":* Hunt, *Secret Agenda,* 85. (Chuck Allen's reporting in 1974 first focused public attention on Strughold's role in Nazi experiments and revealed evidence of his participation in the Nazis' infamous Nuremberg conference. A number of critical pieces of evidence against Strughold were unknown to Allen at the time and would come out publicly only years later.)
      adding traces of silver: Brandt "Medical Case" files, United States Holocaust Memorial Museum.

104   *"Ralphie!" he would chirp:* Author interview with Ralph Blumenthal, former *New York Times* reporter.
      The collaboration produced a story: Ralph Blumenthal, "Drive On Nazi Subjects a Year Later: No U.S. Legal Steps Have Been Taken," *New York Times,* November 23, 1974.

105   *"a distinguished scientist of international reputation":* Speech on the floor of the House of Representatives by Congressman González, defending Strughold, on June 12, 1974.
      immigration officials assured González: Letter from INS Commissioner Leonard

Chapman to Representative González, July 12, 1974; on file among Gonzáles's personal papers at University of Texas Briscoe Center for American History.

7. Out of the Shadows

106   *Tom Soobzokov sat out on the front porch:* Interviews with Lidia and Maira, longtime neighbors of Soobzokov. They asked that their last names not be used.

   Jewish protesters bussed across the river: Paterson Police Department files provided to author, and New Jersey newspaper accounts.

108   *"They've got the wrong man":* Author interview with Aslan Soobzokov, son of Tscherim "Tom" Soobzokov.

   "On my side is God and truth": Herb Jaffe, "Jerseyan Downplays Nazi Probe," *Sunday Star-Ledger,* March 12, 1978.

   "My family, friends, and kids": Judy Smagula, "Soobzokov Is Pleased by Report," *North Jersey Evening News,* May 29, 1979.

109   *He would go out to the port:* Deposition of Erdejib Emtil in *Soobzokov vs. CBS* libel suit.

   The local Teamsters union called him: "Union Cites Immigrant for Aiding Refugees," *Paterson Evening News,* January 24, 1966.

   "a story of persecution": Walter, "Refugee Moslems Convert Store into Mosque," *Paterson Evening News,* December 1, 1958.

110   *"rumors concerning Soobzokov's activities":* FBI report on Soobzokov, October 18, 1977; Soobzokov file, Nazi War Crimes Interagency Working Group, Declassified Records of the Federal Bureau of Investigation (Record Group 65), National Archives and Records Administration.

   "trying to expose a former Nazi killer": Internal FBI memo, October 14, 1977, citing a letter sent to the FBI on February 8, 1973, about Soobzokov from Hamed Bolotok of West Paterson, New Jersey; FBI Soobzokov file.

111   *His FBI handler never really trusted:* Author interview with John Reid, former FBI agent, who was Soobokov's handler in the 1960s as a bureau informant.

   into the boy's file: CIA memo, 1958, FBI Soobzokov file, regarding a twelve-year-old boy named Robert Barski, son of a Russian immigrant.

   a tip about one of Soobzokov's reputed: Howard Blum, *Wanted!: The Search for Nazis in America* (New York: Touchstone, 1989), 51.

112   *a few interviews with Soobzokov's accusers:* FBI investigative reports on interviews with Soobzokov's accusers, including internal memo, FBI Newark field office, August 20, 1975; Soobzokov FBI file.

   "'your führer *is Soobzokov'":* Ibid., 56.

113   *"un-American slanderous remarks":* Plaintiff's documents in Soobzokov libel case.

   brought along a powerful friend: Blum, *Wanted!,* 77.

   DeVito knew nothing of all the drama: Alleged Nazi War Criminals: Hearings Before the House Subcommittee on Immigration, Citizenship, and International Law of the Committee on the Judiciary, 95th Congress, 1st sess., part 2, 1977 (Washington: US Government Printing Office: 1978), 67.

114   *"This case is made to order!":* Blum, *Wanted!,* 33.

"hoping this will all blow over": CIA internal memo of July 12, 1974, CIA Soobzokov file.

"Latest Development in the NOSTRIL case": CIA internal memo, February 10, 1975, on "Latest Development in the NOSTRIL case"; CIA Soobzokov file.

115   *"pinch" them for money:* Ibid.

"He has certainly made plenty of enemies": Ibid.

116   *no evidence that Subject was involved in war crimes:* CIA Soobzokov file. Only later in the investigation did the investigators reach a deal with the CIA to get access to what the agency termed "sanitized" records from its 1950s files on Soobzokov. But some of the most incriminating documents — the polygraphed interviews for his security review, including Soobzokov's admissions about his wartime role — were withheld.

"You don't understand these things": Author interview with Harry C. Batchelder Jr., former assistant United States attorney on Soobzokov case.

117   *The charges in the book were "absolutely false":* Transcript of *MacNeil/Lehrer Report,* "Nazis in America," PBS, February 1, 1977.

119   *a shoddy product:* Allen personal papers.

walked into a gothic mansion: Allen personal papers.

120   *"wore his German uniform":* Herb Jaffe, *Star-Ledger* (New Jersey), coverage of Soobzokov case, 1977–78. Jaffe covered the Soobzokov case exhaustively for the New Jersey newspaper.

"You can wake up now": Allen personal papers.

"Soviets Provide Data": Jaffe, *Sunday Star-Ledger,* September 10, 1978.

121   *"When does World War II end":* Editorial, June 21, 1979, *Independent-Prospector* (New Jersey).

"You are a nazi butcher": FBI records on Soobzokov bombing obtained by author under Freedom of Information Act.

It was a homemade bomb: Paterson Police Department report, June 1, 1979.

122   *"The State Department was undoubtedly":* Internal Justice Department memo, "Prosecution memo re Tscherim Soobzokov," October 17, 1979, Joseph F. Lynch to Walter J. Rockler; obtained by author.

123   *The CIA produced:* CIA Soobzokov file, and "Draft Working Paper: Chapter Sixteen," undated internal CIA report tracing the history of the agency's involvement with early Justice Department Nazi prosecutions, including the Soobzokov case (declassified and released publicly in 2007), 4–19.

124   *the CIA hadn't let the Justice Department know:* Author interviews, and CIA, "Draft Working Paper."

Prosecutors did not believe: Author interview with Allan Ryan.

an impromptu party: Author interview with Maira, longtime neighbor of Soobzokov. She asked that her last name not be used.

"I was never afraid": Coverage in New Jersey newspapers statewide after dismissal of charges against Soobzokov, July 10, 1978.

8. "An Ugly Blot"

125   *Holtzman was livid:* Author interview with Elizabeth Holtzman, former member of Congress.

sat Holtzman down for a briefing: CIA, "Draft Working Paper," 18.

"sanctuary to suspected Nazis": Ibid.

126   *"It is doing nothing":* Holtzman interview; and Elizabeth Holtzman, *Who Said It Would Be Easy?* (New York: Arcade, 1996), 90.

laid out for her neatly: Holtzman interview.

127   *reporters in San Diego:* Author interview with Bob Dorn, former reporter for *San Diego Evening Tribune;* and Bob Dorn and Martin Gerchen, "Area Man Accused of Nazi War Crimes," *San Diego Evening Tribune,* October 14, 1976.

evidence that he had collaborated: An immigration panel ordered that Laipenieks be deported for his role in aiding the Nazis in Latvia as a police interrogator, but an appellate court threw out the deportation case in 1985. The judges found that while Laipenieks had admitted to helping round up Communist "sympathizers" for the Nazis, it was not proven that he had personally persecuted Jews. He died in the United States in 1998.

"Thank you once again": Feigin, *The Office of Special Investigations,* 119.

128   *"I'm not sure I'd tell you":* Bob Dorn, "CIA Denies Giving Aid to War Crimes Suspect," *San Diego Evening Tribune,* November 30, 1976.

a remarkable series of congressional hearings: Hearings Before the House Subcommittee on Immigration, August 3, 1977, and July 19–21, 1978.

"I can only ask 'why?'": Ibid., July 19, 1978.

129   *The two weren't on speaking terms:* Saidel, *The Outraged Conscience,* 87.

130   *the 1950s-era loophole was finally sealed:* Jeffrey N. Mausner, "Apprehending and Prosecuting Nazi War Criminals in the United States," *Nova Law Review* 15, no. 2 (Spring 1991); and Feigin, *The Office of Special Investigations,* 40.

lost three of the five cases: Ryan, *Quiet Neighbors,* 60.

as listeners in the courtroom gasped: Author interview with Andrew Krieg, former reporter for *Hartford Courant,* who covered the Florida trial of Feodor Fedorenko, where the mistaken identification took place. The trial judge threw out the case against Fedorenko in 1978, based in part on the shaky eyewitness testimony. But an appeals court reversed that decision. In the biggest legal win in the history of the Justice Department's Nazi office, the Supreme Court upheld Fedorenko's deportation in 1981 and affirmed the authority of the Justice Department to deport Americans who took part in Nazi atrocities. Fedorenko, a guard at Treblinka and at a Jewish ghetto in Poland, was deported in 1984 to the Soviet Union, where he was convicted of war crimes and executed three years later.

131   *a disgruntled former tenant:* Ryan, *Quiet Neighbors,* 60. The Chicago immigrant, Frank Walus, was originally ordered deported in 1978 because of his apparent role as a Gestapo member in Poland who personally murdered Jews. But prosecutors were forced to drop the case after new evidence confirmed it was a matter of mistaken identity. The collapse of the case was the biggest black eye in the Justice Department's Nazi prosecutions prior to the Ivan the Terrible prosecution more than a decade later.

"legal lepers": Ryan, *Quiet Neighbors,* 61.

Ryan had won a crucial case: Ryan was the appellate lawyer in the Justice Department's victory before the Supreme Court in the deportation of Feodor Fedorenko. (See Ryan, *Quiet Neighbors.*)

"that's one more win": Author interview with Allan Ryan, former director of the Office of Special Investigations at the United States Justice Department, quoting Philip Heymann, former assistant attorney general at the Justice Department.

It didn't get him the job: Author interview with Philip Heymann, former assistant attorney general at the Justice Department.

"A little seasoning": Walter Rockler, recorded interview (2000) for Feigin, *The Office of Special Investigations.*

132   *"We shot them":* Author interview with Art Sinai, former deputy director of investigations at the Office of Special Investigations.

a surprise visit: Sinai interview.

133   *"We'll help you out":* Ibid.

the FBI wasn't willing: Internal memos, 1979–80, between the Justice Department's Office of Special Investigations and the FBI regarding access to FBI records on Nazi suspects; obtained by author.

"their specific identity is not being disclosed": Confidential memo, November 21, 1979, from the FBI to Justice Department OSI officials, informing them that the FBI was not willing to turn over information on sixteen Nazi suspects who were confidential FBI informants. Allan Ryan, then at OSI, said in an interview with the author that he believed higher-level Justice Department officials lodged objections to the FBI decision. But there is no record that the FBI's decision to withhold information on the suspected Nazis was ever reversed.

"every case will be vigorously pursued": Justice Department press statement, January 16, 1980, after creation of Office of Special Investigations to probe Nazi cases.

"To hell with you": Rockler interview.

134   *"There may be reason":* Justice Department memo from John Loftus, prosecutor in Nazi office, April 25, 1980.

the FBI destroyed: Undated memo (1980) from the Justice Department criminal division to the FBI directing the bureau to explain to a judge how the Trifa Manifesto had been destroyed.

put out dozens of articles: Feigin, *The Office of Special Investigations,* 237.

a rogue investigation: Letters from Neal Sher, former director of OSI, to the FBI objecting to its handling of the Koreh case and the delay in disciplining agents, 1994–96; and Feigin, *The Office of Special Investigations,* 231–33.

135 *"so outrageous":* Sher letter to FBI Director Louis J. Freeh, November 23, 1994.

Koreh grudgingly acknowledged: Sher letters on Koreh; and Feigin, *The Office of Special Investigations.* Ultimately, Koreh acknowledged publishing the Nazi propaganda in Hungary and was ordered deported in 1997. The Justice Department agreed not to seek his removal from the country because of his failing health, and he died three months later. The FBI censured his daughter, Veronica Koreh Maxwell, and suspended his son-in-law, Kenneth Maxwell, for a week for their conduct in the investigation in defense of Koreh.

9. The Sins of the Father

136 *Gus von Bolschwing didn't think much of it:* Gus von Bolschwing interview.

"Did you know": Author interview with Jeff Mausner, former Justice Department prosecutor at Office of Special Investigations; and Gus von Bolschwing interview.

must be a bizarre mistake: Gus von Bolschwing interview.

138 *impossible for her to believe:* Author interview with Diane Lavoie, daughter of Vladas Zajanckauskas.

139 *"don't ever lose hope":* Steven Levingston, "The Executioner's Trail," *Boston Globe Magazine,* November 8, 1998, p. 13.

he walked down the school's hallway: Aslan Soobzokov interview.

140 *Aslan left his air base:* Ibid.

colored his earliest memories: Author interview with Rad Artukovic, son of Andrija Artukovic.

made his very first court appearance: Patt Morrison, "A Good Son," *Los Angeles Times Magazine,* May 18, 1986, p. 11.

141 *"a kangaroo court":* Rad Artukovic interview.

"I hate your dad": Ibid.

142 *wanted badly to believe:* Gus von Bolschwing interview.

144 *gave an interview in 1973:* Ralph Blumenthal, "Bishop Under Inquiry on Atrocity Link," *New York Times,* December 26, 1973.

finally pushing ahead with deportation: Trifa voluntarily agreed to give up his citizenship in 1980 but lived at the Romanian church's two-hundred-acre estate in Grass Lake, Michigan, for another four years while American authorities tried unsuccessfully to find a country that would take him. Trifa made clear that he would not go just anywhere. "You know, I'm not looking for any place too hot, or too cold," he said in an interview in 1984 at the Michigan estate. "I will not stay in a grass hut in the middle of Africa, either. I will be 70 in June. I'm looking for a place with a high standard of living, with culture." (Howard Blum, "Stateless Rumanian Archbishop Looks for a Country," *New York Times,* February 2, 1984.) He ended up moving to Portugal in

1984, although Portuguese officials insisted later that they were not aware of his role with the Nazis in Romania when they agreed to let him in. He died in Portugal in 1987. His American followers brought his body back to Michigan and buried him at the church estate.

went looking for witnesses: Author interview with Eugene Thirolf, former prosecutor at the Justice Department.

145   *Mendelsohn was in a car:* Author interview with Martin Mendelsohn, former official at INS Nazi unit and Office of Special Investigations.

raised "obvious questions": CIA, "Draft Working Paper," 31.

"Most of our cases": Ibid.

147   *"I am deeply disturbed":* Justice Department transcript of von Bolschwing deposition.

150   *"I would say":* "Nazi Who Surrendered U.S. Citizenship Dies in Capital," *Sacramento Bee,* March 7, 1982.

151   *was satisfied that no one in his own family:* Paul Chutkow, "From the 'Music Box' Emerges the Nazi Demon," *New York Times,* December 24, 1989.

Prosecutors suspected eighty-three-year-old Istvan Eszterhas: Author interview with Eli Rosenbaum, former director of Office of Special Investigations at Justice Department.

"correct what the father has done": Sharon Waxman, "In a Screenwriter's Art, Echoes of His Father's Secret," *New York Times,* March 18, 2004.

10. A Good Party Spoiled

152   *wandered off to the bookstore:* Rosenbaum interview.

translation of a memoir: Jean Michel, *Dora: The Nazi Concentration Camp Where Modern Space Technology Was Born and 30,000 Prisoners Died* (New York: Holt, Rinehart and Winston, 1979).

153   *a book called* The Rocket Team: Frederick I. Ordway III and Mitchell R. Sharpe, *The Rocket Team: From the V-2 to the Saturn Moon Rocket — The Inside Story of How a Small Group of Engineers Changed World History* (New York: Crowell, 1979).

154   *"I cursed at having to leave the party":* Ibid., 72.

155   *"You ever heard of a guy":* Rosenbaum interview.

156   *"100% Nazi, dangerous type":* "Arthur Rudolph," file, Nazi War Crimes Interagency Working Group, Declassified Records of the Central Intelligence Agency (Record Group 263), National Archives and Records Administration.

singing the "Horst Wessel Lied": Rudolph interview, September 24, 1982.

asked a boyish-looking member: Ibid.

157   *slave-labor factory at Dora:* The underground camp at the site where the prisoners were held was known as Dora. The adjoining factory, connected by tunnels, was known as Mittelwerk, or sometimes Mittelbau.

158   *Rosenbaum got up the nerve:* Rosenbaum interview.

159   *A Lithuanian tailor in Massachusetts:* The Justice Department brought a deportation

case in 1984 against the tailor, Juozas Kisielaitis. He left the United States voluntarily for Canada rather than face a trial over the war crimes accusations. Feigin, *The Office of Special Investigations,* 587.

he killed himself: Author interviews.

160   *"Rudolph* is *a rocket scientist":* Rosenbaum interview.

Rudolph had even brought: Audio recordings and transcript of Justice Department interviews with Rudolph, San Jose, California, October 13, 1982, and February 4, 1983.

161   *"I didn't ask for a lawyer":* Rudolph interview, October 13, 1982.

166   *"I couldn't do a darn thing":* Ibid., February 4, 1983.

168   *he needed to hold on to his pension:* Interview with Rosenbaum; and author interview with Marianne Rudolph, daughter of Arthur Rudolph.

She still couldn't believe: Marianne Rudolph interview.

he would show them: Author interview with Frederick I. Ordway III, a friend of Rudolph's.

169   *"It was just bad luck":* Ibid.

Rosenbaum got a tip: Rosenbaum interview.

11. "An Innocent Man"

170   *"was he a Nazi or not?":* Author interview with Floyd Abrams, attorney for *New York Times* in Soobzokov libel suit.

pay Soobzokov $450,000: The settlement figure is contained in legal documents provided by Aslan Soobzokov. Floyd Abrams refused to discuss the terms of the libel settlement because the record was sealed.

171   *he tried to borrow money:* Aslan Soobzokov interview.

"How can I go back?": Ibid.

rights to "the story of my life": Letters between Tscherim Soobzokov and his attorney, Michael Dennis, May 23, 1980; obtained by author.

"to carry out their false and evil designs": Letter from Tscherim Soobzokov during libel litigation; obtained by author.

Abrams and the company's other lawyers: Interview with Abrams; and Floyd Abrams, "Foreword: Settler's Remorse," *Michigan Law Review* 105, no. 6 (April 2007), 1033.

172   *shot to death in the nearby woods:* Witness deposition in *Soobzokov vs. CBS et al.*

too hot to touch: Correspondence regarding the Soobzokov libel suit; part of personal papers of Benjamin B. Ferencz, on file at United States Holocaust Memorial Museum.

"brainwashed" him: Depositions in *Soobzokov vs. CBS* libel suit.

173   *"I don't know nothing":* Deposition of Hadgmet Neguch in *Soobzokov vs. CBS.*

174   *"I'm not going to pay money to a Nazi":* Abrams interview.

Soobzokov got a check: Documents in libel suit provided by Aslan Soobzokov.

175   *he was just pacing:* Author interview with Lidia, longtime neighbor of Soobzokov. She asked that her last name not be used.

noticed a taxi: Lidia interview and Paterson Police Department reports.

176   *the doorbell awoke her:* Lidia interview and Paterson Police Department reports.

177   *they found yellow wiring, screws:* Paterson Police Department reports and FBI crime-scene investigative reports obtained by author under Freedom of Information Act.

"we applaud the act": Kinga Borondy, "Soobzokov Is Critical," *North Jersey News,* August 16, 1985.

"He was doing what his country asked": Kinga Borondy, "Residents Talk of 'a Nice Man,'" *North Jersey News,* August 16, 1985.

178   *he was shaken:* Author interview with Howard Blum; and Blum, *Wanted!,* 263.

a call came through: Lidia interview and Paterson Police Department reports.

Soobzokov nodded yes: FBI and Paterson Police Department reports.

"I can't believe they did this": Aslan Soobzokov interview.

179   *been also accused of collaborating with the Nazis:* Like Soobzokov, Sprogis beat the Nazi charges in court. An assistant police chief in Latvia during the Nazi occupation, Sprogis admitted his involvement in arresting Jews and confiscating their property, but in 1984 a judge threw out the deportation charges against him, finding that his duties were "ministerial" and did not involve his personally carrying out Nazi persecution. Feigin, *The Office of Special Investigations,* 101–3.

"a brave and noble act": "Police Suspect Link in Blasts at Homes of Men Tied to War Crimes," Associated Press, September 7, 1985.

180   *were practically identical:* The FBI also linked two bombings in Southern California in 1985 to the Soobzokov and Sprogis bombs that same year. One of the bombs killed the leader of an Arab American group, Alex Odeh, in Orange County, California. The bombings remain unsolved.

12. Backlash

181   *a one-man PR assault:* Buchanan declined the author's requests for an interview.

182   *men like Tom Soobzokov:* Patrick Buchanan, letter to the editor, *New York Times,* April 7, 1987.

"how a handful of American Jews": Ibid.

Sher was pacing: Author interview with Neal Sher, former director of Office of Special Investigations at the Justice Department.

183   *turned Sher's stomach:* Ibid.

fifteen thousand postcards, letters, and calls: Feigin, *Office of Special Investigations,* 279.

184   *"I cannot help but feel":* Letter of resignation from Saulius Suziedelis, Justice Department historian, to Neal Sher, April 22, 1986.

the White House defended: New York Times, "Grace Action Noted by U.S.," March 5, 1982.

185   *Reagan's jaw-dropping, public insistence:* Lou Cannon, "Honoring Wiesel, Reagan Confronts the Holocaust," *Washington Post,* April 20, 1985.

"It couldn't be more important": Sher interview and Holtzman interview.

He wanted Meese's secretary: Sher interview for Feigin, *Office of Special Investigations.*

start drafting his letter of resignation: Sher interview.

The twenty-one-page decision: Karl Linnas vs. INS, Second Circuit Court of Appeals (790 F.2d 1024); decision issued May 8, 1986.

186   *Linnas had never really challenged:* Feigin, *The Office of Special Investigations,* 271.

     She didn't think that this was by accident: Holtzman interview.

187   *It was the most attention:* Rosenbaum interview.

     "We would like to make sure": Author interview with Reagan administration official, who asked that his name not be published.

     Their government had already decided: Rosenbaum interview.

     The first thing Rosenbaum did: Rosenbaum interview.

188   *"God bless America!":* Newspaper stories and wire service reports, April 21, 1987. Linnas died ten weeks later of heart failure in Russia before the start of his war crimes trial.

     a typical headline: "Former Nazi Death Camp Guard Relieved from School Job," Associated Press, January 26, 1984. Reinhold Kulle, a guard at the Gross-Rosen concentration camp, had been working as a janitor at a suburban Chicago school. He was deported to West Germany in 1987.

     a scathing Nazi office investigation: Ryan, *Klaus Barbie and the United States Government.*

189   *"a pact with the devil":* Editorial, "Barbie and Dishonor," *Miami Herald,* August 18, 1983.

     had secretly been an intelligence officer: Feigin, *The Office of Special Investigations,* 313.

     as tortured a Nazi history as Austria: In 1991, Austria formally acknowledged for the first time the country's role in support of the Nazis. The revelations about Waldheim were seen as one motivation for the admission.

     What struck Meese as much as anything: Author interview with Edwin Meese III, former attorney general in the Reagan administration.

     "I just worked there and followed orders'": Feigin, *The Office of Special Investigations,* 313, quoting former Justice Department official Stephen S. Trott.

190   *Austria barred Sher himself:* Feigin, *The Office of Special Investigations,* 316.

     Waldheim sent a handwritten note: Ibid., 321.

     must be a mole: Rosenbaum interview.

191   *secretly collecting all the office trash:* Feigin, *The Office of Special Investigations,* 166.

     "Jewish Zionist special interest groups": Anti-Defamation League of B'Nai B'rith, *The Campaign Against the U.S. Justice Department's Prosecution of Suspected Nazi War Criminals,* special report (New York: ADL, June 1985), quoting a letter from a critic of the Justice Department, Dr. Edward Rubel, to Secretary of State George Shultz.

     "Let us chase": The Campaign Against the U.S. Justice Department's Prosecution, 11.

     retained a prominent Huntsville attorney: Ordway interview.

192   *to investigate more than a dozen German rocket scientists:* Justice Department "Paper-

clip" internal documents obtained under Freedom of Information Act, and author interviews.

a "promising investigation": Internal Justice Department memos in Strughold investigation obtained through Freedom of Information Act.

with live explosives and chemical weapons: Justice Department "Paperclip" documents, including memos in 1980–83 on accusations and evidence against Strughold.

"participated in chemical experiments": Justice Department memo to Ryan, November 4, 1980.

it would be more difficult: Sher interview.

193   *wrongly thrown out:* Ordway interview. Ordway was one of the White House visitors who met with Buchanan.

He would help them: Ibid.

194   *"an individual of great courage":* Buchanan quotations from newspaper and wire service reports in the 1980s, and Anti-Defamation League, *Anger on the Right: Pat Buchanan's Venomous Crusade,* special report (New York: ADL, 1991).

"betrays an all-too-familiar hostility": Editorial, *New York Post,* September 19, 1980.

was attending an engagement party: Sher interview.

195   *Tannenbaum was notorious:* Feigin, *The Office of Special Investigations,* 107.

196   *They were the last group:* Rockler interview for ibid.

"Give me his address": Feigin, *The Office of Special Investigations,* 109.

He was a sadist: Sher interview.

197   *defend Tannenbaum pro bono:* Rockler withdrew the offer after the Justice Department concluded his defense of Tannenbaum would be a conflict of interest, given his previous post atop the Nazi unit. Feigin, *The Office of Special Investigations,* 110.

"improper, if not outrageous": Ibid., 110.

he wanted it made clear: Sher interview.

the Justice Department allowed Tannenbaum to stay: Tannenbaum died the next year.

"I dreaded the day": U.S. District Court Judge I. Leo Glasser, February, 4, 1988. Cited in Feigin, *The Office of Special Investigations,* 112.

198   *"hanged him with my own hands":* Feigin, *The Office of Special Investigations,* 112.

13. Ivan the Terrible

199   *An Israeli war crimes investigator:* This account of the start of the Ivan the Terrible investigation and of Eliyahu Rosenberg's identification of John Demjanjuk is drawn from author interviews and from a number of published sources, including: Ryan, *Quiet Neighbors;* Feigin, *The Office of Special Investigations;* and Tom Teicholz, *The Trial of Ivan the Terrible: State of Israel vs. John Demjanjuk* (New York: St. Martin's, 1990).

202   *"became an obsession":* Gitta Sereny, "The Man Who Was Not Ivan the Terrible," *Independent* (London), December 7, 1991, quoting former Justice Department prosecutor John Horrigan.

Demjanjuk returned to his home: "Seven Hills Man Is Called Nazi Guard," *Cleveland Press,* August 26, 1977, and author interview with Walt Bogdanich, former reporter for *Cleveland Press.*

"Is not true!": Teicholz, *The Trial of Ivan the Terrible,* 51.

headline in the New York Times: "Ohioan Is Called Nazi War Criminal," *New York Times,* August 27, 1977.

203 *"We cannot afford the risk":* Letter from Congressman Eilberg to Attorney General Griffin Bell, as cited in judicial decision, United States Court of Appeals, Sixth Circuit, (Cincinnati), *Demjanjuk v. Petrovsky,* issued February 24, 1994.

You son of a bitch: Ryan, *Quiet Neighbors,* 107.

"Demjanjuk could not have been Ivan the Terrible": Memo from Justice Department prosecutor George Parker, dated February 28, 1980, as cited in Sixth Circuit in Demjanjuk decision; and Feigin, *The Office of Special Investigations.*

he wrote to his bosses: Ryan said he never saw the Parker memo.

204 *"He had a pipe, a sword, a whip":* Ryan, *Quiet Neighbors,* 124.

He broke into sobs: Ibid.

205 *Demjanjuk's Nazi identification card:* Ibid., 125.

"Who would want to take back": Ryan interview.

Some Israeli law enforcement officials: Feigin, *The Office of Special Investigations,* 154.

206 *"this fellow Demjanjuk":* Rosenbaum interview.

"We know that eyewitness testimony": Author interview with Judge Gilbert Merritt, former chief judge of the Sixth Circuit Court of Appeals.

207 *"how dare you":* "Survivor Identifies the Accused in Israeli Trial," *New York Times,* February 26, 1987, and other news reports.

"A thousand deaths cannot compensate": John Kifner, "Demjanjuk Given Death Sentence for Nazi Killings," *New York Times,* April 26, 1988.

209 *Buchanan took aim:* Nightline segment, ABC Television, July 29, 1993.

unable to pick out Demjanjuk: Feigin, *The Office of Special Investigations.*

210 *"were blinded":* Opinion of Judge Thomas A. Wiseman Jr., Report of the Special Master to the Sixth Circuit Court of Appeals in Demjanjuk case, 1993, p. 198.

"fraud on the court": Sixth Circuit, Demjanjuk decision.

tainted by outside politics: Author interview with Judge Merritt. After leaving the American Israel Public Affairs Committee, Sher moved to a second Jewish-related organization, the International Commission on Holocaust Era Insurance Claims, as chief of staff, but was forced to resign in 2002 over evidence that he misappropriated travel funds from the group. He was disbarred in the District of Columbia as a result of the episode.

211 *"offered fodder":* ADL National Chairman Melvin Salberg and National Director Abraham H. Foxman, letter to the court, November 19, 1993.

"hate mongerers and neo-Nazis": Neal M. Sher, "Judge Gilbert Merritt's Obsession with Jews," *Jewish World Review,* April 5, 1998.

Ryan yelled: Ryan interview.

a look of discomfort: Rosenbaum interview.

212   *"in the toilet":* Rosenbaum interview.

14. The Road to Ponary

213   *MacQueen wasn't finding it:* Interview with Michael MacQueen, former historian for the Office of Special Investigations at the Justice Department.

"Show me something that I signed": Rosenbaum interview.

214   *he discovered a canvas-bound book:* Sharon Cohen, "In Hidden Records of Horror, Guilt of a Nazi Collaborator," Associated Press, December 15, 1996.

he found a red file: Levingston, "The Executioner's Trail."

215   *"Remember we needed a document":* MacQueen interview.

Rosenbaum was so excited: Rosenbaum interview.

the signatures were a smoking gun: MacQueen interview.

MacQueen studied the names: Levingston, "The Executioner's Trail."

Two names stood out: MacQueen interview.

216   *a wooded hamlet called Ponary:* "Ponary" is the Polish derivation of the site of the massacres. Most Jews called it by its Yiddish rendering — Ponar — and in Lithuanian, it is known as Paneriai.

All roads lead to Ponary: Rosenbaum interview.

217   *The CIA had a file:* Lileikis file, Nazi War Crimes Interagency Working Group, Declassified Records of the Central Intelligence Agency (Record Group 263), National Archives and Records Administration.

"the shooting of Jews in Vilna": Ibid.

"under the control of the Gestapo": Ibid.

plus twenty-one pounds of coffee: Ibid.

He had always hoped: Breitman et al., *U.S. Intelligence and the Nazis,* 264.

218   *The agency told the INS:* CIA Lileikis file; memos between CIA and INS about Lileikis.

219   *twice in the same week:* Rosenbaum interview.

he did know of one: Rosenbaum interview.

220   *Rosenbaum knocked:* Rosenbaum interview and Justice Department records on meeting.

221   *his last name and title:* Arrest order for more than fifty Vilnius Jews, with Lileikis's name at bottom, dated August 22, 1941; Lileikis CIA file.

Lileikis spoke the words: Rosenbaum interview.

222   *"These criminals must now be":* Feigin, *The Office of Special Investigations,* 544.

he laid out the evidence: Rosenbaum interview.

223   *his geezer list:* In later years, Rosenbaum would put Bernard Madoff, imprisoned in 2009 at the age of seventy-one for a notorious, multi-billion-dollar Ponzi scheme, at the top of his "geezer" list. He liked to point out that few questioned the severe sentence for Madoff, despite his age.

Rosenbaum got a call: Rosenbaum interview.

If we have to produce his records: Lileikis's lawyers were later granted security clearances allowing them to examine classified CIA records on their client in private. But the records — and the CIA's involvement with Lileikis — did not become part of the public case.

224 *"She was taken":* "Boston Retiree Accused as Holocaust Perpetrator," Associated Press, September 21, 1994.

His lawyer and his priest: Levingston, "The Executioner's Trail."

He was scared: Author interview with Thomas J. Butters, lawyer for Lileikis.

"Did anyone order you": Levingston, "The Executioner's Trail," and United States District Court Judge Richard G. Stearns, written decision in motion for summary judgment in Lileikis case, May 24, 1996.

225 *"Lileikis is attempting":* United States District Court Judge Richard G. Stearns, decision in motion for summary judgment in Lileikis case, May 24, 1996.

CIA officials wrote: Letter from CIA to congressional intelligence committee, May 25, 1995; CIA Lileikis file.

226 *another Nazi collaborator:* Rosenbaum was trying unsuccessfully to persuade the Lithuanians to take back Vladas Zajanckauskas, who had already been stripped of his citizenship. The Lithuanians refused, and Zajanckauskas died in Massachusetts in 2013.

he arranged for a side trip: Rosenbaum interview.

227 *the place was eerily quiet:* Author interview with Carole A. Jackson, U.S. State Department official, who accompanied Rosenbaum on the Lithuanian trip.

228 *Hundreds, certainly:* Rosenbaum interview.

Perhaps even more than ten thousand: Ryan interview. When he was director of the Justice Department's Nazi unit in the early 1980s, Ryan held that some ten thousand Nazis and Nazi collaborators might have come to America. He based that estimate on the overall numbers of immigrants from Nazi-occupied countries and the prevalance of collaborators named in Justice Department investigations. In author's interview with Ryan in 2013 for this book, Ryan said his earlier estimate was probably too low.

Rosenbaum peered one last time: Rosenbaum interview.

Epilogue

229 *secret internal history:* Eric Lichtblau, "Secret Papers Detail U.S. Aid For Ex-Nazis," *New York Times,* November 14, 2010.

230 *was being investigated:* Author interviews with law enforcement officials.

"no statute of limitations": Certification of extradition of Johann Breyer; issued by U.S. Magistrate Judge Timothy R. Rice, United States District Court, Eastern District of Pennsylvania, July 23, 2014.

231 *"he's been hiding":* Batame Hertzbach, as quoted by Matt Pearce and Maya Srikrishnan, *Los Angeles Times,* June 21, 2014.

231   *auditors tallied up*: Eric Lichtblau, "U.S. Paid Residents Linked to Nazi Crimes $20
Million in Benefits, Report Says," *New York Times,* May 30, 2015. The audit review,
conducted by the Social Security Administration's inspector general, came in response to an Associated Press investigation published the prior October.

one of the final postwar Nazi trials: The sentence against Gröning, handed down
by Judge Frank Kompisch on July 15, 2015, is still pending, and it is unclear how
much time if any he will actually serve in prison. Gröning first admitted his role
at Auschwitz publicly in 2005, in interviews with the German newsmagazine *Der
Spiegel* and the BBC, but he was not charged for another nine years — until John
Demjanjuk's prosecution in Germany cleared the way for other Nazi investigations.

INDEX